spirits
are
drunk

SUNY SERIES IN CHINESE PHILOSOPHY AND CULTURE
DAVID L. HALL AND ROGER P. AMES, EDITORS

the
spirits
are
drunk

comparative
approaches
to chinese
religion

jordan paper

STATE UNIVERSITY OF NEW YORK PRESS

Published by
State University of New York Press, Albany

© 1995 State University of New York

For information, address the State University of New York Press,
State University Plaza, Albany, NY 12246

Production by Marilyn P. Semerad
Marketing by Bernadette LaManna

Library of Congress Cataloging-in-Publication Data

Paper, Jordan D.
    The spirits are drunk :   comparative approaches to Chinese religion
/ Jordan Paper.
        p. cm. — (SUNY series in Chinese philosophy and culture)
    Includes bibliographical references and index.
    ISBN 0-7914-2315-8 (alk. paper). — ISBN 0-7914-2316-6 (pbk. :
alk. paper)
    1. China—Religion.   I. Title.   II. Series.
BL1802.P37 1994
299'.51—dc20   94-9954
                                                                    CIP

10 9 8 7 6 5 4 3 2 1

The rituals are completed;
The bells and drums have sounded.
The pious descendant takes his place;
The officiating announcer cries:
"The [ancestral] spirits are drunk."
The august incorporator of the dead rises;
The drums and bells escort him [/her] away;
The divine protectors return to their abode.
The stewards and the lord's wife speedily remove
    [the food from the altar].
The uncles and brothers repair to the feast
    [of the food from the altar].

The musicians come in and play
So that blessings will follow.
Your food is set out:
No one is left unsatisfied; all are happy.
Drunk and satiated,
Both lesser and great bow their heads:
"The spirits enjoyed the wine and food;
They will give the lord long life.
Very gracious, very timely,
Everything completed —
Many sons and grandsons,
The [patrilineal] line continued uninterrupted."

—From the *Shi* (ca. 2700 BP): Ode 209

To my "elder brothers" Zhao Keli and
Dharma Master Mingfu, without whom I would
have knowledge but no understanding,
and to my colleague and friend Song Zhaolin,
a companion in the exploration of Chinese
religious behavior.

contents

illustrations

Chapter 3

Chapter 4

Chapter 6

Chapter 7

Chapter 8

preface

The study of religion is intrinsically a Western phenomenon. In Western Europe, religion came to be understood as a discreet feature of culture due in part to the various conflicts between church and state as well as between church and science. The study of religion as distinct from theology resulted from a number of factors: Christian missionary interest in non-Western religions, developments in European and American governments and universities, and the emergence of the social sciences, to name a few. There is no need to rehearse these historical factors that are well known to students of religion. Accordingly, the study of religion in non-Western cultures will inevitably lead to anomalies from a Western perspective. Of the religions of non-Western civilizations, the study of religion in China is perhaps the most anomalous.

Late sixteenth- and seventeenth-century Jesuit missionaries, precursors to the European Enlightenment, created an image of Chinese religion—multiple as a trinity, androcentric and rational—that has dominated the Western perception by religionists (as distinguished from anthropologists and sociologists) to the present. This work will attempt to counter this understanding by presenting alternative models as well as by focusing on those elements often ignored: ecstatic religious experience, both functional and nonfunctional; religio-aesthetics; and female elements. The work will conclude with a reversal of this Christian missionary interpretation of Chinese religion, namely, the interpretation of Christianity from a Chinese perspective. Such an interpretation will corroborate the points made in preceding chapters.

Initially trained as a classical sinologist (e.g., Paper 1971, 1973a/b, 1987b), my methodological approach to the history of religions has been influenced by scholars who work from a social science perspective, particularly the Swedish scholar of shamanism and native American religions, Åke Hultkrantz. Accordingly, the studies incorporated in this work to a large degree focus on religious experience, that is, on behavior rather than belief. To understand Chinese religion from a comparative perspective, I began to study native American religions (e.g., Paper 1983b, 1988, 1990a/b). Hence, the emphasis on comparative examples from native American traditions merely reflects my research; parallels from other religious traditions, particularly the West African kingdoms, could equally well have been utilized.

It should be understood that the following is not intended to be an introduction to nor a comprehensive study of Chinese religion. Readers who are completely unfamiliar with Chinese religion are highly recommended to Laurence Thompson's (1989) excellent concise introduction. Deliberately excluded from this book are analyses of Buddhism, Daoism, and "Confucianism," the subject of many superb recent Western studies. Nor does this work reflect a single methodological approach. Instead, the chapters consist of a series of interconnected explorations into selected major aspects of Chinese religion that have hitherto received relatively little analysis, suggesting new approaches and methods. Rather than explicitly discuss methodology, each study presents these comparative approaches through the example of the study itself.

It should be understood that the following analyses do not reflect the long tradition of Western sinological studies but rather more recent trends in the comparative study of religion in the West. From over a decade of correspondence and conversations with scholars in China (ethnologists, archaeologists and Daoist practitioners) and Taiwan (Buddhist scholar-monks and ethnologists), I feel confident that these studies are also in accord with the understanding and approaches of at least some aspects of contemporary Chinese scholarship.

On a final note, it is obvious, I trust, that a scholar who ranges from prehistoric to contemporary China on a number of diverse topics related to religion and who also does research on cultures other than Chinese cannot bring to any one topic the depth of a scholar who dedicates a life's work to that single subject. My contribution, I hope, lies in synthesis and comparison, combined with limited original research. If this book broadens the range of understanding and appreciation of Chinese religion, as well as the understanding of religion in general, it has accomplished its task.

In Chapter 1, "Introduction: The Study of Chinese Religion," problems with the normative approach in the West to the study of Chinese religion and with the Chinese understanding of "religion" are discussed. These problems are traced back to the earliest reports on Chinese religion by Europeans from the late sixteenth century.

Chapter 2, "The Essence of Chinese Religion," introduces a new method for defining and determining a religion, both diachronically and synchronically, with a focus on ritual studies. This chapter argues that Chinese religion as a singular construct can be delineated with a fundamental coherence that is at least four thousand years old.

Chapters 3 and 4, "Ecstatic Functionaries in Chinese Religion I: Shamans" and "Ecstatic Functionaries in Chinese Religion II: Mediums," are based on analytical studies of ecstatic religious experience within a comparative framework and are concerned with the types of ecstatic experience in China, as well as their functions. The emphases of these analyses are on actual experiences rather than the commentary tradition of the literature. It also will be argued that the standard Western typology and terminology usually applied to Chinese religion neither reflects the complexity of the situation in China nor that in East Asia as a whole. In addition, new methods will be introduced for analyzing early iconography from a comparative perspective to ascertain religious behavior.

Using religio-ecological and comparative methods, Chapter 5, "The Mystic Experience in Chinese Religion I: Transformation," discusses the shift from shamanism to the mystic experience, both in general and specifically in early China. It is pointed out that Chinese terminology in reference to the former continued in reference to the latter. Again the focus will be on analyzing the texts on the basis of actual human experiences rather than the history of textual commentaries.

Chapter 6, "The Mystic Experience in Chinese Religion II: Expression," discusses the continuing importance and function of mystic experience and relevant understandings in China over the last twenty-five hundred years to the present. History of religions methodology is combined with literary studies and art history.

Chapter 7, "The Fundament of Religio-Aesthetic Expression: Stones and Seals," continues the theme of Chapter 6 but shifts the discussion from aesthetic behavior to the materials used in aesthetic pursuits. The chapter focuses on the religio-aesthetic aspects of stones in general and seal stones in particular.

China's patriarchal sociopolitical structure has influenced the entire understanding of Chinese religion, which incorporates many patriarchal aspects but also maintains very important roles for female spirits. This later aspect has been poorly understood. Chapter 8, "Female Spirits and Spirituality in Chinese Religion," explores some potential approaches relevant to feminism with regard to the study of Chinese religion.

There are many studies of missionary activity in China, but relatively few studies of indigenous Chinese Christianity. Chapter 9, "Christianity from the Perspective of Chinese Religion," explores a non-Western understanding of Christianity, examining what this understanding tells us about the fundamentals of Chinese religion.

In a postface, the methodologies utilized in these studies will be briefly summarized, the development of new interests in the study of Chinese religion noted, and further needed studies suggested. Finally, the implications of a revised awareness of religion in China for our understanding of religion in the West is discussed.

Note on Romanization:

All Chinese words will be romanized in pinyin, except for place and temple names and political personages on Taiwan, for which the Wade-Giles or other conventional romanization will be used. One hopes this will lead to clarity rather than confusion. Chinese characters have not been provided, except where essential to the argument, on the assumption that those who read Chinese will almost always know which characters are being translated based on context and romanization, and that those who cannot read Chinese will not benefit from them.

Wasausink
August, 1993

acknowledgments

I would like to thank the journals who gave me permission to use portions of my previously published articles. The following is a list of journal articles, parts of which were incorporated into various chapters: Chapter 2: "The Ritual Core of Chinese Religion," *Religious Studies and Theology* 7 (2&3) (1987): 19–35. Chapter 3: "The Meaning of the *T'ao-t'ieh*," *History of Religions* 18 (1978): 18–41. Chapter 4: "The *Feng* in Protohistoric Chinese Religion," *History of Religions* 25 (1986): 213–35. Chapter 5: "From Shaman to Mystic in Ojibwa Religion," *Studies in Religion* 9 (1980): 185–99; "From Shamanism to Mysticism in the *Chuang-tzu*," *Scottish Journal of Religious Studies* 3 (1982): 27–45; "Samen hsinyang yü shenmi chingyen: Tsai tsaoch'i Chungkuo yü hsientai Ouchipeiwa tsungchiao chung te kuanhsi," trans. Lai Chien-ch'eng, *Shih-tzu hou* (1985) 24 [in 3 parts], 1:28–31, 2:26–31; 3:22–27. Chapter 6: "Riding on a White Cloud: Aesthetics as Religion in China," *Religion* 15 (1985): 3–27; "Art and Religion in Contemporary China," *Journal of Chinese Religion* 15 (1987): 51–60. Chapter 8: "The Persistence of Female Spirits in Patriarchal China," *J. of Feminist Studies in Religion* 6 (1990): 25–40; "Comparative Cosmology and the Concepts of Good and Evil, Male and Female," *Explorations* 8 (1990): 17–28. Chapter 9: "Hung Hsiu-ch'üan tui Shengching hsinyüeh de p'i chieh" (Hung Hsiu-ch'üan's Interpretation of the New Testament), trans. Lai Chien-ch'eng, *Shih-tzu hou* 28 (1989) [in 2 parts] (8, 9); "The Normative East Asian Understanding of Christian Scriptures," *Studies in Religion* 18 (1989): 451–65.

With regard to Chapter 7, appreciation is due to my close friend Zhao Keli, who first introduced me to stones and seals; Zeng Shaojian and Yu Deho, who kindly made their seal stone collections accessible to me; my friend Dong Yiyou, who gave me access to his jade seal collection; Zhou Monan, who gave me access to his collection of stones; Jiang Zhaoshan, head of the painting and calligraphy section of the Palace Museum (Taiwan), who kindly arranged for me to study the seal stones at the museum and to use its library; and the staff of the Far Eastern Department of the Royal Ontario Museum for making their library and collection of bronze and jade seals available.

Much of the research for this book was supported during different periods over the last three decades by the National Defense Education Act Title 6 (United States), the Social Science and Humanities Research Council (Canada), and the Faculty of Arts of York University, which also supported preparation of this book, for all of which I am grateful. Sharon Norman enhanced the book with the drawings for Chapter 3.

Most important, I would like to extend my considerable gratitude to those of my colleagues who encouraged the work over so many years. They are far too many to name, but I am sure they know who they are. However, in regard to particular chapters, I would like to specifically acknowledge Michael Pye (Chapter 1), John Major (Chapter 2), Norman Girardot and Julian Pas (Chapter 3), Mingfu Fashi and David Armstrong (Chapter 4), Paul Levine (Chapter 5), Zhao Keli (Chapter 6), Schuyler Cammann (Chapter 7), my wife, Chuang Li (Chapter 8), and Andrew Wilson (Chapter 9). Robert Weller and several anonymous scholars read the entire manuscript in detail and made a number of valuable suggestions. I take full responsibility for the statements and conclusions—many of them controversial—in these studies.

Note on Translation: Unless otherwise specified, all translations from Chinese texts are my own.

1 introduction: the study of chinese religion

Our use of the word religion *in the singular is intended, then, to convey our interpretation that the character of religious expression in China is above all* a manifestation of Chinese culture. *To attempt to understand* religion *in China as several systems of doctrine is to read Western experience into a quite different set of circumstances.*
—L. Thompson 1989:1

Religion is a fundamental aspect of human culture. In order to fully understand ourselves, we must grasp not only our relationship to the religious aspects of our own culture, but the nature of religion *sui generis*. History of religions (comparative religion) enables us to explore the meaning and the function of religion globally. To begin such study, we should avoid a priori, often conflicting, distinctions. Among many examples one could cite the following: the understanding that people of the past ("homo religiosus") were inherently more religious than those of modern civilizations; that only the religions of literate cultures or only the literate facets of literate cultures are worth studying; that since the religions of South Asia and Europe/West Asia have common characteristics, these characteristics define the parameters of religion. The latter viewpoint ignores the many shared linguistic and mythological features of the two cultural complexes, as well five thousand years of nearly continuous cultural interaction. Outside of this macrocultural sphere, other civilizations in East Asia, Africa, and the Americas developed uninfluenced or but slightly influenced from cultures speaking Indo-European languages.

Chinese civilization, with a considerably longer continuous tradition than that of Europe, for much of its history also encompassed a larger territory and population. China provides an ex-

1

ample of a culture that had comparatively little contact with comparable civilizations in its formative period. Hence, the study of religion in China offers the opportunity to increase our awareness of the nature of religion. Such study, however, has been confused by a combination of historical factors in the field of history of religions.

The fundamental difficulty in studying Chinese religion is that, as in all non-Western languages, there is no traditional Chinese linguistic equivalent of the word *religion*. A secondary problem endemic to the study of nonuniversal religions—that is, religions other than Buddhism, Christianity, Islam, and so on—is separating religion from culture in general. Until recently, the tendency in Western studies has been to force Western assumptions and categories on non-Western traditions and artificially create religions that do not exist in actuality, such as the ubiquitous "three religions" of China. (For more detailed analyses of the effects of Eurocentrism on religious studies see Paper 1991, 1993a.)

The Understanding of "Religion" in China

The term *zongjiao*, borrowed from the nineteenth-century Japanese translation (in turn taken from an obscure Chinese Buddhist text), has been used as the standard Chinese translation for *religion* since the beginning of the twentieth century, particularly, at first, by Christian missionaries. It was primarily applied to Christianity (Catholicism and Protestantism understood as two distinct religions in China) with extension to other religions of alien origin in China, such as Buddhism and Islam. Now, particularly in Taiwan, the term is used for any religion which is to some degree institutionalized

The word *jiao* itself has a considerably longer history in China. It was applied to Buddhism (*fojiao*), an entirely foreign religion in China into the second century C.E., and institutional Daoism (*daojiao*), which partially developed out of failed revolutionary religiopolitical movements at the end of the same century. Hence, *jiao* may be understood as applying to heterodox religious institutions, that is, religious institutions outside of the "orthodox" state (Imperial clan) and clan religion. In the medieval period, when Buddhist and Daoist institutions rivaled those of the state and found favor at court, *kungjiao* (Confucianism) developed as temples devoted to Confucius and related scholars, the patron saints of the civil service examination system, were built in population centers.

Jiao was not applied to the dominant mode of Chinese religiosity, involving most religious behavior: the state, clan, and family sacrificial complex, of well over four millennia in age (see Chapter 2). Hence, the Chinese tend to consider "religion" (as *zongjiao*) to be an alien phenomenon. A standard Chinese response to being queried on "religion" in China is to say that the Chinese do not have one. Few Western scholars are acquainted with the actual Chinese equivalent question: "To whom (or what) do you offer sacrifice?" It is a question that elicits a detailed response on Chinese religious understanding and behavior from many of the same people who state that China has no "religion."

From the standpoint of modern religious studies, it would have been better if other terms had been used to translate *religion*. Following Clifford Geertz's well-known definition of religion (1966), the Chinese term *wen* (modern term: *wenhua* = "culture"), which includes among its meanings, "the matrix of culture," could have been used. *Wen* (etymology: person with tattooing on the breast; Karlgren 1957:131) does mean "writing," derived from its sense of design or pattern, but it also derives from the latter the sense of embellishment and of civilization or cultural pattern. Extending the concept of Geertz from religion as a system of symbols with particular functions to the concept of a symbol itself having similar functions, *wen* could be translated as "religion."

Although Geertz's definition has been criticized by some as being so broad that it does not clearly distinguish religion from culture, this feature could also be understood as its strength. Chinese religion is not a universal religion as Buddhism, Christianity, and Islam but is an ethnic religion. In ethnic religions, such as Judaism for a Western example, religion can only be meaningfully separated from culture for the purpose of comparison with universal religions. Within the relevant cultures, the separation is so artificial and dependant on Christian expectations, it has little if any analytical validity.

Alternatively, from a Chinese perspective, the term *li* (modern term: *liyi*), which includes all formal religious behavior, would have also served well (see Chapter 2). It has been suggested that a new Chinese term, *wenli*, could be coined to approximate the term *religion* as it is used by scholars of religion in the West (Paper 1993b).

The Understanding of Chinese Religion in the West

Without rehearsing the history of religious studies, it is sufficient to note that comparative religion developed from the encounter of Christian missionaries with non-Western religions and has served to perpetuate Eurocentric values. Among the earliest of these encounters are those of the Jesuits with China to the far east of Europe and with native America to the west. Jesuit perceptions of non-European religions were based on their cultural background, missionizing strategy, and political situation. Sixteenth- to seventeenth-century Jesuit *Relations* from these regions, written to encourage continued support of their missions, were highly influential on European intellectuals, especially Leibnitz and Voltaire.

Jesuit missionaries were brought into the Chinese government because of their knowledge of European astronomy as well as the training they sought in written Chinese and the literature essential to Chinese elite status, including texts on ritual. (Explicit official appointment began with Johann Adam von Schall after the Manchu occupation of the capital, and the papacy eventually authorized Jesuits to hold such offices.) The Jesuits needed to be able to participate in state rituals without being deemed heretics. They also needed to identify Chinese religion in a manner that presented them with an opponent to their missionizing, on the order of Judaism in Europe.

Matteo Ricci, the most important early Jesuit missionary in China, developed an understanding of Chinese religion that allowed him to interact with the Chinese government—all such interactions explicitly involving ritual. He deemed the state religion to be based on enlightened monotheism and, therefore, compatible with, rather than to be opposed by, Christianity. The state rituals—including sacrifices to the Imperial ancestors and to nature spirits—were virtually the same as those of the Chinese people, except on a grander scale. Yet Ricci considered popular religion to be idolatrous, although, for pragmatic purposes, rituals directed to the ancestors were tolerated. This interpretation of a non-Western religious complex to suit particular Christian missionary needs led to an incorrect understanding of a quarter of humanity's religion for four centuries.

The Jesuit understanding was opposed by Franciscans and other missionaries who did not become government officials and believed all of Chinese religion to be incompatible with Christianity. The century-long "Rites Controversy" which ensued ended when the Vatican decided against the Jesuit position, resulting in Christian missionaries being expelled from China, until they re-entered behind Western guns in the last century.

It is normal for people to view the world around them from their own cultural perspective and to assume their own cultural values to be universal. Hence, the study of non-western religions still tends to proceed from a normative western European Christian viewpoint; for example, monotheism as a value, priority given to "sacred" texts, focus on faith, assumptions that religions have "founders," an understanding that the goal of religion *sui generis* is transcendence, an assumption that religious institutions are separate from those of the state, and so on. These values are responsible for the continued misunderstanding of Chinese religion.

Separation of Religious from State Institutions

Since the collapse of the Holy Roman Empire, there has been a tension in western European Christendom between state and church, a tension previously present from the founding of Christianity to the collapse of the western Roman state. This conflict and struggle for political ascendancy between powerful institutions is particular to western Europe, in that eastern European

Christianity tended to continue the model of Byzantium, where the heads of the church and the state were the same person (as is theoretically the situation in England).

Ricci, as a sixteenth-century Jesuit, was part of the Counter-Reformation. He understood religious institutions to be separate from and often in conflict with the state. In China, the Buddhist and Daoist institutions could be seen to play this role, although tensions with these institutions were considerably weakened with the last major suppression of Buddhism in the mid-eighth century. (Christianity itself was frequently perceived by the Chinese government as both heterodox and seditious.)

Furthermore, it was essential for Ricci and his fellow Jesuits, if they were to accept government support and office, to understand the state not to be a religious institution per se. The Roman Catholic church of Ricci's time, within a century of the expulsion or forced conversion of Moslems and Jews from Spain, had absolutely no tolerance for Christians' participating in non-Christian rituals and executed those convicted of such participation. For example, Spanish traders at that time in what is now the southwestern United States were charged with heresy by the Inquisition for participating in those native American rituals essential for trade (see Kessell 1978).

Related to the Western view of religion discussed above is one that assumes religious functionaries are separate from government officials. The Jesuits were members of the Christian priesthood, a role that in post-feudal Europe became increasingly removed from governmental functions. Although the Jesuits were well aware of the ritual roles of the emperor and the government officials, they had to turn a blind eye to that understanding. They could not serve a government in which the head of state was the chief priest of society and the officials all had major religious roles. Nor could the Jesuits promote Christianity as compatible with Chinese culture if they understood the head of every clan and of every family to have priestly functions.

Hence, the Jesuits looked only on those institutions outside the state, that is, Buddhism and Daoism, along with popular religion, as opponents. The state religion and that of the literati, as well as local temples dedicated to Kongfuzi, were identified as a distinct sect, one that in essence worshipped a male supreme deity (see Chapter 8), compatible, with minor modifications, with Christianity.

Sacred Texts and Founders

The Judeo-Christian-Islamic traditions are unique in limiting the basis of truth to fixed texts. Buddhism, as an alternative model of a literary, universal religion, considers religious texts to be on a par with the Buddha and with the monastic establishment; the bases of its truth are particular experiences.

The early Jesuit missionaries found three canons in China, and from them identified three religions. However, the Chinese Buddhist and Daoist canons are not fixed, and the Classics (*jing*) primarily functioned to define the ideological basis for the selection of civil officials. The ritual texts in the Classics do not delineate the rituals of popular Chinese religion nor contain its myths, although they are compatible.

In the West, sacred texts are ostensibly understood to be created by the deity who transmitted them via human scribes: Moses received the Torah from God; the Gospels contain the teachings of Christ; Mohammed received the Quran from Allah. For Westerners, it was natural to focus on the Dharma, understood to be transmitted by Shakyamuni; on the collection of Daoist texts, the assumed earliest ascribed to Laozi; and on the Classics, incorrectly considered by Ricci to have been primarily created by Kongfuzi. The latter were understood as the basis of ritual practices that actually preceded Kongfuzi by at least a thousand years. Viewed in this manner, the three Chinese "religions" delineated by Ricci are compatible with the Western model of religion.

As Christianity was named after Jesus Christ, and until relatively recently Islam was in Europe incorrectly called "Mohammedism," in Ricci's time it was assumed that religions by their very nature must have a founder and be so denominated. Thus, with regard to Chinese religion, the term *Buddhism* is quite compatible with *Christianity*. Ricci's Jesuit colleague, Alvaro Semedo, who arrived in China in 1613, assumed Daoism must be named after a founder; hence, he mistakenly thought Laozi was named Daozi ("Tausu," in Mungello 1989:88). Ricci understood Kongfuzi to be "a key to his Chinese-Christian synthesis" (Mungello 1989:17); hence, the creation of the Western concept, "Confucianism" (to be distinguished from the functions of its Chinese equivalents, *rujia* and *kungjiao*, combined in the recent term *rujiao*).

The High God

Israelite religion came to define itself, sometime in the first half of the first millennium before the common era, through allegiance to a single god, later understood as the only god. Christianity, Judaism, and Islam maintained monotheism as their primary value, aspects of polytheism continuing under the guise of angels, devils, saints, and so on. When Westerners admired another culture, they interpreted, if not created, a high god for that culture, so as not to be forced to consider the culture inferior.

Ricci overlaid a Christian patriarchal and European feudal structure on the Chinese religious understanding, creating by 1583 the concept of the "Master of Heaven" (Tianzhu), incorrectly understood as the primary Chinese deity, and using this term as the translation for God (Gernet 1985:26). This application of European ideology to a non-Western culture is identical to the contemporaneous Jesuit creation of the "Master of Life" in regard to native American religions (Paper 1983b). The sixteenth-century Jesuit view of both traditions has persisted to this day among at least some Western historians of religions.

In Ricci's understanding, Chinese polytheism, with its focus on ancestral and ghost spirits and the complementary dualistic female Earth–male Sky nonanthropomorphic deities, was subsidiary to a male singular high god:

> From the very beginning of their history it is recorded that they recognized and worshipped one supreme being whom they called the King of Heaven, or designated by some other name indicating his rule over heaven and earth. (Ricci 1953: 93)

We shall further discuss Ricci's attitude towards female spirits and the continuation and consequences of these views up to the present, in Chapter 8.

Nonrecognition of Popular Practice

In Europe, Jesuits served as confessors to powerful political figures. Ricci focused his mission on the Chinese elite. He followed the Jesuit missionary tactic, which assumed that if the leaders of a society could be converted, they would bring the people they led with them to Christianity. Becoming a member of the Chinese elite himself, both his attitude that the common people were unimportant and his lifestyle left him unconcerned with popular religious practices, which he considered idolatry. Hence, he did not connect the religious rituals of the state and the powerful clans with those of the common people. He did not understand that all these rituals had a common basis and structure.

The Franciscan missionaries, who lived among the common people, developed a very different attitude toward the state rituals, which they saw as idolatry, and the Jesuit participation in it as heresy. Although their viewpoint was ultimately successful in the Vatican, it did not change the European understanding of religion in China. Historians of religions, until quite recently, continued to focus on elite traditions, leaving study of the religious practices of the vast majority of the Chinese to missionaries, sociologists, and anthropologists.

Transcendence and Faith

The Western focus on transcendence in the study of religion put considerably greater emphasis on Daoism and Buddhism in Chinese religion than can be justified by any available measure of their relative importance. The Daoist goal of becoming a *xian* (see Chapter 3) has interested only a small minority of the elite, at least since the medieval period. Popular practices understood to be related to Daoism usually have pragmatic ends. Similarly, the Buddhist goal of nirvana in China became amalgamated with

rituals directed toward departed members of the family and toward material benefits in this life. Again, only a few, primarily of
the elite, oriented their lifestyles to the Buddhist concepts of transcendence. The emphasis on transcendence in the Western understanding of religion has biased religionists away from studying
normative Chinese religious behavior and understanding.

Definitions of religion based on the centrality of faith, a particularly Christian notion, ipso facto determine virtually all
educated Chinese to be irreligious, supporting the Chinese understanding that religion is alien to Chinese culture. For missionaries, China appeared to be ripe for conversion, the elite seen as
agnostic, and the peasants, sunk in ignorant idolatry. That the
Chinese intelligentsia, at least since Xunzi, could consider a major object of religious ritual to be maintenance of the social fabric itself (see Chapter 2) is beyond Western religious and most
scholarly understanding.

Many Western scholars have since interpreted ambiguous
statements attributed to Kongfuzi in the *Lunyu* (Analects) to indicate that he was himself agnostic, the precursor of an attitude
towards the supernatural among the late Zhou elite that matched
the attitudes of many twentieth-century sinologists. "This change
reflects what many scholars have already described as an apparent but unexplained rise of rationalism in Chinese culture in this
period" (Mote 1971:22). What these Western scholars did not realize was that these assumed super-rationalists were also being
ritually possessed by ancestral spirits (see Chapter 4) and putting themselves into trance for aesthetic pursuits (see Chapter 6).

Religious Pluralism

Sixteenth-century Europe understood different religions as essentially hostile to each other; indeed, only with Vatican II in the second half of the twentieth century has this attitude begun to
change. For Christianity, other religions were intolerable because
there was only a single truth. Judaism was anathema because it
was a constant reminder of an alternate understanding of Jesus.
Islam was a hated political and military rival. Indigenous European religions had long been brutally suppressed. It was incon-

ceivable that distinct religious traditions could coexist as elements of a larger religious complex, as was the case in China and other non-Western complex cultures.

Hence, Ricci found religious pluralism where none was present. The long-established Chinese term, *san-jiao*, meaning the "Three Doctrines," was reinterpreted by Ricci to mean "Three Sects," a very different concept. Ricci was well aware that his understanding was not the Chinese one:

> The most common opinion today among those who believe themselves to be the most wise is to say that these three sects are one and the same thing and can be observed at once. By this they deceive themselves and others too. (*Fontani Ricciani* 1, 32 in Gernet 1985: 64)

Ricci was adamant that the literati only adhered to the Confucian "sect" and would never "belong to any other sect." He apparently was completely oblivious to the important role of Daoist and Buddhist ideology and practices among the elite, as is normative, for example, in literati aesthetics (see Chapters 6 and 7). More important, the term *san-jiao*, in effect, excludes the vast majority of Chinese religious behaviors: the sacrificial complex found at all levels of society.

Ricci's sixteenth-century interpretation became a religious studies dogma, persisting to this day. This understanding was reinforced in this century by Soothill's popular volume *The Three Religions of China*, first published in 1913. It begins, "There are three recognized religions in China . . . and the three religions may be considered as three aspects of the established religion of the country." The latter phrase, as well as its inconsistency with the former, has been ignored by the authors of world religions textbooks, where the "fact" of three religions in China is a virtual constant. Texts treating Chinese religion as singular were not published until the mid-twentieth century, the most important being Laurence Thompson's *Chinese Religion, An Introduction*, first published in 1969 (see Girardot 1992).

It is still difficult for most Western historians of religion to understand that religion in China is a single complex of considerable antiquity, held together by the practice of frequent ritual offerings of elaborate meals to departed members of the family and to nature spirits, and embellished by many related subsidiary practices, including fertility rituals and rituals of social bonding. Perhaps it is time that we took Ricci's Chinese critics seriously.

Social science approaches have not only enormously enhanced our understanding of modern Chinese religion, but increasingly of the past as well. For example, applying modern historical techniques to the study of popular culture in the past, Valerie Hansen has recently determined the inception of popular religion as found in modern culture to the Southern Song period (twelfth–thirteenth-centuries), an inception due to socioeconomic transitions. Hansen, trained as a historian, had to struggle with the Western understanding of Chinese religion as three religions, none of them highly relevant to popular religion:

> Something . . . has puzzled me since my first visit to Taiwan. I had assumed Chinese people would categorize their own religious beliefs much as we did. . . . All Chinese, I had reasoned would similarly be Buddhist, Daoist, or Confucian. To my surprise, none of the people I met identified themselves as such. And, as far as I could tell, they all attended the same Buddhist, Daoist, and popular religious temples. (Hansen 1990:ix)

A revision of this widely held understanding would have saved her and other scholars from the constant need to tilt at the windmill of "Three Religions in China."

Recent Trends in Western Studies of Chinese Religion

Until a few decades ago, a Christian profession was a de facto, a priori requirement to study non-Western religions at the major American university history of religions graduate programs; the qualifying examination for a research doctorate (Ph.D.) was identical or similar to the requirements for a theological (M.Th.) or practical ministerial (B.D.) degree. Since the mid-1960's, however, the expectations of religious studies faculties have changed;

graduate students are no longer expected to be qualified Christian ministers to do advanced study in religion.

Shifting from the Divinity School of the University of Chicago to the Oriental Institute in 1961 to study Chinese religion, I was taught by H. G. Creel that Chinese culture was superior to Western culture in that it had no religion. Another scholar of the same generation has articulated this view in a major compilation of Chinese philosophical and religious texts: "Indeed, as compared to Japan and India, the dominant traditions of Chinese thought have been less markedly religious in character, there being a noticeable disjunction between the popular practice of religion and the intellectual activity of the ruling elite, which has a more secular orientation" (de Bary 1960:1:v). The popular practice of religion is considered at the tail end of the same work and discussed only in pejorative terms. Labelled "popular cults and superstition," some being "grosser forms of superstition," "primitive Chinese religion" is understood "to subsist on a low cultural level" and is imbued with a "facile syncretism." But the elite were above the ignorant masses, since "there has been a strong tendency in China for the educated and the uneducated to go their separate ways in matters of religion" (2:285–86).

It took me a dozen years to begin to realize the fallacy of these attitudes. Many of the generation of scholars trained after me, fortunately, have been relatively free of these influences and have begun to analyze its motivating factors:

> What [H. G. Creel and Fung Yu-lan] and many other modern interpreters, seem to project is a sort of generic "protestant" attitude, an attitude that generally abhors ritual and virtually every form of social religious activity, and esteems instead an individualistic striving for a more abstract spiritual exaltation. (Kirkland 1992:79)

It is this orientation toward China that has pervaded religious studies, an orientation radically different from modern social science studies of Chinese religion. The latter approaches actually examine religious behavior in China and find, it would seem, a very different culture. For China is not bicultural,

14 THE SPIRITS ARE DRUNK

although there are of course a range of cultural behaviors. Aside from the Imperial family, the elite were not a hereditary caste. Entree to elite status was based on written examinations, and biographical studies indicate that families tended to maintain this status for an average of no more than three generations. Moreover, there was a substantial middle class of professionals, government clerks, and others, many of whom were part of the social and intellectual millieu of the elite. As will be argued in Chapter 2, the basic religious practices of all Chinese are essentially the same, only the details vary according to region and status.

When religious studies departments multiplied in North America during the late 1960s and early 1970s, some scholars of Chinese philosophy, particularly students and colleagues of the scholar of Neo-Confucianism, Wm. Theodore de Bary, quoted above, declared themselves scholars of religion, without changing their methodology, subject, or attitudes. As Kirkland (1992:83, n.16) succinctly analyzes: Confucianism's

> religious dimension has been Protestantized by interpreters like [Rodney] Taylor and Tu Wei-ming to the point that there seems to be little meaningful explanation for the traditional Confucian cultus. One need hardly mention that Tu's vision of Confucianism is even more thoroughly sanitized, purified of any lingering cultural baggage that might put off the modern individual.

A number of younger sinologists trained in the new, more open religious studies programs also became familiar with social science methodologies. This development has led to new approaches to the study and understanding of Chinese religion by historians of religions, and this has born fruit in the last decade. No longer has the study of Chinese religion per se by default been left only to anthropologists and sociologists (e.g., Ahern 1973, Jordan 1972). Of several historians of religions, one could point to Norman Girardot's major comparative study (1983), Julian Pas' many studies of popular Chinese religion (e.g., 1984), and the fruitful collaboration of Daniel Overmyer with David Jordan (1986). The number of recent excellent studies on Buddhism and Daoism, as well as those in the realm of ritual studies, substantially increases this list.

Traditional Chinese Elite Values and Marxism

The traditional Chinese elite developed out of a protohistoric warrior-priestly hereditary class. These functions were not separated as in the early Near Eastern and Indo-European–speaking civilizations. With the development of kingship, the clan chieftain of the ruling clan became the chief priest of the state. The king or, after the third century B.C.E., the emperor was understood as the one person who could sacrifice to the most powerful spirits.

As the elite shifted from a hereditary class to one based on passing a series of written examinations, the elite functioned as assisting and deputy priests in the performance of the state sacrifices. Their education included texts on ritual; approximately 60 percent of the contents of the Five Classics, excluding texts utilized as commentaries, consists of explicit texts on ritual. Simultaneous with this development was a transformation in the interpretation of the rituals, whose focus shifted from spirits to humans. Rituals from the third century B.C.E. came to be understood in China from an indigenous sociological perspective.

With a reorientation in values from spirits to society, the elite came to view the religious understanding of those not formally educated with a mild disdain, even though their practices differed little in essence from those of the elite. Popular religion, other than the family sacrifices, was understood as *xie* (heterodox). However, when the elite functioned as local magistrates, they were practical enough to follow local understanding for functional purposes. For example, Han Yu (768–824), who was exiled for arguing that the emperor should not follow repugnant alien Buddhist practices, sacrificed to a local crocodile deity when exiled to the far South as a magistrate (*Ji o yu wen*, in Birch 1965:1:253–55).

In periods of Chinese revitalization, nonelite religious professionals such as Daoist priests were treated with suspicion. Monks and nuns not only were understood to violate filial piety, the basis of Chinese ethics, but were also the butt of ribald humor (e.g., "The Monk's Billet-Doux" in Yang and Yang 1957:64–76).

The adaptation of Marxist-Leninist thought strengthened this attitude. The labeling of popular religion as *mixin* (superstition) in the modernization movement of the early twentieth century (Duara 1991) accorded with the understanding of religion as "the opiate of the people," particularly when elite sacrificial practices were not identified as religion. It was expected that with universal literacy and mass education, religion would disappear as other "feudal" remnants had. Professional religious, as in the past, were treated with suspicion and considered unproductive leeches on society.

The temples reopened during the last decade are served by Buddhist and Daoist clergy under centralized institutions subject to government control and earning salaries supplied by the government. Although some are dedicated to the traditional nun and monk's lifestyle (see Chapter 6 for contemporary examples), others wear the garb of the monk or nun on the job but return to home and family after working hours.

Religion in Contemporary China

From a foreign relations standpoint, the convergence of traditional and modern attitudes toward religion created a problem. Western countries consider freedom of religion a mark of modern civilization. Although often honored more in theory than in practice in the West—considering the continued suppression of aboriginal religions in Australia, Canada, and the United States—lack of religious freedom is used to disparage nations considered unfriendly. Hence, Communist China placed freedom of religion in its constitution.

Furthermore, countries contiguous to China are heavily Buddhist, and China could improve foreign relations by projecting a Buddhist image. Buddhism continued in China under traditional state control. As Daoism tends to be understood as an indigenous version of Buddhism, to continue limited Buddhist institutions required limited continuation of Daoist institutions as a balance. Besides, there has been a growing interest in Daoist studies outside of China, along with a growing consideration of

Daoism as *the* Chinese religion, which has in turn influenced its increased internal recognition. With the recent rise of travel by Chinese on Taiwan to mainland China, Daoist centers for the initiation of those from Taiwan have developed into a source of foreign exchange.

Many in the western parts of China are Muslim and China wishes to continue friendly relations with Muslim countries; so Islam continues to be openly practiced in China. Minority cultures within China are allowed to maintain aspects of their traditions and many of their religious practices.

But only institutional religions (*jiao*) and the practices of non-Han minorities are accorded nominal religious freedom. As Chinese religion per se is officially deemed "superstition" rather than "religion," it is not accorded any protection.

All of these aspects of Chinese religion suffered considerably, as did all Chinese traditions, during the Cultural Revolution (1966–76). However, the last decade has witnessed a growing resurgence of religious practices. In this regard, at least two contradictory factors affect Chinese religion per se. On the one hand, Chinese religion centers on a sacrificial complex based on the patrilineal family, but this focus is contrary to the extreme need in China for population control. It would be virtually impossible to carry on the single-child policy while it is considered religiously essential for each family to have a male heir (see Paper and Paper 1994a). On the other hand, the Chinese government has recognized that the destructive aspects of the Cultural Revolution left a culture without a basis for "civil behavior." Aspects of traditional Chinese culture and religion are being revived as a socializing force. The incompatibility of these two needs have yet to be harmonized, and the repeated swings of government policy have left the population unsure about what are politically safe activities. However, the shift away from Communist economic theory and the resultant opportunities, as well as uncertainties, have increased the need for spiritual support, so that the practice of traditional religion is becoming both visible and of seemingly long duration (see Paper 1992).

The Study of Religion in China

In 1964, the Institute for Research on World Religions (Shijie zongjiao yanjiusuo) was developed within the Chinese Academy of Social Sciences (for details, see Seiwert et al. 1989). The organization reflected the Western understanding of Chinese religion discussed above; hence its title and mandate. It was also organized to criticize religion and to promote Marxist-Leninist atheism. However, its activities were soon terminated by the Cultural Revolution. In 1977, the Institute again began to function, publishing several journals. The primary one, *Shijie zongjiao yanjiu* (Research in World Religions), was first published in 1979. Beginning with a single annual issue, by the third year the journal was being issued quarterly. An analysis of the articles contained in the journal serves to delineate the Institute's research priorities and methodologies.

In the first issue, a third of the articles were on Buddhism, a third concerned atheism and Marxist issues and the remainder of the articles were on Islam and Christianity. In summary, all the articles concerned religions of alien origin. The second issue (1980) added several articles on Daoism, one on minorities, and one on the study of religion as a Western phenomenon.

After the first two years, a fairly consistent pattern developed in the distribution of articles. An analysis of the issues from 1979 through 1986, excluding translated articles, indicates that 80 percent of the articles covered five topics: Buddhism (39 percent), Taoism (14 percent), Islam (10 percent), minorities (9 percent), and atheism/socialism and religion (8 percent). Most issues had one or two articles on Zoroastrianism or Manichaeism. More variable were the articles on Christianity and on Chinese philosophy. There were also a few articles on Hinduism, Jainism, Judaism, protohistoric Chinese religion, pre-Buddhist Tibet, Shinto, art and religion, Western philosophy, and primal religion. In the last few years, there have been two new topics which will be discussed below.

Although the Institute for Research on World Religions is the most prestigious center for research on religion in China, several provincial academies of social sciences also have sections devoted to the study of religion, particularly local aspects

INTRODUCTION: THE STUDY OF CHINESE RELIGION   19

(except for the institute in Shanghai, which focuses on Christianity). Approximately a half dozen universities also have units focusing on the study of religion, often as part of a philosophy department, as is the case in many American colleges. Members of these various programs are among those who publish in *Shijie zongjiao yanjiu*.

Generally, those interested in aspects of Chinese religion other than Buddhism, Daoism, Islam, and Christianity work outside of these institutions (except for the Yunnan Academy of Social Sciences). Most articles on the religion of minorities in China are by researchers at the Academy of Social Sciences Institute for Research on Minorities (equivalent to the Western discipline of ethnology) and allied institutions. Those interested in primal religions and protohistoric Chinese religion include researchers at the National Historical Museum.

China has a long history of textual and historical studies, and the World Religions Institute's methodological orientation reflects this scholarly tradition. Although the Institute is part of the Chinese Academy of Social Science, the available social science methodologies are considerably dated. While Marx and Engels are among the founders of Western social science, methodologies available in China until quite recently had been frozen by Stalin's preferences and understanding. From conversations I had in Beijing in 1986, those interested in comparative religion apparently were aware of only Morgan for anthropology (who influenced Engels) and Frazer for history of religions. Now (1992) Durkheim, Lévi-Strauss, and perhaps other social scientists are becoming available to Chinese scholars.

Over the last decade, scholars have been sent to the West from the Institute. Usually, they were given specific assignments that reflected the bias toward alien religions and textual and historical studies. The scholar who is now director of theoretical studies at the Institute studied with Hans Küng, the Liberal Catholic theologian, leading to an assumption that theology and religious studies are one and the same in the West. However, association with Western scholars has increased the awareness at the Institute of other subjects and approaches. These effects are apparent in articles of the more recent past.

In 1984, in the second issue of the Institute's journal there were three articles on shamanism. There are a few scholars in China, both Han and non-Han, interested in analyzing early Chinese culture from this perspective. Such an approach requires comparative methodologies. In the same year, there was an article on Chinese popular religion written by a member of the Institute (X. Ma 1984). Although written from a Marxist perspective, it was the first indication of an awareness of popular Chinese religion at the Institute.

1986 saw the first publication of an article on contemporary Western methodologies in the study of religion: Bellah's concept of civil religion (Yen 1986). The article was written by a specialist on Christianity at the Institute. Also in 1986 appeared an article written by a member of the Institute indicating a revised understanding of religion. In this article (Mu 1986), religion is discussed as a universal human phenomenon, and the dominant aspect of Chinese religion as well as other aspects of indigenous religion are discussed as important subjects of study. The article also indicates an interest in comparative religion through an exploration of those features that distinguish Chinese religion from religions of other cultures.

More recently, early-twentieth-century classics in Western religious studies have begun to be translated into Chinese (so far, works by Schmidt and Malinowski). As these developments continue, far-reaching consequences for the study of religion in China can be expected. Hence, an article reviewing the sociology of religion was published in *Shijie zongjiao yanjiu* (Peng and Zheng 1988).

The Chinese Association for the Study of Religion was formed in 1979 with a rather complex history (see Seiwert et al. 1989). Contacts have been increasing with Western educational institutions and scholarly societies, and the above named association has affiliated with the International Association for the History of Religions (IAHR). In 1992, an IAHR regional conference, sponsored by the Chinese Association for the Study of Religion, was held in Beijing (see Jochim 1992).

In summary, until quite recently, the study of religion in China has been limited by a number of factors: Religion was seen

as both an alien and an undesirable phenomenon; the methodological focus was on textual and historical studies; and available social science methodologies were nearly a century out of
date. However, even with setbacks, the recent opening to the West
seems to be engendering, as this is written in 1993, a new understanding of the possibilities of religious studies. The study of
Chinese religion per se by Chinese scholars should lead to an ex-
citing era of scholarly pursuit in the history of religions.

The Study of Religion in Taiwan

Since 1949, a number of Chinese educational institutions founded
by Christian missionary orders has continued on Taiwan, after
moving from the Chinese mainland. Religious studies were limited to these institutions and to Christian seminaries, where a few
Western-trained historians of religion can be found (e.g., Cai
1989). Both Buddhist and Daoist institutions continued their studies of their own traditions. However, the increasing social importance of new aspects of Chinese religion, the interest of a few
scholars in studies of popular religion from a religious studies
rather than a sociological perspective (e.g., Zhen 1988), and a start
in institutionalizing popular religion—for example, the formation
of a new society of *lingji* mediums in 1989 with 1,940 members
(see Chapter 4)—has led to a recent rise of interest in Chinese
religion as a whole.

In September 1989, the first conference on popular Chinese
religion was held on Taiwan, sponsored by a Chinese university
literature department and by newly formed religious movements
and religious institutions. Confirming the confusion in China
over the Western understanding of Chinese religion noted above,
the conference title, "Zhunghua minzu zongjiao guoji xueshu
huiyi," (Chinese Popular Religion International Scholarly Conference) was originally and incorrectly translated as "International Conference on Taoism." Following input from Western
scholars (including my own), the translation was changed to "International Conference on Chinese Religion." Future conferences
may instigate the formation of religious studies departments in
non-Christian Chinese universities. At present, the major diffi-

culty hindering this development is the association of the word *religion* with sectarian factors. Since "Chinese religion" tends to be understood as either Daoism or Buddhism, both claim control of religious studies.

2   the essence of chinese religion

Common Chinese greeting: "Chi meiyou?" (Have you eaten?)

As discussed in the preceding chapter, our understanding of religion in China is far from clear. Students of religion have applied Western concepts to the Chinese gestalt, creating artificial constructs that fit the Western understanding of religion. An example of this approach is that of the sociologist, C. K. Yang, who in his now classic *Religion in Chinese Society* consciously avoided going beyond the Western model:

> To lay emphasis on nonsupernatural religious forces as a factor in the social order would require extensive examination of the entire ontology and value system of a culture. . . . Any elaborate consideration of this aspect of religion lies beyond the scope of this study. (1967:2)

Over a quarter century has passed since the above statement was written, and there has been sufficient study to create an understanding of Chinese religion in and of itself based on indigenous concepts and practices.

With regard to the normative understanding of the Chinese situation as a collection of religions, Maurice Freedman (1974:20) has written:

> A Chinese religion exists; or, at any rate, we ought to begin with that assumption: the religious ideas and practices of the Chinese are not a congeries of haphazardly assembled elements, all appearances and the greater part of the extensive literature to the contrary.

23

His underlying assumption is not unlike that made by de Groot (1910), who anticipated the methodology of participant-observation. De Groot included the following in his diary entry for 9 June 1886:

> I attend almost every religious festival of the people and take notes. It does not take long and I discover the thread that runs through everything and just about everything becomes crystal clear. (Translated by Werblowsky 1990:65)

Students of Yang and Freedman have produced a number of studies, based on conferences bringing together anthropologists, sociologists, and historians. For example, the published papers from a conference on Chinese death rituals place priority on religious behavior over ideology:

> A proper performance of the rites . . . was of paramount importance in determining who was and who was not deemed to be fully "Chinese." Performance, in other words, took precedence over belief—it mattered little what one believed about death or the afterlife as long as the rites were properly performed. (J. L. Watson 1988:4)

The following analysis only differs from this statement in arguing that it is not ritual alone or a specific set of rituals (e.g., death rituals) that distinguishes Chinese religion, but an essential aspect of virtually all Chinese rituals: the offering and sharing of food.

This interest in the study of religious behavior has spread to historians of religions as well: the works of Julian Pas already mentioned and Hubert Seiwert's (1985) important monograph on religion in Taiwan. A major issue has become the relationship between elite and nonelite cultures.

My own position in regard to the usual bicameral interpretation of Chinese culture (e.g., Stover 1974) was highly influenced by the concepts of Clifford Geertz and a conversation with Michael Saso many years ago, who pointed out a middle class composed of government clerks, professionals (e.g., physicians), merchants, and farmers of moderate circumstances. From this group developed local poetry circles, Daoist priests, and so on. Accordingly, rather than the "great" and "little" traditions of Robert Redfield or other schemes for cultural dichotomies, there is rather a continuum. The basis of this continuum, I would argue, is a fundamental religious understanding, of which there are infinite subtle variations, given the immense diachronic and synchronic spread of Chinese culture.

Catherine Bell (1989:42–43) has determined

> A third-stage approach to Chinese religion [that] can be said to reject both a priori bifurcations as well as synthetic entities that mediate them . . . Third-stage approaches do not isolate religious institutions—or religion per se—as the data of analysis; rather, they focus on symbols and rituals in which they see the dynamics of culture played out. Thus, this third-stage approach presupposes a particular perspective for the definition and understanding of religious phenomena and, correspondingly, implies a distinct theory of religion as a fully embedded cultural system.

Bell's description of a third-stage approach not only fits the approach in this chapter, but also the following chapters of this book.

Chinese Ritual and Cultural Continuity

Contemporary Chinese culture is obviously far removed from that of a century ago, but this facile observation is also true of the other major world cultures. However, few would posit that there is no relationship between the China of today and that of the past. Consideration of these relationships is in part a matter of perspective: historians of modern China tend to see radical transformation; historians of the traditional periods may focus on continuity within the transition. Apparent continuity, as Joseph Levenson (1968:3:112) pointed out regarding aspects of contemporary China, may lead to false analogies "if by ignoring historical context one takes likenesses for changelessness." Yet apparent discontinuity may conceal continuity and genuine analogies, as Richard Drinnon (1980) demonstrated in relating the Puritan massacre of the Pequots on Block Island in 1636 to the American involvement in Vietnam three and a quarter centuries later.

Comparison of chronological periods within a single culture requires distinct parameters that exhibit continuity over time. Such parameters may not always be obvious. The form of a cultural phenomenon may remain stable while its essence radically shifts, or vice versa. An essential feature of Chinese culture is ritual, as noted not only by the Chinese themselves, but by virtually all Western observers of China. In the nineteenth century, S. W. Williams (1883:1:424) wrote, "No nation has paid so much attention to [ceremonies] . . . the importance . . . elevated etiquette and ritual into a kind of crystallizing force which has molded Chinese character in many ways." Arthur Smith (1899:193) wrote, "Ceremony is the very life of the Chinese."

Unfortunately, as discussed in the previous chapter, the tendency to focus on ideology in religious studies has led to an exaggerated emphasis on the *sanjiao* (Three Doctrines), misunderstood in the West as "Three Religions" since the late sixteenth century. This approach ignores most of Chinese religious behavior, which, as will be demonstrated, is singular and relatively homogeneous throughout China proper. Accordingly, Chinese religion is best studied through an examination of ritual patterns.

In this chapter, it will be argued that a singular, specific core of Chinese ritual can be determined and traced from the Neolithic period to the present. This core, in essence, is a communal meal which is often shared with (sacrificed to) spirits, primarily ancestral. An awareness of this ritual core is the key to understanding Chinese religion.

Ritual and Religion in Chinese Culture

Religion is a Western concept, and its identification within Chinese culture is not readily apparent. As described in Chapter 1, the modern Chinese translation, *zongjiao*, tends to be applied in China to basically alien phenomena: Buddhism, Islam, and Christianity. The recent rapid growth of Daoist (*Daojiao*) studies in the West has led some scholars to the view that Daoism is *the* indigenous Chinese religion. However, Daoism has never been dominant in China, although it has been at times quite important, as, for example, when promoted for political expediency by the Tang emperors who claimed descent from Laozi (see Benn 1987). (*Xuanxue* ["abstruse learning," usually mistranslated as "Neo-Taoism"], popular among intellectuals in the early third century, was an outgrowth of *rujia* [Paper 1987b].) Hence, such an identification still leaves a major void.

.The above three models for religion alien to China focus on ideology, while a growing consensus recognizes that in China, ritual rather than belief, or behavior rather than ideology, is of primary importance. G. W. Skinner (quoted in Ho 1975:325) has indicated this in regard to elite culture:

> [Xunzi's] statement called attention to the agnosticism of the elite religion, to the central place of rites within it, to its this-worldly orientation, and to its social purpose. . . . But the rites were no less important for this agnosticism. The emphasis was on the rites themselves, not their object.

Steven Harrell (1979:520) has emphasized the related aspect in popular culture: "The perspective of folk religion is fundamentally *active*; believers experience religious reality directly through purposeful behavior, especially ritual."

In his analysis of the late Zhou (sixth-through-third centuries B.C.E.) transformation of ritual (*li*), Noah Fehl (1971:3) notes, "In part *li* takes the place of, rather than constitutes, what in the western or the middle eastern world is meant by religion or even morality." In other words, *li* is functionally equivalent to "religion" in the West. Similar to Skinner, Fehl (1971:194) attributes this concept of *li* to Xunzi:

> What he offered was a rationalist yet deeply sympathetic analysis of the individual in society, a psychology of *li* and especially of those *li* which, like religion, lead men over the crucial thresholds of birth, marriage and death.

But Fehl (1971:208), by the end of his study, dropped "alternative" to refer directly to *li* as religion:

> A final, and possibly the finest, tribute of Hsün Ch'ing [Xunzi] to Chou [Zhou] culture was partial insight, anticipating Schleiermacher by over two millennia, that religion is primarily a response of the feelings rather than the intel-

lect. It is social, practical and personal rather than metaphysical or theological.

Fehl (1971:191) dates the transformation of ritual to Xunzi:

> ... it was not until the fourth century B.C. that the mind of China turned from a preoccupation with the spirits to an effective concentration upon man and those matters that were in his control.

However, Herbert Fingarette (1972:16–17) places the transition over a century earlier with Kongfuzi (Confucius):

> Spirit is no longer an external being influenced by the ceremony; it is that that is expressed and comes most alive *in* the ceremony. Instead of being diversion of attention from the human realm to another transcendental realm, the overtly holy ceremony is to be seen as the central symbol, both expressive of and participating in the holy as a dimension of all truly human existence. Explicitly Holy Rite [*li*] is thus a luminous point of concentration in the greater and ideally all-inclusive ceremonial harmony of the perfectly humane civilization of the *Tao* [Dao], or ideal way. Human life in its entirety finally appears as one vast, spontaneous and holy Rite: the community of man. This, for Confucius, was indeed an "ultimate concern."

To Fehl's and Fingarette's analyses, however, should be added the Chinese understanding that the concept of "human" included both the living and the dead. Furthermore, it was during the sacrificial rituals that the living and the dead intersect, that the dead become present in the living (see Chapter 4).

Thus, it has been argued with regard to elite culture that *li* corresponds to major aspects of our concept of "religion." This is equally true of popular culture. As Saso (1990:1) has succinctly stated with regard to the modern context:

> Chinese religion can be defined as a cultural system that governs the rites of passage and the annual festivals celebrated by the people of China. It is to be distinguished from Confucianism, folk Buddhism and Taoism, which give ritual norms and ethical values to the religious system, and from Buddhist, Christian and Islamic religious belief systems

which entered China from abroad. Unlike these latter faiths, Chinese religion is not a belief system . . . and has survived all attempts to usurp its preeminent, fundamental position at the roots of Chinese cultural and social life.

Although the understanding of the rituals was radically transformed during the late Zhou period, especially among the elite, the form, as will be demonstrated, continued in the main unchanged. To be determined is the essential nature of the form itself.

Ritual and Myth in Chinese Religion: Digression I

Western scholarship of the past understood ritual in conjunction with myth, the two having been integrally related:

> We find that these early ritual patterns consisted not only of things done but of things said. . . . In general, the spoken part of a ritual consists of a description of what is being done, it is the story which the ritual enacts. This is the sense in which the term "myth" is used in our discussion. (Hooke 1933:3)

Studies have sought to demonstrate that ritual was predominantly religious drama in the ancient Near East (Jacobsen 1975). Although this viewpoint was countered over a half century ago by Kluckhohn (1942), correlation between ritual and myth is still considered to be universal by those unacquainted with the relevant scholarship: "The facet of religious ceremonial that appears to be distinctly human is its seemingly inevitable association with myth" (d'Aquili and Laughlin 1979:160).

Accordingly, in regard to Chinese religion, the use of the word *ritual* has been considered incorrect with the term *ceremonial* substituted, and the study of Chinese religion has often been skewed:

> Those familiar with the scattered earlier research in this field [Chinese "ceremonies"] . . . will recall that there has been a prevalent tendency to make the cosmological dimensions primary, and to subordinate the social dimensions to them. Neither the multi-functional approach . . . nor the considerable emphasis of Chinese theorists on the hierarchy-maintenance and teaching and exemplary functions of ceremony will support such an interpretation. (Wills 1979:56, n. 1)

It is to be understood that Chinese culture is hardly unique in that ritual has primacy over myth. In native American cultures, for example, religious activity (i.e., ritual), as in Chinese culture, may predominate over the exposition of myth:

> There was a lot of ceremony or action than verbal instruction in Indian activities, like the medicine pipe ceremony. In the Protestant Church there is a lot of verbal direction and less action. (Alan Wolf Leg orally articulating the thoughts of Blackfoot elders in Waugh and Prithipaul 1979:5)

Ritual may be phenomenologically defined as "a fixed, usually solemn behavior that is repeated in certain situations" (Hultkrantz 1979:36). These situations tend to fall into two groups: major changes in the life cycle and in the year cycle (in Victor Turner's [1969] terms: "life-crisis rituals and rituals of induction" and "calendrical rites and rites of group crisis"). The types of situations have been well enumerated for China by Wills (1979:47).

Åke Hultkrantz (1979:135), dean of native American religious studies, has found an evolutionary phenomenon in his area of studies that is, I suggest, also germane to Chinese culture:

> A ritual is a system of fixed behavior, and it sometimes tends to move away from the belief system that once motivated it. We know this to be the case in stratified societies where the official cult may have very little relation to the living beliefs.

This encapsulates the circumstances in China, beginning in the late Chou period, in regard to elite rituals. Chinese theorists of the period, especially Xunzi, shifted the emphasis on ritual per se from relationship to supernatural and natural powers to sociopolitical as well as aesthetic-emotional needs. Han (206 B.C.E. to 220 C.E.) theorists, such as Dong Zhongshu, elaborated imperial rituals on synthetic and complex cosmological models that would have borne little relevance for the vast majority of the population.

In popular Chinese religion, the increasing complexity of social stratification terminated vicarious peasant participation in the elite rituals as implied in the *Shi* (Odes, ca. eighth to sixth centuries B.C.E., see Karlgren 1950) and eventually led to the partial adoption of elite clan sacrificial rituals by the peasantry. These developments could only have taken place because myth was not essential to these rituals. The early ruling clans traced their descent from mythic beings or deities, and their deceased clan chiefs became powerful spirits, but family sacrificial meals involved ancestors ranging from legendary figures to those of immediate memory, according to the family's status. Clearly the pattern of activity was essential and mythic origin inconsequential, or the ritual meal could not have become the basic religious pattern of all families, including those in areas into which Chinese culture spread. In the following sections of this chapter, we will briefly trace the development of primary rituals in China to determine their central feature(s).

Protohistoric Clan Ritual

Except for inscriptions on oracular material and mythic remnants whose authenticity cannot be established definitively, our knowledge of protohistoric China, the Shang period (ca. 1500–1000 B.C.E.), is based on material remains. Of these nonperishable remains, bronze vessels for the preparation of sacrificial meals are the most impressive in quantity and quality and in respect to the proportion of the surplus productivity that must have gone into their manufacture (see Chapter 3).

Shang and probably earlier ritual had two foci: divination and sacrifice; indeed, the former may have been less ritual than part of the government's decision-making process (although in China government and ritual were inseparable). The sacrifices, judging from the types of vessels encountered and the limited epigraphic remains, were of prepared (and probably unprepared) food.

Early Historic Clan Ritual

The earliest literary descriptions of rituals are found in the Shi. One ode describes a sacrifice to the soil (Ode 239) of a yellow (probably fermented) liquid, clear wine, a red bull, and oak firewood. All other sacrifices described are clan sacrificial meals. (Marcel Granet [1929] found a number of different rituals described in the odes, but his analyses of many are questionable.) These sacrificial rituals originated, according to Zhou (the dynasty succeeding the Shang) myth, with their mythic ancestor, the Lord of Millet (Houji). Offerings (no. 245) included steamed millet, fat burned over wood, and roast and broiled mutton from a sacrificed ram. The Shang odes mention autumn and winter clan sacrificial meals (nos. 301–3); the Zhou, spring, summer, and autumn (no. 300). The meal was offered by the clan chief (the king) to his deceased parents (no. 282) and the clan ancestors in general.

Among these odes, some of which may have been sung as part of the ritual, no. 200 furnishes the outline of the sacrificial meal. Every aspect of the ceremony, including the preparation, was ritualized. The killing of certain animals at specified locations was followed by the preparation of a banquet with invited guests (no. 280), music and dance (no. 300), and a ritual archery contest (no. 246). A person chosen to incorporate the ancestor (see Chapter 4) first drank and ate from the many prepared dishes (for a list, see Bilsky 1975:74–75) until satiated and then announced the satisfaction of the spirits who subsequently departed. The male members of the clan then ate the sacrificial food (as the female members may have separately), in an atmosphere of merriment. The clan members and, it is assumed, invited guests ate until satiated and drank until inebriated as had the clan spirits. Inebriation demonstrated the bountiful gifts of the ancestors in recompense for the gifts of the living to them (no. 247). It also indicates alcohol-induced trance as an essential aspect of the ritual (see Chapter 4).

Texts other than the *Shi* (the *Liji* and *Zhouli*) confirm this description of the rituals: "The central feature of all rites was the offerings that were given to the deities" (Bilsky 1975:71). The basic features of the sacrificial rites continued into the later Zhou period (ending in the third century B.C.E.; for a description, see Bilsky 1975:117–24).

However, with the slow collapse of the Zhou clan's centralized royal authority, the clan sacrificial meal rituals were adopted by the rulers of the increasingly independent states. Furthermore, the relationships between ancestral spirits and nature deities were dissociated. Sacrifices to the local nature gods increased in importance and were different from the ancestral rites. Blood from the animal victims became a major offering and the animals, grains, wine, and other (humans, silks, jade) offerings were burned, buried in soil, and thrown into rivers, etc. (Bilsky 1975:179).

It was at the end of this period that rituals were consciously developed for their social effects. Aside from the family-oriented sacrificial rituals, popular religion seems to have been considered superstition by the late Zhou intellectuals.

Early Historic Family Ritual

Although carried out by a number of clans in the late Zhou period, the above-mentioned clan-state rituals only applied to a minority of the elite. The *Yili* (for translation, see Steele 1917) presents the rituals of the more numerous, lower-ranked, ordinary elite. The compilation of this work took place (late Zhou period) long after the historical period it theoretically covers (eleventh century B.C.E.), and the classic ritual texts are prescriptive rather than descriptive. Nevertheless, there is no reason not to assume that the general outline of the ordinary elite rituals did not closely reflect actuality. For the ordinary male elite there were three life-cycle rituals: capping (puberty), marriage, and death (including the consequent ancestral sacrifices), all centered on food rituals.

The capping or manhood initiation ceremonial, aside from putting on caps and taking an adult name, involved a number of highly ritualized offerings of various alcoholic beverages and prepared foods to the ancestral spirits, the mother, relatives, and guests. The marriage ceremony was more complex, and the rituals took place over two days, excluding the betrothal, which involved a messenger from the groom's parents bringing a wild goose (perhaps an archaistic detail) to the family of the bride and receiving wine and food.

The marriage ceremony itself consisted of the reception of the bride and her retinue at the groom's ancestral temple, as well as the offering of a second wild goose. The bride was then brought to the new couple's bedroom where an elaborate meal had been prepared. The meal was offered to the ancestral spirits and then eaten by the couple (one assumes the others were having a feast elsewhere in the house). The bed was then readied and the couple left alone. The ritual of the first day concerned the bride and groom; the ritual of the second, the bride and her in-laws.

At sunrise on the second day, the bride visited the groom's parents and offered them food. They in turn offered her wine, which she offered to the spirits with food. The bride then served a meal to her parents-in-law after assisting them in offering it; she ate the remains. Her in-laws then gave her a feast, and the remaining food was sent to her parents.

Death rituals were of two kinds: preparation of the corpse followed by burial, and sacrificial meals. The former involved a complex series of special garments worn by the mourners and complex preparations of the corpse. Food offerings were made at every stage, from the moment of death to the burial itself.

At some point after the burial, a sacrifice consisting of a full and complex banquet was presented to the departed with an Incorporator of the Dead present to eat it. The ancestral sacrifices varied according to the status of the family making the offering, the simplest being that of a single animal (assumed to be a pig, Steele 1917:2:232) of which the various parts were cooked and presented separately. Such a sacrifice also included fish, game, vegetables, relishes, grain and wines. The procedure in outline resembled the description in the *Odes*, the male (and females separately?) members of the family together ate the offered food after the Incorporator of the Dead finished and left. The females and the cook also sacrificed to the stoves on which the meal was cooked, apparently an early indication of the stove deity.

Early Traditional Ritual

The establishment of imperial government following the unification of China under the rule of the Qin state (221 B.C.E.) affected the previous rituals. The sacrificial meals of the ruling clan be-

THE ESSENCE OF CHINESE RELIGION   35

came the primary rituals of the empire, and the sacrifices to nature spirits were centralized and integrated into the imperial religion. In sum, the previous ritual procedures continued but on a grander scale (Bilsky 1975:239–40). Ritual in the subsequent Han dynasty changed slightly, in that the emperor, the chief sacrificer, appeared only after the victim was killed (Bilsky 1975:269).

During the Han dynasty, theorists were engaged in reorganizing and rationalizing the rituals. Along with the use of multiple calendars (both lunar and solar), a complex ritual cycle developed. The rituals can be grouped into four categories: the most important, the winter/year-renewal ceremonies (including the La and Lunar New Year); the spring/fertility complex (including the Ritual Ploughing and sacrifice to the First Husbandman, the sacrifice to the Supreme Intermediary, the sacrifice to the First Sericulturist, and the Lustration Festival that may be the forerunner of the Qingming Festival); the summer/fire-renewal ceremonies (and elements that combined to make the later Dragon Boat Festival, see Aijmer 1964); and the autumn/hunt ceremonies (with the sacrifice to the First Forester). This ritual calendar included at least five sacrificial meals offered to ancestral spirits and three sacrifices made to nature spirits, consolidated into the Deities of the Soil and Millet (Bodde 1975:56).

Relevant extant texts are concerned with the imperial court, and little information on the common people is available. By the Han period, the ancestral cult of the ruling families in the Shang period had diffused throughout most of the population. The social class (both actual and theoretical) system was far more complex than a simple distinction between elite and peasants. The peasants were no longer dependent on their lord's family cult but had their own ritual practices, although, of course, on a considerably more modest scale. Sacrificial food offerings to the ancestral and household spirits were made at least twice a year (Bodde 1975:60–61,293–94) and possibly as many as the five times of imperial practice.

Life-cycle rituals are only mentioned in the historical texts in cases of abnormal occurrences or if mentioned in an imperial rescript. For example, the most frequent mention of marriage customs concerns betrothal gifts between powerful families. However, a proclamation of Emperor Huan (59 B.C.E.) contains the sentence: "In the marriage ceremony, there are major obligations; a gathering for drinking wine and eating is the way to perform the ceremonial" (S. Yang 1976:22). Similarly, in the text that came to determine the normative rituals for the elite, Zhu Xi's (1130–1200) *Family Rituals*, consummation of the marriage takes place after the couple privately dine together while the wedding feast is taking place for the guests (Ebrey 1991:60–61). Two days after the consummation, the bride is brought before the family shrine (63). Clearly, the essential part of the marriage ritual was the wedding feast.

Religious and Secular Ritual: Digression II

There is a tendency in Western scholarship to distinguish between religious and secular rituals, or an intermediary type termed "civil religion." The distinction is not made in China and is meaningless for the functional understanding of ritual in the late Zhou period and developments in the early Han. In the words of Frederick Mote (1977:203):

> To distinguish between the religious and secular in Chinese life in terms of the uses of those words in Western societies is somewhat misleading, both because Chinese religion was essentially "secular" (that is, "of this world" and "independent of any church") and because, it would be difficult to prove that some religious element or point of origin did not underlie all the ceremonial proprieties.

In his superb study of Han court festivals, Bodde (1975: 139,143,146–47) distinguishes between the *La* (solar) and Lunar New Year festivals as, respectively, religious and secular. Although he does not define the distinction, it apparently denotes whether the rituals are between humans and spirits or humans and humans. Bodde (1975:216) provides a Western example in "the religious Christmas and the secular-pagan New Year." This example points out that the difference is actually a medieval Christian one, a sharp distinction between this world (realm of flesh) and the other world (realm of spirit). As well, the example captures the Western attitude that that which is not Christian is secular. (Christmas, of course, is itself actually of "pagan" origin: the Mithraic winter solstice/birth of the sun/year renewal festival adopted by Christianity in the late fourth century.)

In Chinese religion no such distinction is made. The imperial clan, as well as the ordinary family, is composed of a continuum of past, present, and future, of ancestral spirits, the living and the unborn. An imperial sacrifice was as "political and social in its purpose" (Bodde 1975:139) as an official reception. In theory, the emperor was human yet semidivine in function, for he was the Son of Heaven. His political suzerainty over the officials and powerful clans was maintained by his position as the semisuperhuman chief priest of the culture, and it was reinforced by his performance of the sacrifices. The emperor was to Heaven as the officials were to the emperor as the people were to the officials—all such contacts were highly ritualized.

At the Han official New Year Festival, the providing of "a great feast and [distribution of] cooked meats and sacrificial animals" (Bodde 1975:143) and the nature of the reception—"all those seated in attendance in the hall bowed their heads to the floor and then, in order of rank, arose and wished long life [to the emperor]" (Bodde 1975:147)—are related to the feast of clansmen and guests and the wishing of long life to the clan head, following his food offering to the ancestral spirits of the early historic period. It is clear that this feast was an integral aspect of the Zhou sacrificial ritual. Similarly, the description of the late Han *La* festival for the "middle class" outlines the various days spent on preparation for sacrifices, sacrificial meals, and reception of visitors as a continuum, (Bodde 1975:60) not as secular and religious aspects, although Bodde (1975:58ff.) cites this passage as an example of the festival's secular characteristics.

Late Traditional Ritual

When one finds congruence between phenomena at the beginning and at the end of a long chronological period, one can logically assume the relative continuity of the phenomena throughout the period. By the end of the traditional period, nearly two millennia after the early Han period, there is considerable data for an analysis of popular rituals. In a late nineteenth-century compendium of year-cycle rituals in Beijing (northern China), of seventeen major and minor popular festivals (excluding two festivals of Buddhist origin), the customs in eight solely involve food. In a further seven, the customs primarily involve food; in the final two, the customs secondarily involve food. These customs include the eating of special food and/or, for the more important festivals, the sacrifice of food. Furthermore, of these seventeen festivals, thirteen have special food preparations particular to each; indeed, three are named for the special food (data enumerated from Dun 1936).

Imperial sacrifices had undergone some transition since the early historical period, especially in regard to the official veneration of Kongfuzi, but were little changed in essence. At the end of the eighteenth century,

> Of the eleven ceremonies regularly performed every year by the Ch'ing [Qing] Emperor in person, only three, those at the Altars of Heaven and of Earth and at the Temple of Agriculture, fit the cosmological interpretation unambiguously. Three more, at the Spring Plowing and at the Altars of Earth and Grain, linked the sovereign to the land, its fertility, and the foundations of civilization in high antiquity, but with little cosmological content. The other five were an annual sacrifice at the temple of Confucius on the Sage's birthday and quarterly sacrifices at the Imperial Ancestral Temple. (Wills 1979: 48)

Of the three major elite life-cycle rituals of the early historic period, two—marriage and death—continue to be practiced. The initiation into manhood, the capping ceremony, was subsumed into the education system, as it came to signify the graduation from the equivalent of our secondary school. The consequent rituals (see Schafer 1977) would not have been relevant to ordinary people. In the modern context, school graduations would have the same ritual connotation (see also Saso 1990:133).

Death rituals and ancestral sacrificial meals, both of the elite and of the people, underwent little essential change from the earliest sacrifices for which we have data, one interesting addition being the use of name tablets. Food offerings can be distinguished from all other offerings and innovations: "whereas spirit-money, paper houses, paper representations of clothes, a set of real clothes, and other items are all transmitted to the deceased in the otherworld by burning, food is never burned for the dead" (S.E. Thompson 1988:75). Thompson goes on to delineate eight core food prestations in funeral ritual.

Popular rituals were described by nineteenth-century Christian missionaries, whose reports, of course, reflected the values and expectations of their own culture. Perhaps the most complete description of marriage rituals is that of Justus Doolittle (1865:1:65ff.) who wrote on the religious customs of southeast coastal China in the mid-nineteenth century. The first major ritual described was the offering of food and wine by the bride and groom at the family altar. In a footnote, however, Doolittle (1865:1:86) points out that this sacrifice might be omitted on the first day of the ceremonies; hence, it cannot be the essential ritual. The couple then drank wine from interchanged cups (or a single cup) and were fed from a sugar loaf in the shape of a cock. Subsequently, with the bride now unveiled, the couple ate a dinner in their bedroom, while the male guests had a banquet in the main hall (the ancestral temple) of the home. On the second day, the couple came out of the bedroom and sacrificed before the family altar (see above) and the stove deity. Michael Saso (1990:111), in his analysis of nineteenth-century handbooks on ritual, describes this sacrifice as a "post marriage custom."

In the early twentieth century, D. C. Graham (1961) observed virtually the same rituals in Sichuan (western China). In Martin Yang's (1945:112–13) description of northern China, the order is somewhat different. It was not until late in the evening when all the guests had left that wine and food were brought to the bedroom for the couple. "Only after this ceremony are the two really united and the titles of husband and wife assumed."

Yang adds the following:

The three things which sanction the marriage are the bridal chair which brings the bride, the parade from the bride's home to that of her husband, and the ritual homage to the gods of Heaven and Earth and to the ancestors of the husband's family.

However, the social sanctioning of the marriage here clearly is not the same as the ceremony which unites the couple as husband and wife.

Food in Chinese Culture

From the above historical survey, it is clear that the rituals of Chinese religion focus on the communal (including spirits) sharing of food. As a basic human need, food is given a prominent place in the rituals and customs of all cultures. Observers are nonetheless invariably struck by the extraordinary importance of food in Chinese culture. Among numerous examples, one could cite the standard Chinese greeting, which literally means, "Have you eaten?" "In traditional south [and every part of] China, virtually every eating transaction is social" (Anderson and Anderson 1977:370). Conversely, every social transaction involves eating. Many reasons have been given for this cultural focus on food, but the popular explanations do not withstand a comparative analysis, since most premodern civilizations were based on agriculture and many, if not all, traditional cultures have had periods of famine.

K. C. Chang (1977b:11) has pointed to the antiquity of this emphasis:

> Few cultures are as food oriented as the Chinese. And this orientation appears to be as ancient as Chinese culture itself . . . I cannot feel more confident to say that the ancient Chinese were among the peoples of the world who have been particularly preoccupied with food and eating.

Chang (1977:42) notes that the fundamental symbol of political authority in this period, a set of bronze *ding* (three-legged sacrificial heating vessels), were basically cooking pots! The importance of food continues into the traditional period: "All imperial meals possessed a ceremonial quality" (Schafer 1977:133). This characteristic is found in all civilizations where the political leader was the chief intermediary between humans and divinity and thus maintained a semidivine status (e.g., Aztec and Incan civilizations). However, among all members of Chinese culture, scarcely an event or situation marking a person's life failed to involve eating of some kind. Worship was the ritual feeding of the dead or of gods. Birth, marriage and death were accompanied by food. (Freeman 1977:163)

In contemporary traditional China, this basic relationship of food and ritual continues. The following description for Hong Kong would be equally true for all of China:

Meals, from snacks with friends to formal banquets, are the most important concrete expressions of social bonding, actually creating and maintaining them. Food sacrifice is obligatory in all major rituals and serves as a key way of communicating to the gods . . . a sacrifice to the gods is a projection or type of a meal, a subset of ordinary meals in which gods and spirits, rather than the visible, tangible humans, are the fellow diners. (Anderson and Anderson 1977:367)

From a physiological perspective, the sacrifices are the means to "allow people to get high quality protein and varied and diverse vegetable foods" (Anderson and Anderson 1977:381). In rural culture, except among the wealthy, all nonordinary meals, that is, meals beyond subsistence needs, are sacrifices that are scheduled throughout the year, averaging twice monthly, and allow periodic intake of highly nutritious foods.

In urban areas, restaurants proliferate, serving the types of food found in rural family sacrifices, and restaurant meals serve similar social functions. Meetings between persons take place primarily in restaurants. The eating and drinking of ritual-type food and wine provides the context (the ritual) for social (in China, always ritualized) relationships. Friendship is one of the five filial, that is, ritual, relationships, and urban inns have provided wine and food for ritualized meetings between friends since the development of traditional Chinese culture.

This function of restaurants may be due in large part to the nature of Chinese domestic architecture. The Chinese dwelling is both home and temple (see Wang 1974); it is the primary place for the offering of sacrificial meals. Its form can be traced back to the protohistoric period; although in the early period, the temples were used for the rites of the dominant class alone. A simple one-room dwelling is also the family temple. (Although the term *temple* has been limited to clan temples in literature, given that the focus of the room traditionally was a large, elaborate shrine for family rituals which could be held nowhere else, *temple* is an appropriate term for comparative purposes.) In larger homes, rooms are added to both sides of the main hall, the family temple, leading to U-shaped and even more complex structures. This form of architecture is identical for Buddhist, Daoist, state-cult, and clan temples.

The furnishings are again identical in the main hall of a dwelling and a temple. Against the wall facing the entrance is a narrow altar table. In front of the altar-table—and partially under when not in use—is a square table on which offerings are placed during sacrifices. In a home, in front of the offering table is a rectangular or round table for dining. Chairs are placed against the side walls. This room functions as the family temple, dining room, living room, and reception hall, except in the multiple compound homes of the wealthy.

With the development of the civil service system, administrative centers became urban areas with a large population of the elite, often without their families, who remained in the family home. Inns provided a place to receive guests. More important, the rites of friendship may have required a special ritual setting.

Friendship is the one ritual relationship historically unrelated to ancestral spirits, and friendship rituals maintain only the communal aspect of sacrificial meals. Hence, the rites of friendship required a setting other than the family temple. Inns allowed for the ritual sharing of wine and festive foods in a space created for this purpose. These rituals cannot be distinguished as secular from a Chinese perspective, because Chinese theory does not distinguish categories of ritual relationships. All social relationships are, in effect, sacred: "A second aspect of *li* as religion in the *Hsün Tzu* [Xunzi] and the *Li Chi* [Liji] is its function as the bond of society" (Fehl 1971:206).

In all cultures, festive meals are to some degree associated with ritual. The nutritional reasons discussed above alone would require periodic feasting. But in many cultures, the meal has become dissociated with the ritual or reduced to symbolic form. For example, in most forms of modern Christianity, Sunday, as well as Christmas and Easter, dinners are usually eaten away from the worship halls and are dispensable features, and the ritual meal itself has been reduced to the Eucharist. Again, a wedding feast is normative to Christian weddings, but the blessing by the ritual specialist is the sole indispensable feature.

Food is involved in the rituals of all cultures, often in some form of sacrifice. However, in China, from the protohistoric period (and, by extension, at least the late Neolithic period) to the present, a communal meal has continually been the form of ritual central to Chinese religion. In it, food is often shared with (sacrificed to) not only the relevant participants, but spirits, ancestral or otherwise, as well. Reversing Anderson and Anderson's (1977:377) statement, "The religious uses [of food] are definitely extensions of the social one," the central role of ritual concerning food eaten by the participants in elite and popular Chinese religion is probably the cause of the unique importance of eating in Chinese social customs.

Modern Transformations

In a sociological study based on informants from south China, Parrish and Whyte analyzed continuity and change in contemporary Chinese rituals. Traditional festivals continued to be observed in rural Guangdong. The major ones are "celebrated in virtually every village, generally with some family feasting, domestic worship, and sometimes visits to kin" (Parrish and Whyte 1978:283).

> This association of festive events with family gatherings and especially sumptuous meals remains absolutely central in the lives of Kwangtung peasants, and provides a welcome break from the regular routine of back-breaking labor and very simple fare. (Parrish and Whyte 1978:291)

New holidays, based on the Western calendar, involve

> little in the way of family feasting or other celebrations ... and this clearly constitutes a major difference from the

set of traditional holidays, where domestic feasting is the
core activity. (Parrish and Whyte 1978:285)

A study of traditional and new festivals in both rural and urban
Taiwan, no doubt, would result in similar findings.

Parrish and Whyte (1978:259) also found that domestic feasting remains the central feature of weddings as an example of life-
cycle ritual in contemporary Guangdong. They point out that
"weddings do not now involve any worship in the lineage hall,"
but note that even before 1949, weddings did not usually involve
lineage ritual. In a somewhat later study in the same general location, three ritual meals (two major) take place on the wedding
day, and the bride ritually serves tea to the groom's close senior
relatives. Only after the last of these ritual meals do "the guests
show the bride and groom to their bedroom, and the ceremonies
are over" (Potter and Potter 1990:213–14). In the increasing economic prosperity of rural China of the early 1980s it was found
that the number of invited guests to the banquet increased, from
an average of 59 in 1979 to 222 in 1985 (Potter and Potter 1990).

In contemporary Taiwan and increasingly in China, an interesting synthesis of Chinese and Chinese-perceived Western
wedding customs has evolved. In Taiwan, this development was
initially due, in part, to substantial missionary influence and the
orientation of the government and leading officials toward Western culture. The government has adopted the modern Western
practice of registering weddings, and the ceremony has become
bipartite. When the registration is public, a Western white wedding dress is rented. More commonly, the gown may only be
worn in the photography studio which keeps them on hand for
this purpose, because a photograph in a Western dress is now *de
rigueur*. For the wedding feast, the traditional red Chinese gown
is worn (usually purchased). That white is the color of death and
mourning and red is the color of life and auspicious events only
adds to the contrast between the combined traditions. The wedding feast remains the one essential element for a couple to be
considered married by the community.

In urban areas, the wedding feast usually takes place in a
restaurant, partly because modern urban dwellings would be too

small to accommodate the number of relatives and guests. Wedding feasts are one of the mainstays of restaurant business. Jacques Gernet (1970:49) has noted this function of urban restaurants at least as early as the thirteenth century.

Observations in Nanjing, a large city in central China, indicate a similar pattern: "The banquet serves as a focal point for the wedding ceremony" (Levine 1982:9). Restaurant meals continue to be the locale for social rituals:

> It is not uncommon at banquets for unrelated people to swear relational titles such as *xiong-di* in order to establish senior and junior ranking. *Xiong-di* is, of course, the elder brother/younger brother appellation used to establish kinship-like relations between good friends. (Levine 1982:10)

Sacrificial rituals for the dead have been expanded to include nonfamily members with the Chinese Communist emphasis on the Chinese people as a single family:

> At the *Yü hua tai* [revolutionary martyr's memorial] just south of the city [Nanking] . . . I observed people bringing food offerings during the commemoration of a 1927 massacre and placing them at the foot of the memorial stele. (Levine 1982:11)

Seasonal rituals continue to focus on special foods, and family sacrificial meals maintain their function:

> Families retire to their homes and cook special dishes for everyone to eat during the first day of the lunar new year and the one or two days following it. Most normal activities come to a halt as all return home for ritual banquets involving immediate family. (Levine 1982:14)

In a study of the urban situation, based on somewhat earlier data than that of Levine, Whyte and Parrish (1984), in distinction to their earlier study of rural Guangdong, found traditional practices on the wane. Much of their data was collected shortly after the collapse of the Cultural Revolution. Some practices were returning with increased liberalization. A study of the mid-1980s in rural south China found a "revived interest in lineage ancestral cults" and a refurbishing of clan temples that had been previously been converted to other uses (Potter and Potter 1990:258). I observed a very traditional funeral procession in 1986 in Jiangsi Province. In 1992, I found increased public displays of a number of aspects of traditional religion in Beijing and Liaoning Province (see Paper 1992). As Potter and Potter (1990:224) state,

> Since 1981, no efforts have been made to restrict the practice of family-level ancestral cults. The family ancestral spirits are enshrined as before on the traditional altars at the rear of the main hall of each house. Incense is burned, and food offerings are made as they used to be.

The immediate effects of the current reversal of liberalization are unknown; more uncertain still are the long-term effects of changing patterns in family size, urban cremation practices, limited holidays from work, and so on. But note that in rural China there has been a liberalization of the one-child policy to allow for multiple children if a son is not produced. As in Taiwan, modernization has not led to a destruction of traditional Chinese religion, and the tradition so far appears to have survived the thorough repression and destruction of the Cultural Revolution.

With regard to Western-influenced architecture, some interesting transitions can be found in Taiwan. In one type, new urban vertical construction placed the kitchen to the rear of the ground floor and business premises to the front, with the main hall, now furnished as a Western living room, on the third floor. Hence, the structure separates the dining area, now on the second floor, and main hall. The television set is the new focus of the main hall. It is set at eye level when seated where the altar would have been. A compromise with tradition is built into the rear wall of the room, which has floor-to-ceiling cupboards and shelves. Above the space left for the television set is a built-in altar. Before the wall units is a bare, rectangular, Western-style "coffee-table" in lieu of the square table, where the food is still set out on sacrificial days before being removed to the separate dining area to be eaten by the family. In the more traditional premises, the television set is placed to the side of the altar.

The Ritual Core of Chinese Religion

Virtually all cultures have or had sacrificial rituals (e.g., Detienne and Vernant 1989). Contrary to theories of sacrifice arising from the Christian cultural context (e.g., W. R. Smith 1894, Hubert and Mauss 1899, Durkheim 1910, Cassirer 1924), which focuses on the sacrificer and the sacrificed, Chinese religion focuses on the spirits who are to be fed. In Chinese religion, the communion is not between the sacrificed animals, whether or not as symbols of the dead, and society, but between society and those to whom sacrifice is offered (the dead), creating and maintaining a larger cosmic society.

Many cultures, including a number of Melanesian, native American, and African ones, have an annual feast for the dead or ancestral spirits, as did early Near Eastern cultures. However, these rituals have not assumed primary importance as they have for Chinese culture (except among west African cultures where ancestral concepts and sacrificial ritual in relation to kingship have a number of remarkable similarities with those of China). The reasons for this development in China are, of course, highly speculative.

One could posit that in the late Neolithic period, with increasing class differentiation, the ghost sacrifice of the warrior-elite clansmen would become increasingly important. *Di* (power—translated by many as "God") was an amorphous concept, not anthropomorphized, but the mythicized ancestral spirits could be communicated to and became intercessors with Shangdi (supreme power). Indeed, Robert Eno (1990b) has recently argued that the term *Di* meant the ancestors themselves as a collective (see Postface).

By the Bronze period, the clans were arranged hierarchically and ritually; the clan sacrificial meal offered by the king became the state ritual reinforcing, indeed legitimizing, his political authority. The peasants may have had fertility rituals of their own, such as sacrifices to the fields, yet relied on the rituals of their warrior-hunter lords for major benefits. The ancestral sacrifices assumed fertility characteristics and became multifunctional.

From a reverse perspective, Chow Tse-Tsung (1978:64–65) has suggested: "Conceivably almost all of the major sacrifices in ancient China were originally for the purpose of fertility and reproduction, and many of them were probably related to the *chiao-mei*." However, his following statements could be regarded as reinforcing the point stressed here: "As for the exact ritual of the *chiao-mei* . . . according to the *Li chi* ('Chiao T'e sheng') and the *Chou li* ('Ta ssu-yüeh') with white bulls offered to the ancestors."

As the Zhou reign, never strong, broke up with the geographical expansion of Chinese culture in the first millennium B.C.E., the rulers of the increasingly independent states and substates maintained their own ancestral cults. They also maintained separate rituals to nature spirits, perhaps rituals from the different regions into which Chinese culture had spread and/or rituals the peasants had maintained on their own.

Following the creation of a single, successful Chinese empire after centuries of military struggle justified by a mythic concept of an archaic, unified China, all rituals were deliberately centralized in the person of the emperor, who was conceived as a semidivine intercessor with his clan ancestor, contiguous with Heaven itself, for the country (the civilized world) as a whole. A vast complex of rituals was consciously articulated with the focus placed on the archaic ritual of feeding ancestors. Popular rituals were miniature models of the grand imperial ritual. The culture was both centralized and unified.

Throughout the subsequent development of Chinese religion, the sacrificial meal offered to the ancestors maintained its hold and subsumed other rituals to it. For example, the Qingming Festival became the major spring festival; hence, one would expect it to be a fertility ritual. Yet the festival involves the cleaning of graves as well as food and wine offerings at the grave site (bringing together members of the family who engage in an outing and then take the offered food home for a family feast). Also at the grave site is a small shrine to the Deity of the Earth (in or on whom the corpse reposes) where a sacrifice is also made (see Chapter 8). It would seem that the sacrifice to the Deity of the Earth as a spring fertility ritual had been displaced by and subsumed into the religion of family. (In the traditional culture, there are also small shrines in the fields themselves before which offerings are made during the planting season.)

In life-cycle rituals, we observe a similar emphasis on the ancestral focus. Although there are, of course, customs and local rituals surrounding birth, birth ritual is conspicuously absent from the ritual texts. Puberty rituals were exclusively for elite males and involved more the conferring of status than a *rite du passage*. Wedding rituals primarily concerned the gaining of status by the female (who is never a member of her parents' lineage but that of her husband and, hence, is virtually statusless, both socially and ritually, until betrothed). It is the ritual surrounding death that becomes the primary ritual.

The feeding of the dead serves not only as the major life-cycle ritual but becomes the year-cycle ritual as well. The harmonization of life-cycle and year-cycle rituals in the prehistoric period probably accounts for the emphasis on food ritual in Chinese religion. Hence, we find that even rituals not directly pertinent to ancestral spirits primarily involve meals. For example, it has been shown that, from our earliest data to the present, weddings were legitimized by a meal shared by the couple, and although an offering to the groom's ancestors was involved, it was a secondary characteristic. In modern China, the ritual meal continues to be the primary ritual, as it does for all socioritual relationships, and cultural continuity remains unbroken.

Two transformations of ritual in China are of major importance. First was the early shift among intellectuals in the focus of ritual itself from ancestral spirits to human society, perhaps beginning with Kongfuzi. This shift in the understanding of the sacred led to a reinterpretation of religious practice:

> Hsün Ch'ing [Xunzi] discounted completely the effect of rites in the control of all that lies beyond man's natural competence . . . all religious arts have only social and psychological significance. (Fehl 1971:205)

(Both Fehl and Skinner, quoted early in this chapter, may have exaggerated the agnosticism of Xunzi—see the end of Chapter 4.)

The second transformation was the extension of ritual as food sacrifice to ritual as social eating. The two seem never to have been separated in Chinese culture, but the emphasis may have shifted as a consequence of the first transformation. That is, among the educated elite, society was the locus of the sacred, whose essence was celebrated and maintained through ritualized eating, following the generalized form of the prehistoric ancestral sacrifices. Among the uneducated, the ritual feeding of the ancestral spirits combined with ritual meals remained in the main unchanged. This phenomenon continues in the modern period, at least in Taiwan, as David K. Jordan (1972: 177) has succinctly stated, "because the system is flexible and geared tightly enough to the changing realities of Chinese life that it cannot be subverted by gradual social change."

The transformation of Chinese religion in any particular period can be studied through an examination of ritual meals. For example, the assimilation of Buddhism into China and the corresponding reverse influence could be studied through the transformation of Buddhist rituals in China, particularly in regard to food, and the changes, if any, in Chinese domestic sacrificial ritual (e.g., Teiser 1986). Contemporary Chinese religion can be studied by examining the changes in traditional ritual meals (for example, the custom of commemorative meals honoring Socialist and national heroes during the Qingming Festival, assuming they continue given the present rapidly changing economic ideology) and patterns in new ritual meals. As the contemporary (but now weakening) theoretical ideal is a classless society with some of the values of the traditional elite (e.g., change through education, society as "ultimate concern," and despiritized rituals), one might expect a gradual shift from traditional peasant practices to new responses on the pattern of the traditional elite in this regard.

3 ecstatic functionaries in chinese religion I: shamans

In my cloud-coat and my skirt of rainbow,
Grasping my bow I soar up in the sky
                    —*Chuci:* "Jiu ge" in Hawkes 1959:42

As discussed in the preceding chapters, the assumed rationalist transformation of elite Chinese religion is posited to have taken place during the period from Kongfuzi to Xunzi; that is, from the sixth through the third centuries B.C.E. It is generally accepted by sinologists that prior to this transformation, ecstatic religious experience was a major factor in Chinese religion. Although there are a number of technical terms related to ecstatic religious functionaries in the pre-Han Chinese texts, virtually all are translated as "shaman." As will become apparent, a major emphasis of this book is that ecstatic religious experience continued to be of considerable importance in Chinese religion, both elite and popular, and furthermore, we must differentiate between modes of Chinese ecstatic experience.

The term *shaman* derives from Tungus, an Altaic language found to the north of China, related to Manchurian. Shamanism, as an adopted Western-language term, has been variously defined: the narrowest definition would limit shamanism to northwestern Siberia, the broadest would include all ecstatic religious phenomena. The most well known study of shamanism, by Mircea Eliade (1964), does not provide a precise definition but assumes the phenomenon to be archaic and to involve trance flight. Åke Hultkrantz, a Swedish scholar who has studied shamanism among the Saami (Lapps) and various native American traditions, finds trance flight to be common but not a diagnostic feature. Hultkrantz points out that the shaman may summon the

51

spirits to her or him and/or send the spirit off to return and report, rather than necessarily travel with the assistance of the
spirit. His definition is perhaps the most useful. He defines a shaman "as a social functionary who, with the help of guardian spirits, attains ecstasy to create a rapport with the supernatural world
on behalf of his [or her] group members" (Hultkrantz 1973:34).
As we shall see in this and following chapters, this definition
fits specific, but far from all, Chinese terms for ecstatic religious
functionaries.

Shamanism in Early Chinese Texts

It is generally accepted, and there is evidence to support the assumption, that shamanism was important in the religion of the
state of Chu (Hayashi 1972; Major 1978), the major state south
of the Yangtze River in the second half of the first millennium
B.C.E. Of particular importance are the earlier poems (fourth century B.C.E.) in the Chuci, by Qu Yuan of the state of Chu (Waley
1955; Hawkes 1959).

Loosely associated with the state of Chu is the oldest extant
Daoist (daojia) text, the Zhuangzi, the earliest strata of which is
older than Daodejing. The association lies in several anecdotes
contained in the text in which the reputed author is offered the
prime ministership of Chu, an offer repeatedly rejected. In this
text, we can find not only terminology reflecting shamanism and,
in particular, shamanic ascent but the transformation of shamanistic terms to reflect the mystic experience (see Chapter 5).

The Zhuangzi Text

As with most pre-Han texts, our received version of the Zhuangzi
is far from the assumed original. The present text was edited by
Guo Xiang (C.E. 312, perhaps based on the work of Xiang Xiu of
a generation earlier) who reduced a fifty-two-chapter Han dynasty (turn of the era) version into one of thirty-three chapters,
divided into "inner" (chapters 1–7), "outer" (8–18) and "miscellaneous" (19–33) parts. The first section, excepting minor parts,
is generally accepted by scholars to include most of the earliest
material.

In an early study (Paper 1977a), I tentatively concluded that much of the material in the first section would date to the late fourth century B.C.E., corresponding to the period of the traditionally reputed author Zhuang Zhou (otherwise unknown—see *Shiji* 63 for apocryphal biography). Most of the second section, which I would end between chapters 27–29, probably dates to the third century B.C.E., the period of the compilation of the *Daodejing*. The third section, containing the remainder of the work, would predominantly date to the Han period (late third-century B.C.E. to early third-century C.E.). This analysis is in general accord with A. C. Graham's (1979) more thorough and detailed study, particularly in regard to the parts that may have been written by Zhuang Zhou.

The *Zhuangzi* text is a most difficult one in a number of regards. It contains many terms not found in any other text, rendering comparative philology in these instances impossible. The earlier parts at least are written in an idiosyncratic anecdotal style that leads to many potential ambiguities. Even more difficult than reading the text, of course, is rendering it into an utterly alien language and culture. For the purposes of these studies, I am seeking to reconstruct the intent of particular passages at the time they were written, an always somewhat dubious undertaking, considering the difficulties of the text. It should be understood that the readings provided often differ from various traditional understandings. Our earliest extant commentary is over six centuries after the earliest strata of the text and, by its time, was but one of many approaches to the work.

A passage cited later in Chapter 5 where I find a reference to the mystic experience is a case in point. In some aspects of institutional Daoist thought, "Lao-tzu [Laozi] is the personification of the Tao" (Schipper 1978:358). Accordingly, this passage has been interpreted by a major scholar, not as indicating ecstatic experience, but as "one of the first indications of the idea that Lao-tzu is coexistent with the Principle of the Universe" (Seidel 1969:85).

In the following as well as in Chapter 5, text references to the *Zhuangzi* are those of the Harvard-Yenching *Concordance* (1947): the first number refers to the page; the second, to the line(s). Translations from the *Zhuangzi* are my own unless otherwise noted, excepting the utilization of some of Burton Watson's (1968) terms.

Shamanic Ascent in Early Chinese Religion

In the *Zhuangzi*, the ideal person (almost always male in androcentric Chinese culture) is usually described in relation to society and/or government, particularly with regard to his responses with respect to social norms. However, other descriptions occur that relate to the developing concept of the *xian*. In these descriptions are hints that the *xian* originally was a shaman more powerful than the *wu* medium (see next chapter) and other government or semigovernment functionaries.

From the end of the Han period, the term *xian*[a] (see fig. 1 for characters) denotes one who has achieved material longevity (the usual English translation of *immortal* is misleading in that the Chinese concept is not the attainment of a lifespan of infinite duration, but of unusually long duration) and as well connotes from its ideographic content (man and mountain) one who lives remote from civilization in the spiritual fastness of mountains. However, prior to the Han period, there were two characters with similar pronunciation whose meanings apparently became blurred together: *xian*[b] (*Shuowen zhici* [SW] 8A9), meaning "a 'spirit' [in the commentary] who dwells on the upper reaches of mountains," and *xian*[c] (SW 8A9 [later *xian*[d]]), meaning "one who lives for a long time and *xian*[d] goes" (commentary quotes the passage in *Zhuangzi* 12 [see below] as explanation). *Xian*[d] is presented ideographically in SW as a person who *xian*[e] (rises high.) Karlgren (1957:72) gives its meaning in the *Shi* as "to caper about, dance"; hence, Needham (1956:134) makes the suggestion that the term is cognate to *wu*, a suggestion with which I disagree (see below).

| A | B | C | D | E |

FIGURE 1. Characters for "shaman" and related glyphs.

In the early Zhou text, the *Shi*, the function of the term *xian* in a line describing dancing may be to denote the height of the leaps. Since, "to live for a long time" has no etymological relation to *xian*, it may be a later accretion. Therefore, *xian*[a] as *xian*[c] (the form in which the term is found in the *Zhuangzi*) meant a person who had the power to ascend (as a bird) but not a flying mountain spirit as perhaps meant by *xian*[b]. Hence, the *xian* was probably originally a shaman, different from the *wu, ji, yi*, and *zhu*, and only after the search for longevity became common among the elite towards the end of the Zhou period is *xian* used to denote the assumed successful practitioners of the art, perhaps as late as the end of the second century C.E.

The etymology of *xian* has been provided in several studies: Wen Yido (1948:1,153–80) believes the concept to be an alien importation from the West, *xian* meaning the spirit of man leaving the perishing body as smoke during cremation rising to the Kunlun mountains; and Max Kaltenmark (1953:10) as Needham (1956) associates the etymology of *xian* to shamanic dance.

Shamanic Ascent in the Zhuangzi

In chapter 19 of the *Zhuangzi* (48/7–8), we find the dialogue that begins, "Liezi asked Barrier Keeper Yin how the Perfect Person can lie under water without suffocating, can tread on fire without being burned, and can travel above all living creatures without being afraid?" (48/7–8). These are attributes that combined refer to shamanic powers (e.g., Eliade 1964:5—"Master of Fire," "magic flight," etc.). Part of the reply is "and thereby communicate with that which created everything." Here we have partially described the function of the shaman. Although chapter 19 as a whole is later than the earlier part of the work, the above description itself may actually be an earlier version of the related passage in chapter 6, since the former version is more realistic in regard to the cited powers (lie under water without suffocating, not without becoming wet): "The True Man of antiquity . . . could ascend up high without becoming afraid, enter water without becoming wet and enter fire without being burned" (15/4–6). However, the concept of entering water without becoming wet can be found in the ethnographic literature relating to Africa; for example, in a Niger sorcerer's self-report (Stoller and Oakes 1985:163–65).

Aside from this more complete description of shamanic powers, the ascent motif alone in the *Zhuangzi* connotes the shamanic theme. All the direct references are to be found within the earlier strata, the first seven chapters, except for one occurrence in chapter 12; the indirect references are all in the middle section of the work. As discussed above, contrary to Eliade (1964), who makes ascent (or descent) the *sina qua non* of shamanism, the ascent motif is not specific to shamanism (Hultkrantz 1973) nor in itself indicates shamanism; for example, the mythic and symbolic aspect of ascent in Christianity. Nevertheless, it is a frequent aspect of the shamanic complex.

By the time of Zhuang Zhou, Liezi was already a legendary figure, but his shamanic power per se was considered inferior to that of the Perfect Person (*zhiren*), the Spiritual Person (*shenren*), and the Sage (*sheng*), about whom no similar stories accrue: (chapter 1:2/19–20) "Liezi rode the wind and travelled with coolly indifferent skill, but after fifteen days he [had to] return [to earth]." The book, the *Liezi*, contains further material about Liezi, but its probable compilation in the third century C.E. or later necessitates problems in seeking data relevant to the fourth century B.C.E. or earlier (see A.C. Graham 1961).

A mythical rather than legendary figure, the Yellow Emperor, who ascended bodily to Heaven, is also mentioned by his ascriptional ascent characteristics: (chapter 6:16/33) "The Yellow Emperor attained it [the Way] and thereby ascended on a cloud to heaven [or to the cloudy sky]."

In one description of the Spiritual Person, half the characteristics denote ascent: (chapter 1:2/28–29) "The Spiritual Person . . . does not eat the five grains, sucks the wind, drinks the dew, mounts the wind and mist, rides the flying dragon and wanders beyond the four seas [the known world]." The Perfect Man (chapter 2:6/71–73) " is as a deity . . . one who is like this mounts the wind and mist, straddles the sun and moon and wanders beyond the four seas." The first aspect may have been the scriptural basis for the later Daoist (*daojiao*) practice of literally not eating grain, perhaps from a fundamentalist interpretation ignoring the role of metaphor.

The Sage (chapter 12:30/31–32) " after a millennium, weary of the world, he leaves and ascends to the [or as a] *xian*, riding a white cloud up to the celestial village" (borrowing Yip's [1976:210] felicitous translation of the term). The Spiritual Man's (chapter 12:32/76), "spirit ascends mounted on light with his bodily form extinguished." The above two statements seem further removed in time from actual trance flights, and in the last, we are presented with a description more relevant to the mystic experience using ascent terminology (see chapter 5).

Late Zhou and Han art motifs include winged and feathered humans flitting about mountaintops (e.g., *Handbook* 1970:248), but the shaman ascends without the need of wings: (chapter 4:9/31) "You have heard of those who having wings use them to fly, but you have not heard of those who not having wings fly." Hence, the flying human-like spirit of the mountains and the *xian* as ascending shaman are probably separate concepts prior to the Qin dynasty (late third century B.C.E.).

Shamanic Ascent in the Chuci

That aspects of shamanic phenomena were an important part of Chu culture as revealed in the early parts of the *Chuci* and by archaeological evidence is generally accepted. In the "Li sao," whose date would approximate the earliest strata of the *Zhuangzi*, and a number of other poems, the primary reference to shamanism and the focus of the poem is the heavenly ascent. The images used in the early poems ("Li sao," "Jiu ge," "Jiu jang," and "Jiu bien") are quite similar to those found in the *Zhuangzi*: the verbs, rather than relating to the individual directly flying, refer to chariots and horses. In the *Chuci*, those who ascend harness a team of four, mount, ride or drive as a chariot; in *Zhuangzi*, they mount, ride or drive as a chariot, ride as a horse. In both, the "vehicles" are *long* (dragons), an ascent symbol (see below), and natural sky phenomena—clouds, mist, wind. Additionally, in the *Zhuangzi*, the sun and moon (also found in "Jiu Huai") and light rays are included; and, in the *Chuci*, thunder. In both, individuals are said to "ascend to the sky (heaven)," "roam in the mist," and "float on a cloud."

The similarity of terminology in the early sections (we would expect authors of later sections of the *Chuci* to be familiar with the *Zhuangzi*) leads to the conclusion that both have been influenced by similar phenomena. Ecstatic experiences of similar types tend to be given similar interpretations by the experiencer, the details varying according to cultural expectations. Hence, direct influence between Chu culture and the author of the *Zhuangzi*'s earlier strata is not implied. Furthermore, myth itself may develop in similar ways in widely separated cultures, an example being the mention of using a water dragon (horned, legged serpent) as a bridge in "Li sao," (line 177) and the serpent (conceived as horned and legged) serving as a log-like bridge crossed by the souls of the dead in Native American Anishnabe religion (Landes 1968:198–99).

Two other related images of interest in the *Chuci* are, cloud banners and symbolic clothing: "In my cloud-coat and my skirt of rainbow, / Grasping my bow I soar up in the sky" ("Jiu ge" 8 in Hawkes 1959:42). It is not necessary to interpret the images as metaphorical. Qing dynasty court robes realistically depicted dragons writhing upwards from the sea through the clouds (the dragon was emblazoned on court robes at least as early as the second century B.C.E.). It is possible that certain types of shamans wore such garb, at least on ritual occasions. It is also plausible that Chu nobles who had shamanic powers denoted their office by cloud-embroidered banners, frequently mentioned as decorating ascent vehicles.

Conclusions and Implications

In late Zhou times in the area of and south of the Yangtze River, a religious orientation existed and maintained itself at least until early Han times that in many respects was different from that of the region to the north. That aspects of shamanism were incorporated and transformed is clear; for example, specific burial practices, assuming they are interpreted correctly, involved with spirit journeys following death, such as the excavated jade burial suits and the preserved body dating to the early Han period. If portions of the *Zhuangzi* can be ascribed, as often assumed, to a Zhuang Zhou who lived in the fourth century B.C.E., and if this Zhuang Zhou was indeed as some traditions state a native of Song, more difficult to ascertain (other traditions link him to Meng), then we have evidence for the existence or memory of shamanic phenomena north of Chu. The phenomena perhaps continued from Shang culture, since by tradition, the Song ruling clan was descended from the Shang. In this regard, the reference is not to mediums, exorcists, diviners, and healers to be discussed in the next chapter, but to the powerful shaman, the one who ascends into the spirit world, who communicates with the powers on high and thereby personally controls his environs.

In the *Zhuangzi*, the Sage, Perfect Person, True Person, and Spiritual Person, originally referring to those who at least in part had shamanic powers—perhaps the original sense of *de* in this regard—come to refer, more clearly in the later parts, to those who live by a particular asocial, naturalistic philosophy combined with meditation practices. *De* is surprisingly provided in the *Shuowen* a similar meaning to *xian.* Commentators have suggested it may have the sense of ascending to an office. However, none of the extant early uses of the term confirm the *Shuowen* definition, except in a very minor way the *Yi*, hexagram 9, top line, where it might have the sense of mounting a chariot.

As an interesting aside, a manuscript containing notes from the "smaller towns and villages along the North Western borderlands" at the end of 1939, records that the common title for the "spirit representative" of mediumistic possession (see Chapter 4) is *ding-ta-xian-de* (supreme-great-*xian*-power) in place of *ding-shen-de* (supreme-spirit-power) found elsewhere (Söderbom 1940:1). This is a contemporary example of the continuation of the term, *xian*, as a functional spirit and ecstatic religious functionary in popular religion.

The ascent motif which was symbolic of shamanic power becomes a metaphor for the free spirit: (chapter 6:18/61) "Who is able to ascend to the sky, wander in the mists." In the earlier chapters, it is difficult to differentiate metaphor from symbol:

(chapter 7:20/9) "The Nameless Man said . . . 'I'll ride the surreal [?] bird beyond the six directions.' " But in the later sections of the work, the motif is certainly meant metaphorically: (chapter 20:51/6) "Mount the Way and its Power and floatingly wander." In Chapter 6, we will return to this theme of metaphorical use of shamanic terminology in poetry and painting.

The Roots of Late Zhou Shamanism: Shang Religion

The study of shamanism in the late Zhou period is possible because of texts that remained extant. The study of ecstatic aspects of religion in earlier periods is far more difficult. The study of protohistoric Chinese religion is a perplexing and often frustrating task because of the paucity of data of which there are but three types: brief written passages directly related to divination which can but partially be read and which are limited in subject range; texts considerably later in time based on earlier material filtered through centuries of changing culture, none of which can be conclusively linked to the Shang period (ca. 1600–1040 B.C.E.); and archaeological artifacts. Because traditional Chinese scholarship of the immediate past emphasized textual and epigraphical studies, emphasis on the study of protohistoric Chinese thought and institutions has been placed on the oracle text material. David Keightly and others have made enormous strides in researching Shang period government and religion from this material. (Protohistoric China delineates that period of China's past ending in the eighth century B.C.E. for which we have partial literary remains and later, in large part accurate, historical traditions, but no actual historical writings.)

Of the various extant artifacts from early Chinese civilization, the bronzes, because of their unique design and superb craftsmanship, have elicited the most interest among archaeologists and nonarchaeologists alike. Aside from epigraphical and textual research on the Zhou period (1040–256 B.C.E.) inscriptions, the majority of studies have dealt with technological aspects (e.g., Barnard 1961) or decor qua decor primarily by linguists (Karlgren 1936, 1937, 1946b, 1951) and art historians (Bachhofer 1946, Loehr 1968, W. Watson 1962a), with some studies on symbolism (Waterbury 1942). Comparative studies have also been made by scholars whose primary expertise was not Chinese studies (Hentze 1936, Fraser 1968). The latter approach has potential for increasing our understanding of Shang religion in that no culture develops in a vacuum (e.g., Mair 1990), and early human religious symbols share a commonality in conceptual logic, similar ecology, and potential diffusion throughout the span of the upper Paleolithic period.

To the Shang and early Zhou elite, the bronzes were the ritual objects par excellence. More of their surplus economic resources must have gone into the manufacture of the bronzes than into anything else, including the construction of the sacrificial halls. Hence, while the decor of these vessels has its own intrinsic value from the standpoint of design and stylistics, to the people who commissioned and used them, the ritual aspect surely was of overriding importance. Also, the bronze vessels were food-preparation and serving utensils. Since the primary rituals were food offerings (see Chapter 2)—even though similar stylistic elements are found on bone and jade also involved in sacrificial and other rituals—the vessels themselves were of utmost significance. It is for this reason that, aside from implements of war, the majority of bronzes are vessels. This part of the chapter will focus on their decor and its interpretation.

The analysis which follows diverges from traditional studies of early Chinese bronzes. Until recently (e.g., Childs-Johnson 1984), art historians specializing in Chinese artifacts, especially ancient bronzes, focused on decor from the standpoint of stylistic development. In doing so, many scholars have ignored the decor's content and context, viewing the motifs as totally abstract designs. One can take, as an example, the major school of stylistic analysis descending from Ludwig Bachhofer (1894–1976) to Max Loehr and his students, the school in which I was originally trained under Harrie Vanderstappen three decades ago. Some scholars from this school have reached the extreme view that the decor had no meaning at all:

> Neither the dragon nor the bird [the iconographic foci of this and the following chapter] is of much importance for its own sake; any too precise definition of anatomical parts would

jeopardize more important ends. Each motif is valued only insofar as it lends itself to an over-riding ornamental purpose and provides a graceful flow of elaborate curvelinear shapes. (Bagley 1980:5)

In contrast, a historian of religions would consider it most unlikely that the decor on ritual objects central to a religion's practices had no religious significance. Other art historians throughout the twentieth century have discussed the meaning of this decor but without the methodologies available to modern historians of religions. Contemporary Chinese scholars assume the decor had meaning recoverable through the methods of paleographic analysis but do not consider such study of major importance. Nevertheless, they do accept that "the customs of the Shang were closely related to their bronze decor" (C.Y. Ma 1980:10).

In this chapter and the next, a hermeneutical analysis of the primary motifs on the bronze sacrificial vessels from both the Shang dynasty and the early part of the subsequent Zhou dynasty will be presented. The analysis in large part will proceed from the perspective of comparative religion. It will be argued that these motifs symbolize aspects of those ecstatic religious experiences pertinent to the sacrificial rituals.

Christopher Hawkes (1954:162) has delineated a fourfold scale of ascending difficulty and descending validity in archaeological interpretation, beginning with technology and ending in religion: "In general, I believe, unaided inference from material remains to spiritual life is the hardest inference of all." Although, in protohistoric China, we are concerned with text-aided archaeology, the inscriptional remains are little different. We learn from them far more about the political structure than about underlying cultural concepts that are assumed, not stated. Chang Kwang-chih (1978:24) has noted that "the Chinese did not describe or even talk about their own institutions, at least in the existing record, until late Chou [Zhou]," and Noah Fehl (1971:48) has pointed out that "myth and ritual come into literature only seldom before they have ceased to be unquestionably accepted and followed in life." Neither scholar assumes that we should not concern ourselves with these concepts.

We at least know what the Chinese ritual bronzes are and approximately how they were used. Granted that the precise instructions in the later ritual texts are prescriptive rather than descriptive, the earlier material in the *Shi* does provide a general outline of the procedures. Cyril F. Fox (1959:xxvii) has pointed out, in regard to the European Bronze Age, that "archeology is incapable of dealing with myth, but ritual it can . . . recover and analyze and appreciate." For the Chinese Bronze Age, we are in a more fortunate situation, for we have in the early strata of the *Shu* and the *Shi*, as well as in inscriptional data, ancestral concepts and mythic remnants. While we cannot be absolutely certain of the meaning of ritual motifs and their relationship to myth, we can create hypotheses that are plausible within the context of protohistoric Chinese religion.

The Taotie

The most common decor element on the Shang period bronze ritual vessels has been commonly termed, since the twelfth century, the *taotie* (fig. 2). The term stems from a passage in the *Lüshi chunqiu*, a third-century B.C.E. text, whose meaning, "glutton," is unrelated and irrelevant to the design motif. In this study, the term will be used solely to denote a particular design complex which, modifying Consten (1957:300),

> denote[s] mask-like animal faces in frontal view, which lie
> flat on the surface of the vessel . . . with legs, tails, and the

FIGURE 2. Typical Shang dynasty *taotie* design.

intimation of a body added to the sides of the face. Except
for inconspicuous variation in the linear pattern fillings, the
two halves of the face are symmetrical to both sides of a
line—either imaginary or stressed by flange or ridge—that
runs down from the forehead to the nose, [the elements of
the body] are subject to the same laws of symmetry.

The mask pattern alone, occasionally found on late Shang,
usually square, vessels—Karlgren's (1937:14ff) "mask *taotie*" in
distinction to "bodied *taotie*," is excluded from the term for reasons that will later be apparent. This pattern is also to be distinguished from the so-called *kui* pattern, the *taotie*-like creature in
profile which never has a central location on the vessels, although
some *taotie* may in design appear to be composed of two *kui* abutting each other. The *taotie* is usually delineated by a background
spiral, round or square, termed *leiwen*. There are many variations
of the *taotie* due to chronological developments, regional differences, and artisan innovations, but all fall under the above general description.

There are several aspects of the pattern to be emphasized.
First, the pattern always has horns or, rarely, at a late stage of
development, ears in hornlike placement, although the artisan in
typical late Shang usage may convert these horns into other designs. Second, the central element of the *taotie* is, with possible
rare exceptions, a mask without lower jaw. Third, the pattern as
a whole is only found on vessels or serving implements, although
we must keep in mind the perishable nature of most Shang
manufactures and be aware that the pattern may have been used
on other items no longer extant.

The origin of the *taotie* is still a mystery. It has not been
found on extant objects from the Neolithic culture, the Lungshan
or "Black Pottery," that most directly led to Shang culture and
religion; yet the motif is present on some of the earliest bronze
vessels found. However, certain hints arise from recent dis-
coveries, and theories of stylistic development derive the pattern from an earlier, different, but related Neolithic culture, the
Yangshao or "Painted Pottery" culture.

The Banpo site in Sian, Shansi Province, carbon dated to between 4200 and 6500 B.C.E., yielded a bowl on which was painted

a small, horned, tattooed, frontally depicted, human-like head with fringed, elongated triangles off both sides and the top (*Historical Relics* 1972:21; see fig. 3). Another Banpo vessel has a similar design except that the face or mask lacks horns, but projecting from each side are fish, mouths abutting where ears would be (*Xian* 1963:128).

FIGURE 3. Design on Yangshao pottery possibly related
to the later *taotie* design.

Second, attempts at tracing the evolution of fish designs on ceramics from this site demonstrate the possibility of a design derived from the merging of two fish placed lip to lip leading to the painting of one stylized head with triangular bodies on each side, the eyes large and distinct (*Xian* 1963:183–85; see fig. 4). Last, a red pottery bowl with a crudely incised design that may be a *taotie* was excavated at Shijiaho, Tianmien Xian, Hubei Province; although from a Neolithic culture site, this vessel does not necessarily predate the Shang (W. Watson 1960:pl.18a). Hence, it is possible that the origin of the *taotie*, at least stylistically and possibly in part conceptually, may derive from the Painted Pottery Neolithic culture.

FIGURE 4. Possible sequence of fish motifs found on Yangshao
ceramics suggesting development of *taotie* design.

Horned Figures

The horn, one of the distinguishing characteristics of the *taotie*,
is commonly accepted by historians of religions as a symbol of
power, rather than a sign of the sacrificial animal, as has often
been suggested by sinologists. Furthermore, Chang Kwang-chih
(1976:128) suggests that the food served in the vessels was ritually related to the material of which they were made and that
grain was more likely to be offered in the bronzes than meat; besides, the *taotie* is equally common on wine vessels. More indica-
tive of the import of the horn, symbolizing the masculine power
of beasts such as the ram, are the few examples where a horned
human head serves as a major bronze design motif.

The unique bronze drum in the Sumitomo collection (Osaka)
depicts a splayed human figure with characteristic S-shaped
horns (Hentze 1936:fig.189); splayed human figures are found on
a number of Painted Pottery as well as Shang ceramic pieces (e.g.,
ROM:930.20.1). The lid of the famous *ho* in the Freer collection

(Washington, D.C.) consists of a human face with the *taotie* "bottle"-shaped horns (Pope 1967:1,pl.39). The unusual human-headed *taotie* on a square *ding* (late-Shang square *ding* often exhibit stylistic peculiarities) excavated at Ningxiang, Hunan, has C-shaped ears, clawed forelegs, and S-shaped horns (*Historical Relics* 1972:pl.48). Although the horns on a pole finial, formerly of the Meyer collection, function as prongs, the design is clearly of a horned human head (Garner and Medley 1969:1,reel 1, no.2). Similar double-pronged pole finials have been found, but they are more commonly horned mask helmets above a human face (cf. White 1956:pl.23a). Most important, among the clan insignia graphs on Shang bronzes are those that depict plumed or horned humans (Hayashi 1972:169,figs.14d,e; fig. 5).

The horned human image is found in many cultures; a comprehensive listing would require a chapter in and of itself. In North American culture we have more recent graphs very similar to the last mentioned example (fig. 5), which provides us with a comparative understanding of its significance:

> Whenever [horned figures] appear, they denote "superior power" or more than ordinary endowments and talents . . . the majority of them . . . indicate either shamans' spirits or figures of the shaman himself. Hoffman states that the "presence of horns attached to the head is a common symbol of superior power found in connection with the figures of divine forms in many *Mide* songs and other mnemonic records." Both Schoolcraft and Mallery confirm Hoffman's interpretation. (Vastokas and Vastokas 1973:95)

As this meaning of the symbol is relatively universal, the horn aspect of the *taotie* most likely signifies power in a context related to shamanic phenomena.

Masks

A second characteristic of the *taotie* is that the figure is masklike in appearance—a mask that does not cover the mouth, terminating at the upper lip. Shang period artifacts include large, unwearable masks without lower jaws (Kelley and Ch'en 1946:pl.1) as well as ones that could be worn (Loehr 1956:117).

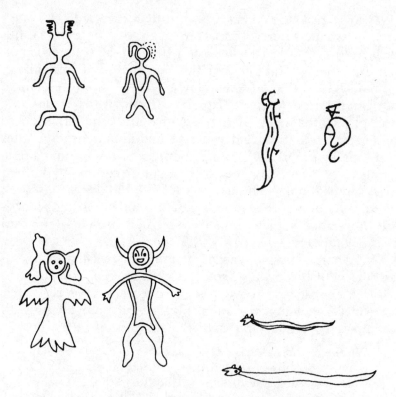

Figure 5. Upper left: Bronze inscription graphs (after Hayashi).
Upper right: Oracle bone graphs.
Lower left and right: Anishnabe (Great Lakes area)
pictographs (after Vastokas).

More than two thousand years later, we find a copper mask being worn by a Chinese general in the eleventh century (Eberhard
1968:330), and until recent times, copper masks were worn by
Tungus shamans (Lommel 1970:pls.75, 76).

It is as an aspect of shamans' or mediums' costumes that
we find the significance of the mask:

> We may conclude that the mask plays the same role as the
> shaman's costume . . . the mask manifestly announces the in-
> carnation of a mythical personage (ancestor, mythical animal,

god). For its part, the costume transubstantiates the shaman,
it transforms him, before all eyes, into a superhuman being.
(Eliade 1964:167–68)

One may add that the mask also enhances the identification of
the wearer with the entity represented by the mask (see Paper
1977b).

In Chinese ritual the mask played an important role. The
officials acting as subleaders during the year renewal *No* exorcism ritual of the Han period (206 B.C.E. to 220 C.E.) wore wooden
animal masks (Bodde 1975:83), while the exorcist wore a mask
helmet (see below). Throughout Chinese history, exorcists usually wore metal masks (Eberhard 1968:372), as still apparent in
Siberian shamans' costumes. By the Song dynasty (960–1279),
performers on the stage used masks similar to those of the *No*
exorcists, leading to the masked performers of Japan as well
(Eberhard 1968:329).

Horned and Plumed Masks and Helmets

Shamanistic ritual frequently involves ritual paraphernalia (drum,
etc.) and symbolic costumes, of which an important aspect may
be a cap or helmet. These headgear frequently exhibit parts of
birds, bears, or horned animals. These elements are variously interpreted in different cultures, but there are certain universal aspects. The person who dons ceremonial garb takes on the power
and assumed attributes of the theriomorphic spirit; it is the power
of this spirit that enables the wearer of the garb to fulfill his or her
function. Specific symbolism has been commented upon in a number of studies: it is usually understood that the bird symbolizes
and/or assists the shaman in trance flight and the horns symbolize hunted or herded animals. The wearing of such ritual animal
garb can be traced to at least the upper Paleolithic in the European
cave paintings and continues in certain cultures to the present day.
At least some Manchurian shaman costumes have a headdress
with metal birds attached by metal springs (on display 1990, St.
Petersberg, Museum of Anthropology and Ethnology). The wearing of horns, especially of the bull, is particularly relevant to war-

rior societies, signifying awesome power which the wearer assumes by donning the helmet.

In the previously mentioned *No* ritual, the *fangxiangshi* ("exorcist") wears what seems to be a bear-mask helmet (Bodde 1975:78). In the Shang period, there is clear evidence that horned and/or plumed mask helmets were worn (e.g., W. Watson 1962b:pl.12; Loehr 1956:fig.68). These helmets came to just above the eyes of the wearer (fig. 6) and frontally depicted the horned (in some cases these "horns" may be tiger's ears) animal to the upper lip, exactly as does the *taotie* mask (for representative jade images, see Dohrenwend 1975).

One wonders if the capping ceremony (see Chapter 2), the *rite de passage* of male adolescents at least as early as the Zhou pe-

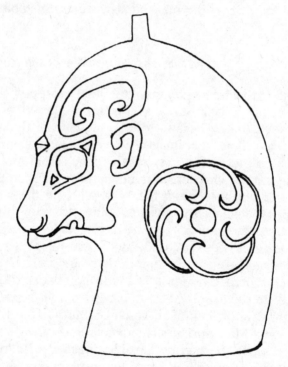

FIGURE 6. Shang period bronze helmet (after Loehr).

riod, might be related to the wearing of the horned or plumed helmets of the Shang period, although Eberhard (1968:72–74) believes
the ceremony comes into Zhou culture from the south. Children
in parts of China still wear tiger mask caps (coming to just above
the eyes as did the Shang apparatus but with lower jaw) for spiritual protection. The understanding of the helmet's power was
maintained well into traditional China; in the Han period, during
court audiences, the emperor wore what was called a "Communicating with Heaven Crown" (Bodde 1975:142–43).

Identification of the Taotie Body

Hence, the *taotie* is a horned, jawless mask with body or remnant
of body symmetrically attached to each side; the latter being the
circum-Pacific split-animal design. But what animal in particular
is it? A number of answers have been proposed, enough to lead a
scholar to write quite understandably: "None of these interpola-
tions remains convincing, and it is possibly mistaken to assume
that it had any such precise significance to the makers of the ritual
vessels" (W. Watson 1974:28). Nevertheless, if this decor complex
is of ritual significance, it must represent a concept of significance;
to understand it, we must identify the concept.

The horns on the design led to early supposition that, as previously mentioned, it represented the sacrificial animal. This for
the reason stated above and because of other characteristics
(fangs, claws, and long tail) is unacceptable. Another early theory
was that the *taotie* represented a large, ferocious feline—a tiger.
Rostovtzeff (1929:70) believed it was a horned lion-griffin derived
from Persia. This theory is in part still present. William Watson
(1974:27) writes, "The *t'ao-t'ieh* mask hovers between the tiger,
the greatest plague of men and animals, and the ox, its natural
prey." Such an approach disregards significance of design on
ritual objects.

Identifiable feline monster figures do occur on Shang bronze
art (and form a motif complex that will also occur in Oceanic and
native American art). However, these figures have protruding
upright, slightly pointed ears, as do the images of owls where
the *taotie* horn occurs (e.g., the combined owl and tiger on a *guang*

in the Fogg Museum of Art; Mizuno 1959:pl.54); indication of a lower jaw may also be present. They may have split body as well, but do not take the central position on the vessel.

Interestingly, these feline figures also occur in an obviously shamanic context: a human being is seemingly being devoured by the tiger, probably preliminary to the tiger becoming a guardian spirit (jaguar in Mesoamerica; bear in northwest coast North America). In one clear example, the surmounted human has the first known example of the protruding-tongue motif (Fraser 1972:646; Hayashi 1972:172; Li Chi 1957:pl.1). By at least the late Zhou period, the tiger as spirit is an expeller of demons (Bodde 1975:129). There is an exception to the above generalizations, however, on an unusual late Shang bronze *hu* with two *taotie* friezes. The lower one has bovine horns, and the upper, subsidiary, has feline ears instead of the horns (W. Watson 1962b:pl.5).

Other speculation devolved on the crocodile (Consten 1958). This theory is readily disproved by a unique vessel excavated at Shilou, Shansi, in 1959, that also indicates what the *taotie* actually represents. The vessel, a Shang *guang* (fig. 7), in the shape of a creature with bottle horns, open-toothed mouth, and up-turned snout flowing from a tubular body on slight legs, has a design on the side of an unmistakable, clearly delineated, scale-patterned crocodile juxtaposed to a typical *kui* depicted with a long, serpentine, diamond-patterned, reptilian body with open mouth, upturned snout, forked tongue, and bottle horns (*Trésures* 1973:pls.82&D39).

Further evidence that this vessel itself represents the appearance of the *taotie* may be found in narrow bones with carved decor which show a horned *taotie*-like head (except with lower jaw) above an unmistakable serpent body with clawed forelegs (White 1945:pl.59; and ROM 937.21.12; see fig. 8). (For a complete analysis of this decor complex, see Z. Chen 1969, who also interprets the design, based in part on comparative mythology, as a horned and legged serpent.) One can speculate that the long vertical format allowed a more precise representation than the horizontal format of bronze vessel design. The *kui*, at least, is the horned serpent, sometimes depicted as legged.

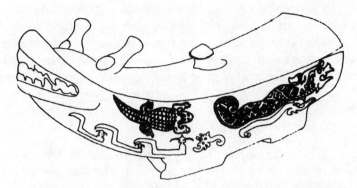

FIGURE 7. Shang period bronze *guang* unearthed in 1959.

FIGURE 8. Design on
Shang period bone
fragment (after White).

The serpent is a ubiquitous figure in the mythology of most cultures. In native American religion, the figure (fig. 5) is usually depicted as horned and occasionally with four legs (and in Northwest Coast art with upturned snout, large teeth, and prominent eyes; but here a more direct although undetermined relationship with East Asia would not be surprising). Dwelling in the earth with access to lakes, they may appear as half snake, half fish (the fish is often a fertility symbol):

> [In the Algonkian world view, it] may frequently issue from the earth, penetrate the earth, and it may also peer into heaven. Although the serpent is primarily a creature of the underworld, the great serpent was nevertheless also a powerful *manitou*, the guardian and tutelary spirit of many Indians. (Vastokas and Vastokas 1973:95)

As mentioned above, Ruth Landes (1968:198–99) quotes from William Jones's 1900 notes on Ojibwa religion that the log-like bridge crossed by the soul of the dead on the way to the shadow world is a huge serpent.

Although the original import of the Shang oracle script graphs now associated with *long* ("dragon") are far from clear, some unmistakably depict horned serpents, in one case with legs; a gaping downturned "mouth" is a feature of others (Sun 1963:446–47; see fig. 5). The legged, horned serpent is a unique and controversial graph. Some epigraphers consider it a tiger because of the legs and undulating rather than fully serpentine body. The down-curved T-shaped horns also occur on tiger graphs. It is interesting that these tigers are extraordinary or "spirit" tigers; they are never found being hunted as are the nonhorned tigers. These graphs are found in a variety of contexts, including their apparent use as the name of a tribe, geographic name, or a kind of illness; interestingly, one occurs in the context of rain ritual (ROM, unpublished, according to James Hsü). One scholar considers the *long* interchangeable with the snake (Lou 1957), but there is a graph for a snake which lacks the horns and gaping mouth.

On the earliest bronzes with *taotie* decor (Loehr Style 1 and 2, Erh-li-kang style, and the vessels excavated at Liulige, Hui

Xien, Honan Province), the horns are similar to the written graph form identified as *long* with T-shaped, down turned horns (d'Argencé 1966:pl.IA&B; W. Watson 1960:pl.44). This design style logically leads to the inverted C-shaped horns of the late Shang period (Loehr Style 5, late Anyang phase; for comparative sequence, see Loehr 1968). The inverted C horn seems to have been combined with the feline and/or owl ear in some very late Shang pieces, but this may be considered a relatively unusual variation by the late Shang artisans in a period of free innovation and stylistic creativity. The bottle-horn *taotie* resembles another *long* graph with "caped" horns (White 1945:62). The gaping-mouth graph with inverse S body resembles not only the form, but often the positioning of the *kui* pattern.

Vessels with *taotie* having diverse horn shapes as well as other stylistic differences, even to representing other creatures— such as the elephant on a few rare pieces—are all of the late Shang period. By this time, the design had been developing for at least three centuries, and in a period of geographic dispersion, relative cosmopolitan culture, sophisticated technique, and apparently greater centralized wealth, it is not unexpected that creative talents would innovate on a relatively standard design; creativity in such a cultural climate could overwhelm conservatism. And yet in the outlying regions, design motifs may have maintained themselves over a longer period of time as well as demonstrated stylistic variation. A late Shang, non-Anyang (the late Shang capital) *zun* found at Funan, Anhui Province, has a *taotie* with clearly upturned snout and T horns with downcurved ends, between which are perhaps plumes (*Historical Relics* 1972:pl.49) quite similar to early Shang pre-Anyang phase vessels (W. Watson 1962b:pl.2a).

The Long

Since the *taotie* and *gui* designs are dragon-like in appearance, it is always a temptation to identify this motif with the word (*long*) the Chinese later used for a creature invariably translated as "dragon." Consten (1958:225) suggests, "It is better to drop the world *long*, because it belongs with the medieval [Chinese] dragon." While it is certainly the case that Buddhism brought to China the *naga*-king, pearls, and so on (Zimmer 1946), we should understand that the water association with the serpent is a most antique image among mythological conceptions, and further, the *long* appears as an important image in the earliest Chinese literature.

Outside the inscriptions on Shang oracle bones and carapaces and early Zhou bronzes, the earliest Chinese text extant is the basic part of the *Yi* (Book of Changes), originally a divination manual. In the first hexagram reflecting supreme sun-sky power, the statements associated with the individual lines refer to the *long* who, first hidden beneath water, is found in cultivated fields and flying in the sky. This concept, dating from at least the early Zhou period, is basically the *long* concept of later Chinese culture: a fantastic, horned, powerful, masculine, serpent-like, legged and clawed fertility spirit that inhabits the bottoms of deep pools in winter, who during the thunderstorms of spring rises into the sky, and who among other aspects is the bringer of rain and a symbol of the emperor (to be distinguished from nonhorned serpents which as spirits are usually female). Eberhard (1968:257) clarifies the diverse types of dragons in Chinese culture and distinguishes the *long*, "the pure cloud-dragon," from the evil, crocodile-like *jiao* of the southeast coast and the river dragon resembling an ox of the west and center.

In an ode that would date to the first half of the Zhou period, we have the line "*long*-banners blazing bright" (*Shi*, Ode 283, following Waley 1960:22), indicating the use of the *long* as a powerful emblem at least by this time. Later texts indicate that the early understanding of the *long* continued into the late Zhou and early Han periods: "When the *long* arises, variegated clouds follow" (*Huainanzi*,3/3a in Bodde 1975:129); and "Prodigies of water are the *long*" (*Guoyu*, Lu B.9:5/7a in Bodde 1975:108). At the end of the Zhou period, among the titles given the "First Emperor" was *Zilung*, "Original/Ancestral Dragon." By the early Han at least, the *long* was among the symbols representing the emperor.

These references from Zhou texts lead, on the one hand, to the conclusion that this mythic complex had fully developed in China by the end of the Zhou period (third century B.C.E.), prior to direct influence from India, although the diffusion of particular aspects in either direction would not be unexpected. (For a comprehensive survey of the dragon image in China, albeit preceding modern critical scholarship, see de Visser 1913.) On the other hand, the religious significance of both the nonhorned and the horned serpent tends to be common in diverse cultures, and the development of the complex can be understood from the very nature of the symbolism.

The serpent is both a terrestrial and an aquatic creature and in shape is not unlike the fish. The two images are at times combined. As a terrestrial creature one finds female connotations, as the nonhorned snake has in the Mediterranean and other regions, including China; but the phallic shape of the animal allows an alternate understanding. Depicted entering and exiting holes in the ground in a number of native American cultures, the horned serpent symbolizes the male fertilization of the female earth, the action of rain descending from the sky, the solar or masculine spirit world.

Hence, the horned serpent, the horn a sign of masculine potency, is a creature that symbolizes the fertilization of the fields by rain and becomes a spirit conceived as residing in the earth during the dormant season—in the Chinese mode hibernating not in the ground but at the bottom of pools—and rising with vital masculine energy during the spring thunderstorms as a waterspout to the sky to serve as a rain-thunder deity until the coming again of winter. Such a figure comes to symbolize the emperor of Chinese civilization, the person of supreme paternal, masculine potency who, as intermediary between humans and the procreative powers, Earth and Sky (Heaven), performs the ritual to bring rain, and who himself as intermediary between humans and Heaven symbolically sends his spirit from the terrestrial realm to the abode of ancestral spirits in the sky.

In regard to this latter aspect, we have scattered hints which indicate that the *long* may have had a particular relationship with the ruling clan of the Shang period. H. G. Creel (1937:180), in an early work discussing Shang culture, noted that "the 'Dragon Woman' is a mysterious figure of whom we know little more than the name." The Zhou period state of Song, according to tradition, was ruled by descendants of the Shang aristocracy who maintained their customs; in the *Zuozhuan* (Xiang 28.1), an early historical text, the constellation named *long* was associated with Song. In the *Shanhai jing*, a text of uncertain date that may incorporate very early material, it is written that Chi, the founding ancestor of the Zu (Shang ruling) clan, ascended to Heaven riding two *longs* (K. C. Chang 1963). A number of scholars have the impression, although there is as yet no proof, that the culture of the southern state of Chu may relate to the earlier culture of Shang. In the *Chuci*, "Jiuge" (Yun zhong zhun, line 7), there is reference to a *long* vehicle for heavenly travel. Hence, we have the possibility that on the one hand the Shang clan emblem may have been the *long* and, on the other, that as early as the Shang, the *long* was a means of ascending to the sky. The latter is a common shamanistic motif as previously discussed: the shaman on his or her spirit flight riding a transporting agent, often a bird, sometimes a swift horse, here the ascending *long*.

The Meaning of the Taotie

Although our knowledge of Shang culture is limited by the relative paucity of remains, due to such factors as the decay of most artifacts, including all written records except those on late Shang oracle bones and carapaces, in the last few decades there has been an increasing output of considerations of Shang religion. While a large number of questions remain unanswered, the broad outlines are becoming clear. The religion, at least of the elite, would fall under the heading of "sacred kingship" typical of cultures that have made the transition to settled grain agriculture with sufficient surplus to maintain a nonproducing class—the warrior clansmen whose chief mediates between the powers and humans.

Further back than the Shang we cannot as yet go, save our knowledge that major elements of this religion existed in the preceding Neolithic culture and that the Shang people themselves were aware of an earlier related civilization, the Xia. Agriculture existed in northern China at least as early as the fifth millennium B.C.E., as perhaps did a rudimentary writing system (Ho 1975:393ff.), yet many elements of Shang civilization as we know it (e.g., bronze casting and the chariot, the latter perhaps due to Indo-European influence) did not precede the second millennium B.C.E. Therefore, it is likely that the religion of the Shang maintained, especially in regard to symbolism, aspects of earlier religions. To argue from an analogous example, Christianity in the present time still maintains symbols from Europe and the Near East far older than Hellenic and late Israelite culture, that is, of religions practiced more than three thousand years ago.

There is substantial literary evidence for the presence of shamanism during the mid- to late Zhou period (see above). Since shamanism is and was common both to the north and to the west of China, it is probable that aspects of shamanism were part of the religious complex of one or more of the cultures that led to the development of Shang civilization.

The classic forms of shamanism are found within gathering-hunting, or its close corollary, reindeer and bison herding, cultural ecologies and are often considered significantly different from the religious phenomena germane to an agricultural cultural ecology (Hultkrantz 1957:296). While Shang (and certain other civilizations at a similar stage of development) had an agricultural ecology, its elite were not farmers but warriors, an occupation derived from hunting. Hunting itself was their alternative activity. Considering that the religion of the surrounding semi-nomads was probably—due to both ecological and later historical circumstances—shamanistic, and given their lifestyle, shamanism cannot be considered either unknown or totally alien to the Shang elite. Furthermore, although with sacral center, complex astrology and rituals, and political functions, the Shang clan-chieftain become sacred-king is a highly institutional role, his function, via divination and sacrifice, to communicate with his ancestors to mediate with the powers is not too distant from the shaman, as defined at the beginning of this chapter.

The bronze artifacts under discussion were exclusively food storage, preparation, and serving vessels for ritual purposes. The ritual was to nourish the ancestral spirits of the clan, stemming from a prehistoric belief that these ancestral spirits required freshly sacrificed animals, that they were literally to be fed blood (*xue-shi*; Ho 1975:322). The function of the vessels was to serve in the preparation and presentation of this food to the departed spirits of previous clan chieftains whose present locale was skyward (of the two human souls, on death, one remains in the vicinity of the corpse in the Yellow Earth/Springs underground, and one ascends to the sky). It is assumed that the decor of implements with specific sacral functions is usually related to their function; hence, the decor of these vessels most likely would pertain to the transmission of food to spirits above.

The early Neolithic period of China presents evidence of use of a horned-face or mask motif, possibly with *taotie*-type body. A fish design seems to be transformed into the split-animal style with central head and large eyes, and the fish and serpent are often related symbols. Shang bronze decor includes a number of obvious horned-serpent motifs, typical on the interior of the *pan* shape, as well as legged, horned, serpents at least later called *kui*. The form of the *taotie* is so similar to the *kui* that its origin has been interpreted as the combination of two *kui* nose to nose (Yetts 1939), but this theory is not generally accepted, the consensus being that the *taotie* is a single, holistic unit (Karlgren 1937:77). Hence, the *taotie* is a design complex consisting of horned mask over split-animal body, being a legged, horned serpent, similar in form to the written symbol associated with *long*. The design complex is often delineated by the *leiwen* spiral pattern, so named because the Shang graph for storm or cloud is a similar spiral pattern. The combination of *long* in storm cloud is a later common Chinese design, and its existence on the bronzes is certainly more than coincidence.

The *taotie* has previously and understandably been interpreted as a storm god (Yetts 1925:431), and Schuyler Cammann (1953:198–99) speculated that the image "might have been conceived to symbolize a supreme sky deity" and pointed out that this meaning continues in regard to the modified Tibetan version. However, the vessels were not, as far as is known, primarily for the ritual of rain or fertility sacrifice, nor would this explain the mask aspect. Another interpretation has it that "the *taotie* were spirit-guardians, emanating divine power, warding off evil spirits" (Waterbury 1942:3). Such an explanation does not take into account the function of the vessels or the specific components of the design complex. Other theories that emphasize the lack of or changing expressions are, I believe, of limited value (e.g., Michihara 1975:360ff.).

Returning to the ritual function of the vessels, it is important to note that these rituals in the period under discussion were carried out by the king himself, assisted by ritual specialists. Only the son or brother could sacrifice to the spirit of the deceased former kings. Therefore, the clan chieftain of the dominant clan of these charioteer archers was both chief warrior and chief priest of the culture. All power, spiritual and physical, reposed in him. As we have noted before as typical of shamanic garb, such power was often symbolized by a special headdress, usually with horns and/or feathers. For example, among the rock engravings of Camonica Valley in northern Italy is one that depicts a procession. Some persons display weapons, others, headdresses, but only one displays both, and that person alone is astride a horse (Anati 1960:214,fig.97). If we jump three millennia in time, we can find similar scenes in the nineteenth-century paintings and early photographs of the headdressed, armed riders, the native American war shamans of the plains.

The power of the horned human is ubiquitous in hunting and herding cultures. We are familiar with the symbol in our own culture, although in ours the horned figure represents the anti-Christian power of the previously dominant European cultures, the Christian symbolism centering on other important images, such as the fish and the tree. That essential element of the *taotie*, the horn, is not a frightening image, but an awesome one. It does not represent the sacrificed animals as has been suggested (although this may be the reason why horned animals were sacrificed), but the power of the king himself, or perhaps more generally of the clansmen.

The form of the mask on the *taotie*, closely related to the mask helmet of the period, could logically derive from a much earlier practice of wearing an animal skull minus the jawbone, which detaches easily. Furthermore, removal of the mandible is a virtual necessity for the animal skull to fit properly over the human head. Hence, a secondary possible derivation is from ritual involving skulls. In later recorded Chinese rituals, the sacrificial animal's head was the messenger between humans and the spirits: "The presentation of the [head] was [intended as] a direct [communication with the departed]" (Legge 1885:v.27,444). This reading is supported by later Chinese ritual practices.

Perhaps even more relevant would be the concept of the mask itself, which at least later will function as the seat of the souls of the dead. Since we are aware of wearable bronze masks during this period, is it possible that the Incorporator of the Dead (see Chapter 4) at the sacrifices wore such a mask? This interpretation is supported by the independent findings of Childs-Johnson (1987). Hence, we have at least two possibilities: the *taotie* mask derived from the mask helmet signifying power and authority, or it derived from a wearable mask symbolizing the spirit of the dead to whom the sacrifices were offered. In either case, the horned mask of power combined with the ascending serpent or dragon figure graphically represents the function of the vessels to deliver food to the ancestral spirits. In part it also represents the chief sacrificer, the Shang king himself, the institutionalized shaman-chief, whose essence was the ability to interact with the spirit realm and who, upon death, will ascend to Heaven to merge with the spirits as a clan ancestor, able to communicate with the vague powers beyond the ken of humans.

Chang Kwang-chih (1981) also analyzed the shamanistic aspects of Shang ritual decor, but he separates the concept of the *taotie* from the *long*. He (1983) understands the motif to represent the shaman's passage to the other world, but he delineates the design motif more generally than I do. Sarah Allan (1985–87) understands masks and the dragon to relate to the "watery underworld of the Yellow Springs." Elizabeth Childs-Johnson (1987) reinforces the mask aspect of the design's interpretation, but she does not concern herself with the body of the design.

The *taotie* as a design complex demonstrates the maintenance of shamanic concepts in a period of incipient civilization. The spirit flight in an agricultural setting with sacrificial ritual becomes transmuted to the flight of the spiritual aspect of the offering up to the ancestors. When unity is finally established after the collapse of the Zhou hegemony, the political ruler will incorporate the imagery of the archaic past, becoming not only chief priest but superhuman, a being between humans and spirits, wearing the emblem of the *long*, the potent, legged, horned serpent writhing upward amid lightning flash and crashing thunder from Earth to Heaven to send down the fertilizing rain and communicate with ultimate power.

Conclusions

In middle to late Zhou texts, there are passages that meet the expectations of virtually all definitions of shamanism. An analysis of Chinese ritual vessel decor from the late Neolithic period through the Shang period suggests that these phenomena extend well back into the prehistoric period of China. None of this evidence relates to the actual use of shamanism in early Chinese culture. All passages which explicitly concern ecstatic religious functioning rather relate to mediumism, the topic of the next chapter. Hence, our understanding of shamanism in Chinese culture remains to date hypothetical at best, although continued studies of Chu texts and material remains may yet provide a clearer picture of the situation.

4 ecstatic functionaries in chinese religion II: mediums

The dead of past generations place people in trance and use them to speak.

—Wang Chung, first century C.E.

A number of early Chinese terms relating to ecstatic religious functionaries were introduced in the preceding chapter: *xian*, *wu, ji, yi*, and *zhu*. All of these terms have been translated by the majority of scholars with the same word, "shaman," from the Tungus *xaman*, that has become part of the vocabularies of European languages. For some of these scholars, the assumed early functions and operative modes of the *wu*, particularly in regard to dance connected to rain-making, is understood to define shamanism. This reasoning has an intrinsic circular logic and renders any comparative study of ecstatic aspects of religion in China meaningless. For example, in a recent study (an excellent paper on a different topic) reflecting this now standard approach, we find the following authoritative statement regarding Chinese shamanism:

> The tradition of shamanism, according to which the basic functions of the shaman were to secure rain at the proper time and proper amount . . . Shamanistic dances were also used to expel evil or any sort of demonic influences, which could cause serious diseases, among other things. (Despeux 1989:238–39)

The general tendency to refer to all ecstatic religious functionaries as shamans blurs functional differences. For example, the linguist Jerry Norman (1988:18-19), in an otherwise compelling argument that the Yue (pre-Han southeastern China) were Austroasiatic speakers, writes, "The common Min word 'shaman' or 'spirit healer'" is cognate with the Mon *don* "'to dance (as if) under daemonic *possession*'" (emphasis added). Similarly, other scholars have used terms relating to ecstatic religious experience interchangeably, assuming that the terms *mediums* and *shamans* refer to identical phenomena: "The next spirit the *medium* encountered ... The *shaman* continued on her trip ... " (Potter 1974:11, emphasis added. In a recent publication, the author used "spirit medium" consistently: Potter and Potter 1990). The conflation of these terms is also common for Korean (see Chapter 9) and Japanese scholarship: "The possession type is the only type of shamanism known in Japan" (Miller 1989).

Early Chinese culture, which considered precise terminology (*zhengming*) to be of major importance, however, is not likely to have had multiple terms for the same phenomenon. A close reading of the texts in which these terms are found indeed indicates different practices and functions to varying degrees. Before proceeding, it is necessary to differentiate two major types of functional ecstatic religious behavior that are frequently confused as in the above examples.

Shamanism and Mediumism (Spirit Possession)

In Chapter 3, Åke Hultkrantz's (1973) definition of shamanism was provided. This definition is based on three determinative criteria: (1) social function, (2) assistance of guardian spirits, and (3) ecstatic state, variable in intensity. Hultkrantz's second criteria actually consists of two parts: relationship with guardian spirits, and assistance by them. It is the latter aspect that distinguishes shamanism from mediumism or spirit possession.

Like Eliade and Hultkrantz, Gilbert Rouget (1985:18), who has researched the other major form of functional ecstacy, mediumism, considers that "shamanic trance and possession trance constitute two very different—and indeed opposite—types of relationship with the invisible." The difference is in large part one of volition: shamans request the spirit(s) to come and assist them; mediums are usually involuntarily possessed, at least at first, by spirits who control them. In mediumism, the spirits use the bodies of the mediums to communicate with the medium's community; in shamanism, the spirits respond to the needs of the community as expressed to the spirits by the shaman. In both cases, the religious functionary is in trance, but the shaman remains aware and in partial control of the situation, while the medium is understood by her or his community to have relinquished all control to the spirit.

Adapting Hultkrantz's definition of a shaman, we may define a medium as *a social functionary whose body only, the person's awareness suppressed while in an ecstatic state, serves as a means for spirits to assist and/or communicate with members of the medium's group in a positive manner.* Hence, possession by malevolent spirits or malevolent possession is excluded from this definition. Also, this use of the term is not necessarily germane to the "mediums" of spiritualism that developed in mid-nineteenth-century America and Europe, as not all are involved with possession trance.

In classic mediumism, mediums do not or, at least, claim not to remember what occurred while in trance, since only their bodies but not their minds were present. In a number of cultures, including that of China, it is common for a second person to interpret the words or writings of the possessed medium. This is an activity the medium is incapable of performing after the trance, because he or she is unaware of what has taken place. In China and elsewhere, mediums often require assistance for their physical safety. When the spirit leaves the possessed person, the mediums frequently collapse. They are caught by others before they strike the ground, since there is often a slight delay in regaining consciousness.

There are also geographical differences: classic mediumism is found in sub-Saharan Africa, South Asia, and Indonesia; classic shamanism is found in northern Eurasia and native America (North and South). One theory suggests that mediumism involves a different neurophysiological state than shamanism (P. A. Wright 1989:28): it may be the case that mediumism is distinguished by temporal lobe disinhibition (Mandell 1980).

Reality is rarely as neat as theoretical models, especially when these models fuse together. Definitions should facilitate study but not limit our analysis. Both shamanism and mediumism not only coexist in East Asia but may merge in some instances, particularly in Korea. There mediums may be aware of their trance experiences (see the descriptions in Kendall 1985). A particularly thorny issue is possession among shamans. In this regard, the question of control is crucial.

According to Daniel Merkur (1985:73),

> This conception [of the spirit speaking though the shaman's mouth], in Igluli shaman's esoteric language, of the shaman as *puuq*, the "container" of the helping spirit, is not to be considered a type of possession. In the Icy Cape idiom, the shaman's chest is the "house" of his helping spirit. The shaman remains in control of both himself and the spirits that manifest through his body.

In speaking with native American shamans and from personal experience, a number of ways of psychologically interacting with helping spirits can be delineated. For instance, one may summon the spirits and communicate with them in their psychic proximity; one may send them off yet be where they go; one may fuse with them for various functional purposes; one may allow the spirits to speak through one while being present. In the last two cases, this is not spirit possession, for one maintains one's identity and awareness and controls the actions of the resultant fused entity. (Among native North Americans, at least, a distinction is made between a spiritual and a physical fusion, the latter considered a mark of evil sorcery.)

People who are primarily shamans may occasionally have mediumistic experiences, and there are those, in cultures where this is possible, who function in both modes. A videotape by Romano Mastromattei (see also 1989) of a Nepalese ecstatic functionary during a fourteen-hour séance indicates the person at times to be functioning as a shaman and at other times as a medium. (In neighboring Tibet, religious functionaries [dpa'bo] do so via possession trance, see Berglie 1976.)

The Anishnabe shaman discussed in the next chapter told me of being possessed several times but disliking the experience, because she was not in control of the trance. If shamans themselves are aware of the differences, we must assume their actuality.

Merkur (personal communication) has suggested that the origins of the two types of trance functionaries may be related to religio-ecological factors. Hultkrantz (1965; 1966) has linked shamanism to hunting cultures, a relationship with therio-morphic spirits essential for survival; Merkur suggests linking mediumism to horticultural cultures. Settled or semisettled horticulture creates a relationship between the land and the ancestral spirits who brought the land under cultivation. To be possessed by ancestral spirits in a culture where persons identify themselves with clan (usually matrilineal) and locale would be a positive rather than a negative experience (see description of Bellona religion below). This model certainly fits Africa and China, although there appear to be no native American examples. Hence, diffusion appears also to be a factor. Since horticulture seems invariably to be a female occupation in mixed economy cultures, the males hunting, raiding, and so on, the development of mediumism in conjunction with horticulture in Africa, the Near East (in regard to biblical references to female mediums) and South Asia would explain the fact that in many mediumistic cultures women predominantly function as mediums. The major exception, as in Zhou China, is where patrilineal clan leaders derive their authority from their function as medium-priests.

At the end of this chapter, there is discussion of the possibility of a southern locus for pre-dynastic Zhou culture, or at least a linkage of mediumism to the spread of wet-rice cultivation in China. Korean myths pertaining to mediumism reinforce this hypothesis. In these linked myths, a goddess arriving by sea brings wet-rice horticulture, supplanting the male-oriented hunting culture (see C. K. Chang 1988:40). In that northern Altaic-speaking hunting cultures are predominantly shamanistic and the continuation of pre-Buddhist/*rujia* Korean culture is mediumistic, with most mediums being female, these myths appear to indicate the transformation of shamanism to mediumism with the advent of wet-rice horticulture.

Shamanism and mediumism do not exhaust ecstatic religious states. As will be discussed in the next chapter, the mystic experience is a nonfunctional ecstacy. Many cultures understand states of possession that are harmful to the person possessed and the community, hence, the need for exorcism. Healing may involve ecstatic states, usually mild, that do not involve relationships with spirits. Various types of meditation lead to ecstatic states, such as trance flights, that may or may not involve spirits but have no social function. Morton Smith (1978) delineated both the magician and the divine person, other types of social functionaries to have been found in the Near East. And, of course, most persons in Western cultures will be familiar with the roles of prophets and visionaries in the Bible. The list could be considerably extended.

Virtually all the functions of shamanism and mediumism can occur without the necessity of ecstacy. Divination, for example, also takes place, as it has in China as far back as we can trace its culture, through the manipulation of various instruments. For example, pyroscapulamancy was of major importance to Chinese government in the second millennium B.C.E. It seems to be a very ancient practice as it is found throughout the circumpolar regions, including northeastern native North America. Healing, as we know from modern Western culture, can take place without ecstacy, although perhaps not as efficiently. Again the list can be extended.

We cannot assume the existence of shamanism or mediumism simply on the basis of fulfilling socioeconomic needs, such as rain making or other forms of weather control, as in the example provided at the beginning of this chapter. However, if rain making in China did involve ecstatic trance, it undoubtedly was mediumistic. It would make little sense to expose the *wu* to the sun's rays during a drought, for which there are numerous references in the early literature, unless the *wu* was possessed by the responsible spirit. It is the spirit who would be expected to suffer, not the possessed person. This reasoning accords with the later practice of exposing images of the deity in times of prolonged drought. A linkage of rain dances with mediumism also accords with contemporary ethnographic accounts from Africa (Stoller 1989:34). (A discussion of rain-making techniques and dances in native American cultures is complex and would require a book in itself.)

The Problem in the Modern Chinese Context

In the preceding chapter, it is argued that shamanism is implied in protohistoric Chinese iconography and explicitly referred to in early Chinese texts. Subsequent texts discussing religious functionaries seem to refer primarily to mediumism, although trance flights continued as a meditational rather than a functional practice. Nevertheless, some social functionaries by temperament, if not by culture, continued to act as shamans.

In 1983, in Taiwan, the scholar-monk Mingfu enabled me to speak to a practicing shaman from southern Taiwan who prefers to remain anonymous. When consulted by clients, the shaman did not ask a spirit or deity to travel to the realm of the dead to ascertain the cause of the problem, nor did he serve as a means for the deity or the ancestral spirits to speak to the client as is the normative Chinese practice. Rather he called his assisting spirit, who, taking him by the hand, guided him to the realm of the dead. There he spoke with the departed spirits of the client's family. On returning to normal consciousness, he pretended that the spirit was speaking through him, but actually spoke himself. He pretended because present-day Chinese culture only understands mediumistic trance; that is, the client would not accept the advice if the spirits did not directly impart it. The necessity of his subterfuge indicates the pervasiveness of mediumism in Chinese religion.

The above description is in complete accord with the models for shamanism of both Eliade and Hultkrantz. The shaman, however, seemed not to understand the more common mediumistic trance and assumed, because he faked the voice of the spirits, that all mediums were frauds!

Various fusions between the two modes of ecstatic functioning are relatively common and difficult to categorize. For example, Julian Pas (1989:43) has described the writing in trance of a popular text, a common means of mediumistic communication in the highly literary Chinese culture (see Chapter 6), in which

> while his physical body is in trance, his hand, holding the wooden implement, or *luan-pi*, is being moved by a divine

spirit, named Yü-hsü t'ung-tzu. At the same time, his spirit or yang soul leaves the body temporarily and is taken on successive trips to the netherworld under the guidance of a very popular Buddhist figure, Chi-kung.

Here, we have described a situation that simultaneously fits the definition of a medium and that of a shaman.

Another type of amalgamation between shamanism and mediumism, also taking place in Taiwan, is described by Emily Ahern (1973:228–35). The "medium" (Taiwanese: *tang-ki*) in this situation did not enter trance as he often did, but placed individuals in trance and then directed them to the spirit realm, where the living may visit the deceased. On returning and coming out of trance, the journey is remembered. Although the person traveling is not possessed, he or she is under the control of the *tang-ki*.

The Enigma of Protohistoric Chinese Mediumism

As will be detailed below, Chinese religious functionaries undoubtedly act mediumistically. This can be traced with certainly back to the late Zhou period. Concerning the earlier period of three thousand or more years ago in north China, it is certain that there were ecstatic religious functionaries, but how they functioned is an unanswered question. As discussed in the preceding chapter, there is indication, far from conclusive, of shamanistic functioning in the Shang period from remnant terminology in later texts and the iconography on ritual vessels. Given that Shang culture of the north China plain was contiguous with the southernmost Siberian cultures, which undoubtedly maintained circum-polar shamanism at the time as they do now (see Siikala 1978, 1991), an assumption of familiarity with shamanism is not farfetched.

As with Shang religion, analysis of early Zhou iconography provides tantalizing evidence for aspects of Zhou religion. The decor on ritual vessels suggests that mediumism is denotative of Zhou culture in its earliest stages.

Early Zhou Ritual Decor

The second most common decor motif—the *taotie* (see Chapter 3) being the most common—on early Chinese bronze ritual vessels is the bird. In this regard, we must distinguish manifold uses of bird motifs on the bronzes, such as owl-shaped *zun* vessels, and focus on the bird motif placed where the *taotie* is otherwise found. Bird motifs can be traced to China's early Neolithic art, and the Yangshao spiral design has been stylistically traced from a bird's head similar to later Shang representations (Shi 1962:321). The bird is an important element of Shang mythology, a "dark bird" being the means for the deity Ku to impregnate the ancestress of the Shang clan.

However, of particular interest to this study are the differences in the bird motif on Shang and early Zhou vessels. The *taotie* tends to be far less frequently used in the decades following the transfer of power and soon disappears. In its place on the same vessel shapes, we find opposing birds or spiral-bodied, elephant-headed figures. The former relates to a Shang decor element more common on friezes above the *taotie*. These early Zhou opposing birds are different from the Shang design in that they have a large rear sweeping crest, and often the bird's heads are turned to face backwards (see fig. 9a). The spiral-bodied facing figure can be understood to represent a flying elephant-headed bird (see fig. 10ab). Also found on bronzes of this period are representations of the elephant trunk alone. For a discussion of the specific bronze vessels and their decor that are at the basis of the following analysis, please refer to the Appendix.

 ### Shang Birds: Owl and Crow (or Swallow)

Bird designs are found on late Shang period bronze vessels, but, except in the few cases of very late Shang vessels usually considered to be predynastic Zhou in origin or commission, they do not appear in place of the *taotie*. There are a number of vessels in the shape of an owl, and at least one with an owl depicted on the side, but the doubled image as in the *taotie* does not appear

A   B

FIGURE 9.
A: Outline of half of a typical early Zhou bird replacement of *taotie* motif
with rearward-turning head, sweeping double crests
and split tail, as found on a *zun* in the University of Pennsylvania
Museum and a *zhi* in the British Museum.

B: Bird with rearward-turned head, double crest, and split tail found
on sixth to fourth century B.C.E. silk (Hermitage 1687/101).

A   B

FIGURE 10.
A: Outline of half of typical elephant-bird design with trunk, crest, and
spiral body as on *zun* excavated in 1971 (Shanxi Provincial Museum).

B: Outline of half of design with clearly depicted elephant head on
winged, feathered body on foot of *gui* (Art Institute
of Chicago no. 27.316).

(e.g., Fong 1980:pl.26). A noncrested bird appears frequently as a subsidiary frieze design element or as a lid handle. Interestingly, none of these designs appears on Zhou period vessels.

In current Chinese folklore, the cry of the owl is feared as a harbinger of death, as it is elsewhere—for example, in West Coast native North American cultures. In the *Shi* (Ode 264), the bird is briefly mentioned with a connotation of evil. Yet these connotations probably do not apply to the owl's plastic depiction on Shang sacrificial vessels, since such symbols of a feared and evil harbinger of death would be irrelevant to the offering of food to revered ancestral spirits who are already dead.

From a comparative standpoint, one can find other symbolic understandings of the owl. In the Anishnabe religion of aboriginal North America, the owl is also related to death, but not in a fearful manner: "[The sign on a birchbark scroll] represents the Ko-kó-ko-ñō(Owl) passing from the Midé-wigân to the Land of the Setting Sun, the place of the dead, upon the road of the dead" (Hoffman 1891:171). This concept of the owl as a vehicle from the realm of the living to the realm of the dead, the abode of the ancestral spirits in early China, seemingly corresponds closely to the Shang concept of the *long*, as analyzed in the preceding chapter. Of course, such correspondence is suggestive rather than conclusive. The owl motif itself predates the Shang period: for example, a jade pendant in the form of an owl manufactured with Neolithic techniques and dated to the early second millennium B.C.E. (Hansford 1968:pl.1).

The noncrested bird is often identified as a swallow; it has been noted that "the swallow is everywhere regarded as sacred" (Thomas n.d.:1:528). According to the origin myth of the Shang ruling clan, they were descended from a woman, Jiandi, into whose mouth a *xuan-niao* (dark bird), usually considered by commentators to be the swallow, dropped an egg (K. C. Chang 1976:167–68). This identification of the *xuan-niao* with a swallow is first cited in the *Lüshi chunqiu*, a third-century B.C.E. work.

Sarah Allan (1981:291) notes, "The black bird which gave birth to the Shang thus seems originally to have been undiffer-

entiated with regard to species, but in color matches the sunbird."
The crow or raven is considered the sunbird from the mid-Zhou
period on (see below). Allan (1981:311) persuasively argues "that
the Shang rulers had a totemic relationship with the ten suns
which were also thought to be birds." Either swallow, crow or
raven fits the noncrested bird design on the Shang bronzes,
but the crow as the ancestral sunbird now seems the more likely
identification.

The Feng

The *feng* (usually translated as "phoenix," without the specific
Western connotations of the term) is a fabulous bird traditionally depicted as a multicolored cross between a peacock and a
pheasant (Yetts 1912:24). The character occurs on the Shang oracle
bones (Karlgren 1957:no.625), where it is considered to signify a
wind spirit (C. Y. Ma 1980:8). Pheasants are indigenous to northern China, and the warmer climate of the Shang and early Zhou
periods would have allowed for peafowl. In Japan, the pheasant
is generally viewed as a messenger to the Shinto deities (Volker
1950:133), and in central India, the peacock is a clan symbol to
which offerings are made (Frazer 1915).

On a Chinese silk covering a saddle blanket that was found
frozen in a Siberian tomb and dendrochronologically and carbon
dated to the sixth to fourth centuries B.C.E., three birds are depicted: a small, single-crested bird with a partridge gait; a single-
crested, long-tailed, pheasant-appearing bird with a pheasant
gait; and a bird somewhat different in appearance from the other
two with a double-crested, long split tail and back-turned head
(Hermitage collection 1687/101; *Frozen Tombs* 1978:pl.39; see
fig. 9b). The last is identical with the earlier Zhou bronze decor
motif and confirms that the bird depicted is, at least in part, a
type of pheasant or a game bird similar to a pheasant.

In the later, traditional period of Chinese history, the *feng* is
the female complement of the *long* and serves as an ascent vehicle for female *xian* (shaman, see Chapter 3). For example, after
Xiao Shi, the legendary flautist ascribed to the sixth century B.C.E.,
taught his wife, Lungyu, to play the flute, they both ascended to

the sky, he riding a *long*, and she a *feng*. However, the early meaning of the *feng* seems distinct from the later one. There are two major aspects of the early Zhou *feng* image: sun cock and ancestral spirit.

W. Percival Yetts (1912:24) points out that the "Vermillion Bird," the *feng*, presides over the southern quadrant and represents the sun and warmth of summer. The *niaoxing* (bird star or constellation) identified with the *zhuqiao* (the Red Bird) at the center of the southern palace (the Vermillion Bird) was one of the two most important constellations that may have been recognized by the Shang (Needham 1959:242). This bird was written on the oracle bones with a crested bird glyph (Needham 1959:244). (Some scholars have argued that this interpretation is mistaken, that the oracle glyph read as *niao* does not signify "bird" and *xing* does not signify "constellation"; at present, there is no definite consensus on reading the glyphs.) In myths of New Britain in Melanesia, parrots and cockatoos, both crested birds as in the early representation of the *feng*, represent the sun (Luomala 1940:39–40). Wolfram Eberhard (1968:430) suggests that the divine cock in the sun and on the sun tree may be the models for the *feng*.

The identification of birds with ancestral spirits is common and extends from Africa—"The Shilluks of the White Nile believe that the souls of their kings become white birds after death" (Seligman n.d.:11,461)—to Polynesia—"Morioris of Chatham Islands, southeast of New Zealand, call the tree carvings, which represent the ancestors, 'birds'" (Skinner 1923:70). Waterbury (1952:89) suggests that there had been a cult of bird deities that existed outside of the official religion that may have been Tunguistic in origin. However, the evidence does not necessitate the interpretation of a separate cult: "The present-day Jakuts, Tungus and Dolgons still set up rows of wooden birds on poles at burial grounds. They represent the mundane form of the spirit and other dead souls whom the dead men once helped or served" (Harva 1938:314).

The odes of the *Shi* are but a century or two younger than the later bronzes under discussion and incorporate earlier material. In the odes, particular birds are auspicious in regard to their appearance:

Flying are the *chui* birds, in great numbers they come;
the lord has wine, fine guests feast and second him.

(Karlgren 1950:Ode 171)

Crosswise fly the *sang-hu* birds, finely marked are their wings;
the lords are joyful, they will receive Heaven's blessings.

(Karlgren 1950: Ode 215)

We do not know what kinds of birds these were, but the *feng* is mentioned in one ode:

There is a curving slope; the whirl-wind comes from the south;
the joyous and pleasant lord comes and diverts himself and so
    lets forth his airs.
You are great and high, like a *kuei* scepter, like a *chung* scepter,
    with good fame, fine to look at;
joyous and pleasant lord, to the four quarters you are a regulator.
The phoenixes [*feng*] go flying, *xwâd-xwâd* their wings; again they
    settle and then stop;
a great crowd are the king's many fine officers, the lord gives
    them their charge; they have love for the Son of Heaven.
The phoenixes go flying, *xwâd-xwâd* their wings; they even reach
    heaven;
a great crowd are the kings' many fine officers, the lord appoints
    them; they have love for the common people.
The phoenixes sing on the high ridge, the eloeococcas grow on
    that east-facing [literally: sunny-side] slope;
they are dense and luxuriant; (they sing) harmoniously and in
    unison.

(Karlgren 1950: Ode 252)

In this context, it is unclear as to whether the *feng* is a solar spirit per se, but it is a spirit that arrives at auspicious occasions, including sacrifice, with south- and sun-facing attributes.

The *feng* on the ritual bronzes must be understood in the context of sacrifice since that is the function of the bronze vessels. Bernhard Karlgren (1946a:215) has pointed out that, to the Zhou, "the gods did not accept sacrificial gifts from such as were not of their kin." The Zhou ruling clan offered ancestral sacrifices at four altars: to Ku, the formal father of Houji (the Lord of Millet—his mother was impregnated by stepping in the footprint of *di* [here, as per Eno 1990b, ancestors]); to Houji, the clan ancestor; to King Wen, the father of King Wu; and to King Wu, who founded the Zhou dynasty.

The *Shanhai jing* (Classic of Mountains and Seas), a late Zhou or early Han repository of fragmentary myths and legends (some early) mentions that Dijun, whom Yuan Ko believes was a bird-headed deity, gave birth to Houji. Yuan Ko (1957:144) argues that Dijun was the direct ancestor of the Shang as well. In Han period texts, the mothers of the mythical founders of both the Shang and the Zhou dynasties had the same husband. Chow Tse-tsung (1978:83–84) notes, "If this is true, the royal houses of the two dynasties must have originated from the same ancestor or clan." But the merging of the two ruling clans into a primordial single one seems to be a relatively late concept, perhaps a conflation of two separate traditions with bird or even sunbird linkages.

Bird-headed spirits are mentioned in references at least as early as the mid-Zhou period: "Prince Mu of Ts'in [Chin] (658–619 B.C.) in clear daylight, in the middle of the day, was in a temple, when a Shen god (Spirit) entered the door and stood to the left. He had a human face and a bird's body" (*Mozi* in Karlgren 1946a:244). There are examples of human-headed, bird-bodied jade figures dated to the early Zhou or the Shang period (e.g., Chicago Field Museum of Natural History no. 91153 and Freer Gallery no. 42.6), but the dating of early jades is less certain than that of bronzes. On late Zhou bronze vessels, human-headed figures are depicted with bird bodies and human legs with snakes in horn location on the heads (Waterbury 1952:pls.16,17A). These can readily be linked to Yujiang, Agent of the North, mentioned in the *Shanhai jing* (K. C. Chang 1981:541).

Also, the *Shanhai jing* says that one of Dijun's wives, Xi Ho, gave birth to ten suns (K. C. Chang 1976:157). The ten suns as sunbirds are linked to the Fusang tree, both in the early parts of the *Chuci* (a fourth century B.C.E. southern Chinese text) and the *Shanhai jing* (see Loewe 1979:50–51). This is of interest, for the Fusang tree is linked to the birth of Houji in the *Chunqiu yuanming bao*, possibly a first-century B.C.E. work, cited in the *Taiping yulan*: "Chiang Yüan, the ancestor of Chou [Zhou], visited the Closed Temple in the place Fu-sang, trod on a big footprint, and gave birth to Hou Chi [Houji]" (Chow 1978:60). Allan (1981:312–13) also points out a strong connection between the mulberry tree as the Fusang tree and the Shang origin traditions. Should this relatively late citation maintain a detail from earlier myth, then there is a connection between the Zhou ruling clan and the sun. The *Shi*, (Ode 235) states:

> Wen Wang [King Wen] is on high, oh, he shines in heaven; though Chou [Zhou] is an old state, its (heavenly) appointment was not new; the house of Chou became amply illustrious, was not the appointment of God [*di*] timely? Wen Wang ascends and descends [as a spirit, to accept sacrificial gifts], he is on the left and right of God [*di*]. (Karlgren 1950)

In the Appendix, it is pointed out that, on one unique vessel, the plume from the bird's head ends in an anthropomorphic design (see fig. 11a) similar to the early Zhou glyph for "king" (*wang*, fig. 11b). I suggest that this glyph indicates that the bird (or elephant bird) symbolizes the Zhou dynastic ancestor, King Wen. This vessel was manufactured several generations after King Wen died; indeed, it has been argued by Ch'en Meng-chia (Fong 1980:209) that the vessel was made by a grandson of King Wen (Marquis Zhi, the son of Duke Shao). H. G. Creel (1970:505), in discussing the relationship between *tian* (Heaven) and King Wen in regard to receiving sacrificial offerings, points out, "T'ien [*tian*] [may be a] group of ancestral Kings as a body, among whom King Wen is an outstanding individual." This interpretation of *tian* is similar to the interpretation of *di* by Robert Eno (1990b). If the glyph does refer to King Wen, then the bird decor on the early Zhou sacrificial vessels signifies the *feng* who represent the Zhou ancestral spirits as they descend, as in Ode 235, to eat and drink the sacrificial offerings presented in the vessels.

Elephant-Bird

The elephant-headed bird and elephant-trunk motifs are contemporaneous with the *feng* motif; the two designs arise and disappear at the same time on similarly shaped vessels (see Appendix).

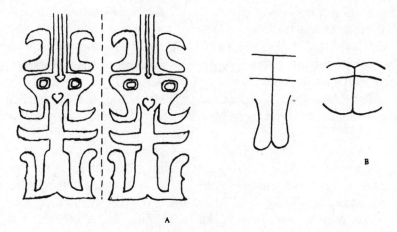

FIGURE 11.

A: Figures at ends of descending plumes (of design in fig. 1a) on vessel
excavated in Lianoning Province in 1955, discussed as
anthropomorphized glyph *wang* (king).

B: Two versions of the glyph *wang* (king) as found on Zhou bronze
vessels in the National Historical Museum, Beijing.

It is tempting, therefore, to assume that the two designs had similar significance, but there is far less material available for interpretation of the elephant-bird and elephant trunk than for the
feng.

A reference to a *long-feng*-elephant concept does exist in Chinese literature but provides not even a hint as to its meaning. The
Shanhai jing (3:47), in the section on the north, states that on Yang
(solar-masculine power) Mountain,

> there are birds whose appearance is that of the female pheas-
> ant, are decorated with the five brilliant colors [a common
> description of the *feng*], and can change their sex. They are
> called *xiang-she* (elephant-serpents). Their cries can be heard
> for a distance.

Unfortunately, no mention is made as to why these magical birds
on Yang Mountain who are described as *feng* are given a name
that could readily describe the figure depicted on a bronze in the

Buckingham collection (fig. 10b): an elephant-headed, trumpeting, serpent-like bird.

Carl Hentze (1936:83ff.) has argued that a design motif on Yangshao culture pottery represents mammoth tusks and symbolizes the spring sun. However, the mammoth disappeared from northern Asia at least eight thousand years ago, and the particular artifacts described were from Xindien in Gansu Province (see G. D. Wu 1938:105–6). They are from an Aeneolithic culture dating no earlier than the close of the second millennium B.C.E. (K. C. Chang 1977a:408). These same design elements Karlgren considers represent thunder in conjunction with solar symbols, but he does not link them to elephant tusks (Karlgren 1930:50).

Aside from elephant tusks mentioned as tribute, the only reference to elephants or elephant decor in ritual is in the *Liji* (Record of Ritual—a second century B.C.E. work supposedly representing earlier ritual):

> The ruler appeared at the top of the steps [of the ancestral temple] to the east; his wife was in the apartment on the west. The great luminary [sun] makes his appearance in the east; the moon makes her appearance in the west . . . The ruler fills his cup from the jar with the elephant on it; his wife fills hers from that with clouds and hills. (Legge 1885:410–11)

The text interprets the decor as representing a sacrificial victim. Although elephants were occasionally sacrificed in the Shang period, by the time the work was written, the elephant had long disappeared from northern China, and its original significance already may have been lost. Indeed, the elephant probably disappeared from northern China by the late tenth century B.C.E., although Eberhard (1968:262) thinks they may have remained in the Yangtze River area. One of the Jiangbo tomb vessels excavated in Shansi Province in 1974 is in the shape of an elephant (*Zhongguo* 1976:pl.40). However, except for the upraised trunk, the animal depicted is only vaguely elephantine; the body resembles a pig. This appearance could be due to poor craftsmanship—none of the Jiangbo vessels is of high quality—or to lack of observation of an actual elephant—the Shang elephant vessels were quite realistically sculpted. A phenomenological interpretation of the complete passage from the *Liji* clearly indicates that the elephant decor signifies solar-masculine-celestial power in contrast to the symbolism of the moon-feminine-earth symbols represented on the vessel used by the ruler's wife.

Except for the few early Zhou vessels where the complete elephant is depicted, the elephant trunk is raised and curled back, the posture of a trumpeting elephant (which would correspond to the loud sound of the *Shanhai jing* description). Hence, the elephant could represent celestial thunder, which, along with the solar symbol of the late tenth-century vessels, may suggest celestial *yang* power—as does the *long*—and the abode of ancestral spirits.

In South and Southeast Asia, the elephant symbolizes storms and rain and is also linked to serpents, the horned serpent being a ubiquitous rain image. Edouard Chavannes (1910a:no.342) observes that elephants, especially white ones, are the mount of Indra. According to Eveline Porée-Maspero (1962:1:3), "It should be noted that the Hindus also sometimes call elephants *nagi* [serpent], perhaps because of the resemblance of the trunk to a serpent." In Thailand, the royal white elephant was thought to have the power to bring rain, and, in Cambodia, a dream of an elephant was the forecast of rain.

More tenuous would be an interpretation that links the elephant-bird, like the *feng*, to ancestral spirits. However, according to legends well established at least by the fourth century B.C.E. (e.g., in the *Mengzi*), the sage-ruler Shun had a younger brother named Xiang (elephant), and Shun is provided with links to the *feng* by his birth and clothes (Yuan Ko 1957:157ff.). Shun gave Xiang an area called Youbi ("having a nose"), a name which Yuan Ko points out could signify an elephant's trunk. In the *Later Hanshu* version, which may incorporate an earlier variant tradition, the "bi" of Youbi is written with a character implying an elephant's trunk. Eberhard (1968:266) believes Youbi was located in southern China where, at least as early as the third century C.E., there was a temple for Xiang that was considered effective in bringing clouds and rain. Eberhard (1968:26) links an aspect of one version of the legend—"Shun plows wet-fields and hangs together with thunder swamp"—with the "elephant which, in turn, is connected with wet-field agriculture, rain and fertility." Unfortunately, the early Zhou relationship of Shun to Xiang, if any, is unknown, but the linkage to thunder, given the uniformity of the upraised trunk in regard to the motif, is fairly certain.

Crow

The *feng* design disappears from Chinese ritual bronzes within a century of the Zhou conquest, and the elephant-trunk motif disappears slightly later, along with the vessel shapes on which these decor elements occurred. Sometime after the tenth century B.C.E., the *feng* begins to take on what will become its traditional feminine ascent connotations and no longer will have solar connections nor be symbolic of the Zhou dynasty clan ancestors, both of which have masculine connotations. Included with the Jiangbo vessels, among which are what may be the last of the elephant-trunk decor vessels, is one in the shape of a three-legged bird, which commentators have noted may be linked to the later three-legged sun crow but appears to resemble more closely a turtle-dove (*Zhongguo* 1976:pl.41). However, the shift from sun cock to sun crow may be as late as the fourth century B.C.E.; in the *Shanhai jing*, the sunbirds on the Fusang tree are identified as crows (Loewe 1979:128). Certainly, by the end of the Zhou period, the solar symbol is the crow in the sun, as illustrated in the second-century B.C.E. shroud excavated at Mawangdui.

The raven or crow as sun symbol is a circumpacific motif found in Siberia as well as among the northwest coast native American cultures: in the Tlingit origin myth, Raven, a white bird burned black, releases the sun (see Swanton 1909, Boas 1902 and 1916). Indeed, the raven or crow sun symbol is connected to the sun-shooting myths that Eduard Erkes (1926) has shown to have East Asian–native American correspondences. If Allan is correct in identifying the *Xuan-niao* as sun crow, then sometime between the tenth and the fourth centuries the sun cock introduced by the Zhou ruling clan was replaced by the earlier Shang concept of sun crow. An early date for the sun crow in northern China would more logically coincide with the northern circumpacific distribution of the motif.

Mediumism: A Zhou Innovation?

To summarize the preceding, the decor on the early Zhou sacrificial bronzes is distinctly different from that of the Shang. This decor, which continues for approximately a century, consists of two related motifs. One is a crested bird identical to a probable game bird embroidered on a mid-Zhou silk. The second is a trumpeting, elephant-headed, flying bird. Both designs replace in position and orientation the *taotie*, the primary design on the Shang sacrificial vessels. On one vessel, the crest plumes end in an anthropomorphized glyph, *wang* (king). The crested bird is most likely the early version of the *feng*, an important feminine religious symbol from the late Zhou period to the present. The early version of the *feng* is a masculine, solar-ancestral spirit, in part, the Zhou equivalent of the Shang sunbird symbol, the crow. The elephant bird has celestial characteristics—thunder as well as sun—and may have ancestral connotations. From this analysis of early Zhou ritual decor, tentative conclusions concerning Zhou religion can be developed.

According to the Chinese myth of dynastic succession, the initial three dynasties, the Xia, the Shang, and the Zhou, were three successive cultures, each built on the other. In this model, Zhou religion would be a borrowing of the Shang and not readily distinguishable. Chang Kwang-chih (1976:191) has stressed that there is "no evidence [in the archaeological manifestations of the Shang and Zhou civilizations] whatsoever for any discontinuity, implicit or explicit." Cheng Te-k'un (1963:293) wrote,

> The Chou [Zhou] people started their existence very close to the Shang people. They followed the Shang culture in practically every respect. Their material remains show hardly any difference from those of their predecessors. We may even go as far as to say the typical Shang culture continued to flourish until the fall of the central power at the end of the Western Chou.

Modern archaeology, especially with the use of dendrochronologically amended radio-carbon dating, has indicated that in
actuality the three cultures chronologically overlapped and were
all descended from different loci of late Neolithic culture (K. C.
Chang 1980:350–52). That in the eleventh century B.C.E., the Zhou
ruling clan conquered the Shang ruling clan is not questioned,
but the idea that the Zhou were only recently civilized by copy-
ing the Shang is another matter. Certainly there were important
differences between the religions of the two related cultures.

The ritual practices of the two seem to have been basically
the same: sacrifices were made by the ruling clan chieftain, the
king, with the assistance of leading members of the clan and other
allied ones, and consisted of a banquet offered to the clan ancestors as well as other spirits and powers (see Chapter 2). Theologically, however, there appear to have been differences. Chang
Kwang-chih (1976:193) has pointed out that, in the Zhou period,
"Shang Ti [Shangdi] now becomes divorced from any identification with the Shang ancestors and the world of gods and the
world of ancestors become two distinctly different worlds."
Chang places the reason for this shift to political expediency since
the Shang ruling clan (Zi clan) had identified its ancestors with
Shangdi, and the Zhou ruling clan (Ji clan) would not, of course,
accept the Zi clan's conception of its power and the influence of
its ancestral spirits. The religious difference, however, may be
more farreaching.

Not only do the Zhou appear to have placed more sacrificial emphasis on the clan ancestors, but the Zhou clan ancestor,
Houji, the Lord of Millet, implies greater emphasis on agriculture by the Zhou than by the Shang. This interpretation would
only be enhanced if the original written form of "ji" was a different character meaning a way of tilling the soil rather than millet (Wen 1948:1:73–80).

From the standpoint of ritual decor, there are clear differences, although the vessel shapes are generally the same. The
major sacrificial vessel decor of the Shang, the *taotie*, is found on
some of the earliest bronzes made shortly after the conquest—
for example, a *gui* dated to the eighth day after the Zhou conquest and excavated in 1976 in Shansi Province has the *taotie*

decor but also has bird handles and the high, square Zhou foot (Fong 1980:pl.41)—but this may be because the artisans in Anyang, the conquered Shang capital, were ordered to produce bronzes too quickly to allow for the craftsmen to create motifs other than those with which they were familiar. The Shang bird motifs are not found on Zhou vessels, and, assuming that the vessels with the earliest bird motifs replacing *taotie* motifs were made for predynastic Zhou rulers (see Appendix), the primary early Zhou motifs, the *feng* and the elephant bird, are not found on Shang vessels:

> The sudden rise of the bird motif to a position of dominance on several families of bronze vessels in the early Chou [Zhou] period, whatever its significance in terms of dynastic change or religious orientation, was an important aspect of the revolution in both style and iconography. (Pope 1967:1:327)

Although the *feng* has been interpreted as a wind deity in the Shang period and, rather tenuously, a thunder deity in the Han (see Fehl 1971), the argument for a solar connection is stronger, as it is based on comparative as well as internal evidence. Alternatively, Kennedy's (1982) hypothesis of game birds eating toads containing hallucinogenic toxins and serving as biomediators is appealing. However, while this hypothesis may be considered in regard to the symbolism of the crane as a familiar of the *xian* (see Chapters 3 and 6), it is less plausible in regard to pheasants. Sympathetic as I am to a pharmacologic substratum of myth, here, I believe, the symbolic explanation is still the most feasible.

Of equal importance to the solar connection is the potential connection of the *feng* to ancestral spirits. This argument is based on a connection between a single verse in the *Shi*, from the Zhou sacrificial odes, and a vessel that has been archaeologically excavated. This single case argument has been pointed out to me by David Keightly as weak, but I would counter that the opposite may hold with respect to ritual motifs. Commonly understood symbols are not commented on within a culture and could be most ambiguous to those without. For example, how would the simple

Protestant cross be understood by future archaeologists if the Gospels and Christian theology had been an oral tradition? It is the odd example that is explicit and, if linked to mythic material, may explicate the larger number of implicit symbols.

The interpretation of the *feng* as symbolic of ancestral spirits, bolstered by important comparative associations, matches the previously noted Zhou emphasis on ancestral spirits in comparison with the Shang. If the link between Hou Ji and the Fu-sang tree is early, then we have the connection between the solar and ancestral attributes of the *feng* as suggested in the *Shi* (Odes 235 and 252). In Ode 235, the character translated as "shines in heaven" literally means "bright," and the character contains the sun radical. The *feng*, therefore, may represent the Zhou ancestral spirits to whom sacrifices are made—such as King Wen—in their descent to receive the offerings. These ancestral spirits have a solar connotation, the most visible symbol of celestial power, essential to agriculture. One might speculate that the origin of the tradition of the (northern) Chinese ruler facing south is that only he can face the ancestral spirits symbolized by the sun.

Allan has linked the Shang ancestors totemically with the ten suns symbolized by ravens, which may be the noncrested birds found on the Shang sacrificial vessels. She (1981:321) suggests that "this system was specific to the Shang and lost its integrity when the Shang . . . were conquered by the Chou [Zhou] whose mythology only included a single sun." Hence, the Shang may have had both the ten sun birds as ancestral totemic spirits, symbolized by a crow or raven, and possibly also the single astral crested sun cock (*niaoxing*), while the Zhou had but the single sun cock, which they identified with the ancestors.

Approximately one century following the Zhou conquest, both the decor and the shapes of the bronze vessels noticeably change. The *feng* disappears as a design motif and apparently shifts in significance from a masculine concept in its relationship to the sun and ancestral spirits to, by the end of the Zhou period, a female complement to the *long*. In this period, the crow becomes the recognized sun symbol. Perhaps the Shang motif was maintained in the state of Song, with its Shang-descended rulers, and possibly in the state of Chu, which is linked to Shang culture by a number of scholars, and eventually displaced the Zhou sun-cock motif as the various cultural traditions merged. In any case, the crow displaced the solar aspect of the *feng*, freeing the image to take on the missing and increasingly important feminine power-symbolic complex. However, the time span involved, over half a millennium, does not lead to any degree of certitude in these regards.

The elephant-bird motif remains an enigma to me. The physical interpretation of the design motif I consider certain, and such a concept is attested to in Chinese legends. In general, it would seem that the design is an amalgamation of the masculine fertility bull/bison/elephant symbolic complex with the masculine solar/celestial *feng* symbol of early Zhou culture. It is plausible that the motif developed in a different location than the *feng* or was that of a subbranch of the Zhou Ji clan. However, at this time, archaeological data and inscriptional analysis are inconclusive. Future finds may clarify the situation.

The change in ritual decor from the Shang to the Zhou periods indicates more than a relatively simple change in symbolism. For a long period preceding the present, China has had the presence of both shamans and mediums. This complex situation could simply be due to the immensity of China and the synthesis of a number of divergent cultures over several thousand years. However, if the *feng* does represent the ancestral spirits in their descent to the sacrifice, there is a major conceptual difference from the Shang concept of the *taotie* that probably represents the ascent of the sacrifice to Shangdi and the ancestral spirits above.

Remnants of shamanistic experiences and concepts continued in late Zhou culture (fourth century B.C.E.), especially in the *Zhuangzi* and the *Chuci* (see Chapter 3), but there is substantial evidence indicating the presence of mediums in the late Zhou texts as well (see below). The character translated as "descend" in regard to mediums in these texts is the same as the one in Ode 235, previously cited. Perhaps Shang culture was shamanistic, and predynastic Zhou culture mediumistic, the two orientations merging after the first century of Zhou rule. This, of course, is quite speculative, and, in part, would hinge on whether the meaning of *shi* (Incorporator of the Dead, see below) had the same exact meaning in the Shang as in the Zhou period, when the *shi* functioned mediumistically.

A second-century C.E. Chinese text explains the mask, important to early Chinese rituals, both Shang and Zhou, as the seat of the departed soul (Eberhard 1968: 330), an understanding pertinent to mediumism. Elizabeth Childs-Johnson (1987) has added an important epigraphic consideration to this analysis. She has suggested that one of the major Shang dynasty terms for ancestral spirits, *gui*, is an image of a spirit worshipper donning a spirit mask. This mask is closely related to the mask represented in Shang decor. Although in the preceding chapter, the Shang evidence was argued to indicate shamanism, the possibility of mediumistic trance in Shang ritual as well cannot be discounted. Further research is needed in these regards.

These various hypotheses raise another interesting issue. All the Zhou symbols have a southern locus, in distinction to those of the Shang. Shamanism is a Siberian and circumpolar phenomenon; mediumism is common to Southeast Asia and Oceania. Crow is a northern circumpacific sun symbol; sun cock is Southeast Asian and Oceanian. *Xiang* (elephant) has a southern Chinese locus, and may be linked to wet-rice agriculture. The Zhou homeland was in the Wei valley, southwest of the last Shang capital, but, according to their traditions, the Zhou had only moved there within the century before the conquest of Anyang. There are hints in the *Shiji* (the second century B.C.E. history) that the Zhou were "barbarians" before they moved into the Wei valley; that is, they had customs different from those of the Shang. It is possible that their origin was actually further south, perhaps linked to the still undetermined source of wet-rice agriculture, connected to the mythic adoption of mediumism in Korea.

The Polynesian people of highly isolated (until 1938) Bellona Island of the Solomons on the fringe of Melanesian culture are organized into patrilineal clans. The priest-chief was possessed in rituals by the founder of the clan who spoke through him. "The priest-chief's primary task during rituals was to act as the embodiment of the ancestors of his patrilineal descent group. He was thus the ritual symbol of the entire group" (Monberg

1991:187). The ancestral spirits interceded for the priest-chief with the sky god:

> On Bellona there was thought to be a hierarchical line of communication in which people conveyed wishes to their ancestors, who in turn related them to district deities, who then assumed direct communication with the sky gods, who again fulfilled the wishes of humans for fertility and other gifts. (Monberg 1991:212)

If we interpose the title *wang* (king) for priest-chief and use the Chinese term *tian* (sky, sky deity) for the sky god, we have here a description that would fit early Zhou religion. If the Zhou ultimately had a more southerly locus, then it would be expected that they would share common traits with Oceanic religions, which are also distantly derived from those of southeastern China.

Historic Mediumism

In contemporary China and for at least the last thousand years, mediums have arisen from among the poor and socially disadvantaged. This accords with I. M. Lewis's (1971) understanding of ecstatic functioning as a means for individuals to gain a degree of social prestige not otherwise available. Nonetheless, I differ with his terminology, which follows the British anthropological practice of calling all ecstatic functionaries "shamans."

Since the adoption of Zhu Xi's understanding six hundred years ago as the official, orthodox one, rationalistic interpretations became normative for the educated elite. Except for sacrificial rituals and private meditation, all modes of overt religious behavior were considered superstition. This is an attitude reinforced today in China by the combination of Western science and Marxist-Leninism. However, it is clear that prior to this shift in interpretation, mediumistic practices were not limited to the lower classes.

Elite Mediumism in Early China

The preceding section argued that the *Odes* indicate spirit possession as part of elite sacrificial rituals. The ritual texts provide sufficient information (as pointed out by my former student, David Armstrong 1994) that in the late Zhou period, the *shi*, (Personator of the Dead, as usually translated) in elite sacrificial rituals was possessed by the ancestral spirits to whom the sacrifice was being offered (noted also in Küng and Ching 1989:28–29). Accordingly, it seems preferable to translate the term, which is also the common one for a corpse, as "Incorporator of the Dead."

The sequence of preparatory steps carried out by the *shi* prior to the sacrificial ritual, as well as the rites themselves, ensured an ecstatic state; that this state was mediumistic is definitely indicated by the context. After divining an appropriate day for offering sacrifice, the primary sacrificer, the Descendant (son or daughter-in-law of the deceased, depending on the appropriate gender), and the other participants fast for seven days to "bring [the mind] to a state of fixed determination" (*Liji* in Legge 1885:28:240). On the fourth day of the fast, the *shi* was chosen from among the participants (grandson or granddaughter-in-law of the deceased) by divination, "inviting the spirit *in his person* to take some refreshment" (*Yili* in Steele 1917:2:160, emphasis added).

The *shi*, once selected, underwent an immediate increase of status and was treated as if he or she were already the ghost of the ancestor, "in passing whom it is required to adopt a hurried pace" (Legge 1885:28:292)."When an officer sees one who is to personate the dead he should dismount from his carriage. . . . The ruler himself . . . should do the same" (Legge 1885:27:87).

Meditation intensified for the *shi*, who was instructed to remember and visualize all aspects of the deceased: "How and where they sat, how they smiled and spoke, what were their aims and views, what they delighted in, and what things they desired and enjoyed" (Legge 1885:28:240).

Given that the *shi* was already into the fourth day of a fast, albeit probably only partial, one can assume that alternate states of consciousness similar to those produced by hallucinogenic substances were engendered.

> Mental imagery is intensified through ritual procedures for
> inducing altered states of consciousness that manipulates

both physiological and psychological variables through the auto-hypnosis of the participants. (Noll 1985:447)

Furthermore, "The hallucinogenic vitalization and the synaesthetic perception of the mythological events by various sensory systems immensely strengthen the power of symbols to reorganize the personality" (Andritzky 1989:84).

On the day of sacrifice, the *shi* was driven to the clan temple in a chariot and deferred to as if he or she were the deceased, although the text still refers to the *shi* as "one who is to incorporate the dead." During the sacrifice, the *shi* several times ceremonially offered food and wine to the dead, which the *shi* then ate and drank. Only after drinking nine cups of alcoholic beverage (Legge 1885:28,246), did the *shi* communicate blessings to the Liturgist (master of ceremonies), who in turn announced these blessings to the other participants (Steele 1917:2,172). It is the inebriation of the *shi* that leads to the descent of the spirits into her or his body:

> The representative [Incorporator of the Dead] feasts and drinks felicity and blessings descend on you.
> (repeated refrain, Karlgren 1950: Ode 248).

> The pious descendant goes to his place,
> the officiating invoker [Liturgist] makes his announcement:
> "The spirits are all drunk";
> the august representative [Incorporator] of the dead then rises,
> the drums and bells escort away the representative;
> the divine protectors (the spirits) then return (leave the temple).
> (Karlgren 1950: Ode 209)

Jiu, the fermented beverage, was at that time made from millet. Although there is no record of its alcoholic content, one can reasonably assume it would be similar to beer made from cereals. In homemade lagers and ales made from barley, it is difficult to keep the alcoholic content to less than 5 percent, and 7 to 8 percent is not difficult to achieve. Given that by the time these texts were written, the Chinese had had at least two thousand years of experience in fermenting grain, an estimated range of 5 percent to 8 percent would be a conservative figure.

Volumes of early Zhou bronze sacrificial cups in the Royal Ontario Museum were measured to near the rim (assuming one fills an opaque cup nearly full), giving an average of 5.5 ounces (170 ml.) for the *gu* and 5.25 ounces (155 ml.) for the *zhi*. Of course, the ritual texts were not put together in their final form until the Han period, but the capacity of Han ritual cups tends to be even larger. Hence, a conservative estimate is that the *shi* consumed between 2.4 and 3.9 ounces of pure alcohol (equivalent to between 5 and 8 bar shots of eighty-proof liquor).

When consumed over a ninety-minute period, six standard drinks or 75 grams of ethanol will generally cause slightly blurred vision and other signs of intoxication in the average Caucasian male weighing between 68 and 80 kilograms (Fisher et al. 1987). East Asians are in general genetically predisposed to be more affected by alcohol than Caucasians (Wolff 1972; Scwitters et al. 1982). Given that the alcohol consumption, although ingested with rich food, took place after a seven-day fast, the inebriation of the *shi* was ensured.

Alcohol, along with other drugs, is a common inducer of trance in a religious context. William James (1902:297) noted, "The sway of alcohol over mankind is unquestionably due to its power to stimulate the mystical faculties of human nature." The alcohol, the seven-day fast and continuous meditation, including three days of visualization, the treatment of the *shi* by others as the deceased spirit, the sacrificial ritual, usually with drums and bells, and cultural expectations all combined to lead undoubtedly to the possession of the *shi* by the recipient of the sacrifice. Hence, it is not the ritual office alone that leads to the assumption of mediumistic trance. For example, in Andean religion, the *mihuq* (eater) consumes the food for the dead member of the family in sacrificial ritual but is not understood to become the dead spirit. Rather, "he gobbles down the dinner while intoning [Roman Catholic] prayers that direct the food to the dead recipients" (Allen 1988:152).

The grandson or granddaughter-in-law of the deceased became the means for the spirit of the deceased to descend to the sacrifice, to eat and drink the offerings, thereby becoming inebriated and extending blessings to the clan. One wonders if the experience of the elite in becoming inebriated, to allow the incorporation of the clan's deceased spirits, gave rise to the understanding that the spirits must become inebriated to offer their blessings. Since these sacrifices were the most common elite religious ritual and given the relationship of the *shi* to the spirits, one can reasonably assume that most members of the elite at some time in their lives had such an experience, most commonly in late adolescence. This experience undoubtedly enhanced the identification of elite individuals with the clan.

Shi continued to be possessed by clan ancestors at least into the Chinese medieval period. In the "Ancient Text" addition to the *Shu* (*Yinzheng* [Book of Documents]), probably written in the third or fourth centuries C.E. (Creel 1970:448), we find the rulers of ancient Xia being discussed pejoratively "as if they were in the office of the *shi*, being without hearing or awareness." Here we have an explicit description of the normative mediumistic state. However, by the eighth century, the elimination of the *shi* seems to be the one significant change in the sacrificial rites (Ebrey 1991:xviii).

Mediums as Officials in Early China

Although throughout most of the twentieth century, scholars have identified the *wu* with shamans, J. J. M. de Groot (1910: 1191) writing near the turn of the century, far more accurately understood the *wu* to be possessed by spirits or gods, and termed the complex "Wu-ism":

> These instructive lines [in the *Guoyu*, see below] thus state explicitly that the wu and hih [*xi*] were possessed by shen, that is to say, by divinity or spirituality, and that this descended into them in consequence of their own powerful imagination.

The word *wu* was used in the Shang period, but its meaning is controversial. Chow Tse-tsung (1986) suggests that the term etymologically derives from the jingling of jade pendants worn by the *wu* during ritual fertility dances, dances based on treading in the footsteps of the deity who impregnated the mother of the mythic founder of the Zhou dynasty. Dances tracing footsteps of mythic beings became a major aspect of Daoist rituals and meditation practices. Chow further traces the term to the founding ruler of the Shang based on the etymology of names and places, but whether actual shamanism or mediumism is involved is far from clear.

Victor Mair (1990), arguing from linguistic (*wu* pronounced *m^yag* in the Shang period) and archaeological evidence (a seemingly Caucasian carved head with a sign similar to the graph for *wu* on the forehead), posits that the *wu* was a religiocultural borrowing along with the chariot from early Indo-European culture, that the *wu* is equivalent to the Persian *maguŝ*. Given that early Chinese culture was bordered by shamanism on the north, present since before 30,000 B.P. (Bering Straights crossing by paleo-Amerindians) and mediumism, at least since horticulture in Southeast Asia, and that the Chinese did not exist in a religious vacuum, it is unlikely that the function of the *wu* was borrowed from the West, although the term may have been. Furthermore, given a general scholarly consensus that ecstatic religious functionaries were an essential aspect of protohistoric Chinese government (David Keightly, various unpublished papers; K. C. Chang 1983), although the details are debated, such borrowing is improbable. In any case, the functioning of the *magi* is not the same as that of either mediums or shamans (see Smith 1978).

Sarah Allan (1991:77), arguing from an epigraphical analysis, finds that the logograph may refer to the four directions, particularly in the context of sacrifice. In at least some instances, the graph seems to refer to performing sacrifice as well as divination with regard to sacrifice.

The situation regarding the Zhou period is much clearer. The *wu* were among a number of officials involved with religious rituals and other practices. The *Zhouli*, in various places, discusses hierarchically ranked officials including female and male *zhu*, assisted by male and female *wu*. In the Han period, the two terms were combined into a single compound, *wuzhu*. Ranked above at least the *wu* were their *shi* (masters—not the same Chinese word as the Incorporator of the Dead). The functions of the *wu* included exorcism, rituals regarding burial and the dead, prognostication through spirits, and so on. *Yi* (physicians) were apparently also perceived to be related to or connected with the *wu* (see de Groot 1910:1203). In later Chinese culture at least, mediums also enabled deities to heal through the use of their bodies.

Wu are mentioned in a number of Zhou and Han texts (for citations, see de Groot 1910:1187–1211), the most precise regarding the ideal is a passage in the *Guoyu*, "Chiyuxia":

> Those among the people whose souls were not flighty and were able to be reverential and inwardly upright, their wisdom could interpret the upper (Heaven) and lower (Earth) realms; their sanctity was able to enlighten the distant, proclaiming it with clarity; their intelligence was able to illuminate it (good spirits); their cleverness was able to understand and eliminate it (evil spirits). For this reason, the bright spirits descended into them; if (they descended) into a male, (he) was called *xi*; if into a female, (she) was called *wu*. [The ritual texts instead refer to "male *wu*" and "female *wu*."]

In contrast, the later attitude of the educated towards the *wu* can first be found in the skeptical writings of Wang Chung (C.E. 27–97):

> The dead of past generations place people in trance and use them to speak. When the *wu* pray with mysterious sounds they bring down the souls of the dead, who speak through the mouths of the *wu*. All their words are but boastfulness. (*Lunheng*, chapter 20)

By the Ming dynasty, laws were passed forbidding the *wu* to practice, with severe penalties for noncompliance. These laws were continued by the last dynasty. Nevertheless, mediums have continued to flourish, using different names, to the present. The terms used for mediums vary considerably over time and place and constitute a study in itself.

Mediums in Modern China

Much has been written on Chinese mediumism of the late nineteenth and twentieth centuries (e.g., de Groot 1910, Jordan 1972), and there is no need to summarize these studies here. Mediums, frequently associated with local temples, along with the sacrificial complex discussed in Chapter 2, are ubiquitous aspects of popular Chinese religion. They are (or at least were into the mid-twentieth century) common from far north in Manchuria to the extreme south of Hainan and Guangtung, and from the eastern island of Taiwan to Tibet in China's far west. For example, in notes written at the end of 1939 in far northwestern China, we find, "The spirit man [or woman] claims that a certain Spirit or Hsien [*xian*] will enter into him after which he loses knowledge of what he is saying; he claims he is transformed into the mouthpiece of the Spirit" (Söderbom 1940:3). Mediums are still common among overseas Chinese (see Elliot 1955).

Characteristic of mediumism in southern and southeastern China is one of the means used for engendering or enhancing trance. Many mediums initiate or deepen their trance by beating themselves with spiked balls on a thong or the sharp edges of swords or by thrusting skewers through the fleshy parts of their body. This action not only deepens the trance, perhaps by releasing large amounts of endorphins, but indicates to the congregants that the medium is authentically in trance. As in a deep hypnotic state, not only is the medium oblivious to the pain, which would otherwise be considerable, but both physiological trauma and bleeding almost immediately cease. However, these mediums do not always use such techniques for entering trance, and other mediums in the same region may never use them.

Contrary to the expectations of both educated Chinese and Westerners, the modernization of Chinese culture and expansion of the economy in Hong Kong, Singapore, and Taiwan, have led not to the demise of mediumism, but to its growth. I will give several examples from Taiwan, with which I am most familiar, over the last few years.

The tremendous surge of the economy with a considerable increase in disposable income has led to a flourishing of temples, both the building of new ones and the refurbishing of the old. Many of these temples arise from people's dreams and from the words of spirits spoken through mediums. The services of mediums are required to meet the needs of those who come to the temples for advice and assistance.

The current availability of trucks and other vehicles has eased the difficulties of the yearly journey of local temple dei-

ties to the home temple for family visitation and spiritual re-
charge. Pilgrimage, particularly in regard to Mazu has been geo-
metrically increasing. In 1989, Taiwanese, in over ten thousand
small boats, crossed the Taiwan Straits in defiance of the government and consequent serious criminal charges to bring their local Mazu images to visit the home temple in Fujian Province on
the mainland of China. (The Nationalist government wisely decided to ignore its own dire warnings after the event.) Each pilgrimage from a local temple requires mediums to be available
for the appearance of the deity, as well as chair carriers for the
image who go into trance as the power of the deity increases on
approaching the temple.

Private store-front temples are also flourishing. The combination of a government lottery and the rise of many of the middle
class to the ranks of the wealthy in the booming economy, with
land speculation and a rapidly expanding new stock market, has
given the poor and the lower middle class hopes of striking it
rich also. Rather than depend on simple luck, many seek the advice of the spirits to ascertain the winning lottery number. This
has led to the rise of so many store-front temples that newspa-
pers have reported the noise of the séances to be a serious urban
problem. Indeed, some have combined the lottery-ticket-selling
operation with a small temple on the same premises.

I attended a typical session at a store-front temple in a town
outside of Taichung. The owner of the temple termed himself a
fashi (the latter part of the binomial expression discussed above
as occurring in the late Zhou ritual texts). De Groot (1910: 1244)
noted *fashi* was used by mediums in Amoy (the mainland port
nearest Taiwan) in the early twentieth century. *Fashi* could be
functionally translated as "possession priest," borrowing the term
from Paul Stoller's (1989) study of African religion; Alvin Cohen
(1992:191) translates the term as "Master of the Rites." (The same
term in the Chinese Buddhist tradition means "Dharma Master"
and is an appellation for scholar monks.)

The *fashi* did not himself enter trance, but commanded the
appropriate spirits to enter the two mediums he employed under him, indicating his mastery by cracking a whip he carried
throughout the séance. Until customers arrived, the *fashi*, the two

mediums, and I chatted, uncertain if there would be any call for consultations with spirits that evening. Eventually, clients did show up, some for healing, but most for a lottery number, which was given during the last part of the trance in a private room so the number would remain secret.

The mediums alternated going into trance, the *fashi* calling the spirits considered best for the particular request. The mediums did not wound themselves, but, as in African and Afro-American religions, went from a light to a deeper trance by putting on costumes or other symbols appropriate to the spirits summoned. Each trance also involved a dramatic component suitable to the relevant spirit.

The ending of martial law in Taiwan has led to a lessening of the prohibitions on mediumism and related aspects of popular religion. The Zhonghua Minguo Lingji Xiehui (Republic of China Medium's Association) was one of five religious sponsors of the 1989 International Conference on Chinese Religion (discussed in Chapter 1). Several members of this organization, who had limited formal education, attended every session of the conference, constantly took notes, and made themselves useful at appropriate opportunities. The first trip after the formal conference was to the Huang-i Kung temple outside of Hsin-tien, where the Association was organized. The temple is dedicated to the Dragon King. There we were invited to a "dialogue between scholars and mediums" and lunch.

The Association is quite new, having been founded and given government recognition in 1989. Its stated purpose includes relevant research and study courses to bring the mediums respectable recognition and to bring them into the modern world. A school for mediums began to operate in 1992. The Association has both group (temple) and individual memberships. In the latter regard, the Association functions as a registry of mediums. According to the listing published in September, 1989, there were 62 organizational members and 1,940 individual members (who call themselves *lingji* and *lingmei* rather than *chigung*, etc.).

The meeting took place in the modern basement of the temple, which was arranged with a long head table and three long tables perpendicular to it. The hall was rather plain, except for prominent photographs of the late Chiang Ching-kuo, the son of Chiang K'ai-shek and former president of the Republic of China who shrewdly promoted Taiwanese language and culture; President Lee Teng-hui; and patriotic slogans. Approximately forty participating mediums sat at the middle table, with the scholars sitting at the tables on each side. The majority of the mediums present were women, ranging in age from the twenties to the sixties, of interest because women had been forbidden to function as mediums in China since the sixteenth century, although they continued to do so in far southern China. All were dressed in ordinary, contemporary clothing.

After formal introductions, a microphone was passed in order of seating among the mediums. As each received the microphone, the medium went into an imperceptible to a perceptible (rigid postures, muscular tremors, etc.) light trance. Through the mediums, various spirits spoke to us in a variety of languages: Taiwanese, northern *guanhua* (similar to the speech of northern opera), Japanese, and unintelligible (to the unaware) spirit languages. Many otherwise shy mediums spoke with impressive theatrical diction or sung with magnificent voices. A few spirits wrote long messages to us on paper or a modern blackboard. All of the scholars I talked with afterwards were pleasantly surprised that the "dialogue" was not to be with the mediums as expected but with the spirits who possessed them. During lunch and during the bus ride to other temples there was ample opportunity to speak informally with the mediums themselves.

To test the spirits, one of scholars asked about an undisclosed will and related documents of Sun Yat-sen. (I assume the questioner had been doing research on the subject.) The spirits of various deceased supporters of Sun Yat-sen came through the mediums and began to heatedly argue with each other concerning the topic. Finally, one of the mediums at the head table was taken over by the famous magistrate of the eleventh century, Bao Cheng, who calmed the proceedings and brought order to the scene. The scholar never received a direct answer to his question.

One could go on to discuss the many other aspects of mediumism in contemporary Chinese culture, such as the growth of *shanshu* (morality texts), dictated or written through mediums when in trance (see Pas 1989; Zhen 1988), but I trust the point has been made. Mediumism is not an anachronistic element of Chinese culture but an essential element that thrives in the context of modern culture.

Conclusions

In the formative period of Chinese culture, all textual references to ecstatic functionaries are to mediums, even though there are also references to shamanic experiences but with no mention of function. Male and female aristocrats, including those of the ruling clans, at times functioned as mediums in the most important rituals. Given the frequency of ancestral sacrifices, virtually all of the elite in their youth, both male and female, would have been bonded to the clan by becoming the medium for the descent of the clan's deceased members. Occupations that involved mediumistic experiences were government offices. Iconographic evidence when related to the earliest extant texts indicates that this religious phenomenon may be connected to the predynastic Zhou, that is, into the second millennium B.C.E., if not earlier.

Although the elite came to frown on mediums, mediums became or remained (the situation is unclear) a major element of popular religion. In Chinese popular religion, faith is unnecessary, for the people experience the immediate presence of the deities as they are embodied in possessed mediums. Modernization in and of itself has had no negative effect on this aspect of Chinese culture.

Chinese mediums did incorporate through cultural borrowing aspects of Siberian shamanism (or Siberian shamans may have adopted aspects of Chinese mediumism); for example, initiation through climbing a ladder of swords (de Groot 1910:1248). Nevertheless, substantial differences remain, such as possession itself and the medium usually not remembering what took place while in trance.

Hence, it might be appropriate for scholars of Chinese religion to be more precise in their terminology and cease to call Chinese mediumism (or spirit possession, for those who prefer the term) by the inappropriate term *shamanism*, reserving the word for actual shamanistic phenomena. (Although, as Chinese ethnologists familiar with the differences recently pointed out, even if current Manchurian ecstatic functionaries are mediums, they continue to utilize the Manchurian word, *sáman*.) A reading of some of the basic works on sub-Saharan African and Afro-American religions, as well as Oceanic traditions, would indicate the considerable similarities between common Chinese functional trances and those of mediumistic cultures. Indeed, a comparison from a religio-ecological perspective of early Chinese sacred kingship with that of West Africa, given the many similarities regarding ancestral sacrifice and possession trance, may further clarify the early Chinese religious situation.

The probable high incidence of mediumistic experiences among the elite from at least the mid-Zhou period into the medieval period also demands a reinterpretation of Western scholarly assumptions regarding the religious attitudes of the elite. While intellectuals redirected the understanding of the sacrificial rituals to the social fabric itself (see Chapter 2), this does not necessitate the interpretation that the elite were agnostic regarding the spiritual recipients of the sacrifices.

Several passages in the *Lunyu* (Analects) have been commonly interpreted by Western scholars as implying that Confucius was agnostic; for example, "The Master said, '. . . to keep one's distance from the Gods [*shen*] and spirits [*gui*] while showing them reverence may be called wisdom'" (6:21; Lau 1979:84). However, this typical reading of the text emphasizes a modern Western interpretational framework. "This last passage has been . . . considered to be clear evidence of agnosticism. But this does not accord with the understanding of most Chinese commentators" (Creel 1960:115). The passage can also be literally read: to "reverence the ancestral spirits [*shengui*] while keeping [oneself at a respectful] distance from them can be called wisdom."

The interpretation of agnosticism arises in part from a confusion of two different terms: *shen* (spirit) and *gui* (ancestral spirit). The compound *guishen* is also used for *gui* (but not for *shen* alone): "Jilu asked how to serve *guishen*. The Master said, 'You are not yet able to serve humans [adequately]; how are you able to serve their *gui*'" (11:12). In the *Analects*, the *shen* are potentially dangerous—

"The Master did not speak of the uncanny, brute strength, disorder, and *shen*" (7:21), while the *gui* are family—"The Master said, 'To sacrifice to *gui* that are not one's own is obsequious' " (2:24). Perhaps with regard to *shen* there was a degree of agnosticism— "Sacrifice to *shen* as if they were present" (3:12), an attitude not taken toward *gui*. Confucius, in praising the mythic culture hero Yu, said he exhibited "the utmost filiality towards *guishen*" (8:21).

If the elite when youths were possessed by their ancestral spirits during the sacrificial rituals at the time of Confucius, it is unlikely that they were skeptical as to their existence. Furthermore, as will be argued in the next two chapters, other ecstatic experiences, particularly the mystic experience, increasingly became of interest to the elite. Hence, as in Hellenic and Hellenistic cultures, trance experience was at least as important as normal consciousness in informing their world view.

In Europe, the Protestant emphasis on the text of the Bible combined with the shift of alchemy to the physical sciences created a culture that only considered knowledge directly derived from sense perception under the conditions of normal consciousness to be real or objective. Awareness gained in any other fashion was considered irrational and subjective. *Irrational* became a pejorative term. Western interpreters have read this value into Chinese culture, but such interpretation is belied by the available data.

5 the mystic experience in chinese religion I: transformation

Now I have said something, but I do not know whether or not what I said has really said anything.

—Zhuang Zhou, fourth century B.C.E.

There is a tendency among many students of religion to use the term *mysticism* in a very general fashion, as a catchall for various types of religious experience and behavior (e.g., Eliade 1960:73). In the study of Chinese religion, the word tends to be utilized for the techniques, experiences, and cultural subsets directed towards individualistic ecstatic experiences in elite Buddhism and *daojiao* (e.g., Livia Kohn 1991). Many of these experiences would fall into the psychological category of "altered states of consciousness" (Ludwig 1966). In this book, the various terms usually applied to ecstatic religious experiences are discreetly defined: shamanism (Chapter 3), mediumism (Chapter 4), and, in this Chapter, the mystic experience as a particular type of ecstatic experience. Here the relationship between shamanism and the mystic experience will be discussed, particularly in regard to the initial integration of the mystic experience into Chinese culture. In the following Chapter, further integration of the mystic experience within Chinese culture, particularly among the elite, and its relationship to aesthetics will be explored.

This Chapter includes a speculative study concerning the development of the mystic experience in human history and its relationship to primal and complex human cultures. The study originally arose over fifteen years ago from two stimuli: a reading of Agehananda Bharati's (1976) work on the mystic experience which, admirable in many respects, is understandably weak in dealing with primal culture, and a paper by a former student of mine, then an apprentice Anishnabe (Ojibwe) sha-man, which, in effect, interpreted the mystic experience reflected in Chinese literature as shamanistic. In investigating the reasons for this interpretation, I found that the religio-ecological trans-formation that had taken place, until very recent times, in north-ern Anishnabe culture not only explained the relationship between the two modes of ecstatic religious experience in na-tive American cultures, but was applicable to early Chinese cul-ture as well.

This Chapter, as well, is a further exercise in the compara-tive study of religion. As in the preceding Chapters, observation of comparable developments in cultures closer in time to the present can suggest hypothetical solutions for understanding problems in the development of Chinese religion, particularly of the distant past. The comparative models need not be literate cul-tures nor civilizations, in the technical sense. The religio-ecologi-cal process that I found to have taken place regarding shamanism and the mystic experience relatively recently in a native Ameri-can culture appears similar to changes that can be identified in the early (fourth century B.C.E.) strata of the *Zhuangzi* (see Chap-ter 3). A plausible explanation for the process also fits the socio-economic changes taking place in Chinese culture at that time. Further analysis of the later strata of the text suggests the means for the integration of the mystic experience into the Chinese cul-tural matrix.

The Problem

A partial consensus, still controversial, has developed regarding a definition of the mystic experience, considered not as a set of experiences, but as a particular type of universal (not culturally bound) human experience (see Staal 1975, Merkur 1989). W. T. Stace (1961:131), a philosopher, in a now classic work, analyzed all mystic states to be basically the same although expressed in two modes, the primary characteristics of which are "The Unify-ing Vision—all things are one" and "The Unitary Consciousness." Bharati (1976:25), an anthropologist writing as a participant-observer, presents an operational definition of the mystic experience (or "zero-experience": "any consummative experience within each universe of discourse"):

> [It is] the person's intuition of a numerical oneness with the cosmic absolute, with the universal matrix, or with any essence stipulated by the various theological and speculative systems of the world.

To reverse the above definition: all ecstatic experiences are not mystic experiences (this point is of the essence in comparison to shamanism); only the ecstatic experience of complete loss of self-identity—union with the ultimate in some sense (Bharati) or with Nothing in Chinese and Jewish (Sholem 1954:4–5) mysticism, "ego-loss" in psychological terms (Laing 1967:95)—is properly the mystic (or zero) experience.

The definition is similar to one earlier presented by French sinologist Henri Maspero (1950: 211, 213). Bharati's definition as Stace's use of the term is to be distinguished from more general definitions that would accept a greater number of ecstatic states or interpretations; for example, "The basic definition of mystical experience is the intuitive perception that we are part of a universe that is a unified whole" (Deikman 1977:68).

The term ecstasy is almost as variable in its use as *mystical experience*; for example, the broad definition of Marghanita Laski (1961:5):

> The usage I had in mind was one in which ecstasy named a range of experiences characterized by being joyful, transitory, unexpected, rare, valued and extraordinary to the point of often seeming as if derived from a praeternatural source.

My use of the term is more limited, applying to trance states to which Laski's modifiers often apply. Trance states are subsumed within the term *altered state of consciousness* which is increasingly used by psychologists (e.g., Pelletier and Garfield 1976).

The mystic experience in itself is ineffable (James 1902); any interpretation or description is post-experience (Stace 1961). Hence, any description of the experience is culture-bound, described in complex cultures within the relevant philosophical or theological systems. It is for this reason that many definitions are not universal, but are particular to specific, so-called higher, cultures. For example, Stace (1961) focuses on "unity of evidence from Christian, Islamic, Jewish, Mahayana Buddhist and Hindu sources, also . . . the pagan mystic Plotinus and the modern Englishman. . . ."

This problem brings us to the initial concern of this chapter: Is the mystic experience peculiar to "higher" cultures as theologically oriented theorists tend to assume (Sholem 1954; E. Underhill 1955; Zaehner 1957) or is it a natural human experience as posited by some anthropologists (Bharati 1976) and psychologists?

> Here the "highest" experience ever described, the joyful fusion with the ultimate that man can conceive, can be seen simultaneously as the deepest experience of our ultimate personal animality and specieshood, as the acceptance of our profound biological nature as isomorphic with nature in general. (Maslow 1971:334)

Since among the psychologists, with their emphasis on the individual human being rather than social groups, there are those who have posited this experience as the basis of religion—"Certain transcendental experiences seem to me to be the original wellspring of all religions" (Laing 1967:95)—while theologically oriented historians have posited that the experience occurs within the development of religion—"Mysticism is a definite state in the historical development of religion and makes its appearance under certain well-defined conditions" (Sholem 1954:7)—the question is of considerable importance to the historian of religions.

There is sufficient evidence to substantiate the claim that the mystic experience takes place among those in modern culture who are outside of traditional religions or a theological framework: R. M. Bucke in Bucke (1901), J. A. Symonds in Stace (1961), Jesse Watkins in Laing (1967), the examples collected by Hardy (1979), and the examples cited by the transpersonal psychologists (the late works of Maslow, etc.). Hence, Bharati's (1976:142) opinion, "zero-experiences are natural experiences," is acceptable, although the neuro-psychological state has yet to be identified, as it has been to some degree for the native American vision quest (Jilek 1974:28–31). In this regard, transpersonal psychologists have reported producing this state in deep hetero-hypnosis (Tart 1970, Sherman 1972).

Accordingly, it is concluded that the mystic experience takes place among individuals in all human cultures, including primal ones. Bharati (1976:145) met several non-Hinduized shamans (more likely, mediums) among the Santhals in the Chotanagpur District of northeastern India, at least two of whom he decided were "genuine mystics." But he concludes that, "most shamans are not mystics," given the criterion of identification with the ultimate, even though in vision-seeking cultures a relatively greater incidence of such experiences would be expected: "The quest for an ecstatic experience, when modally pursued in a society, yields a greater number of the mystical events" (1976:145).

Part of the problem of the mystic experience in shamanistic culture is lack of data. Ethnologists tend to utilize a broad, imprecise definition of mysticism to include all ecstatic states. In regard to relevant native American cultures, there are further difficulties. Within these cultures, a vision is generally considered to lose its effectiveness in providing power to the recipient if it is communicated to anyone except one's spiritual mentor (Landes 1968:9; Rodgers 1962:D6) until old age (Jenness 1935:50). Discussions of native American visions, usually from Plains culture, tend to be based on the same few readily accessible published accounts (e.g., Neihardt 1932, Lame Deer, et al. 1972). None of these, for reasons discussed below, concern the zero experience. Joseph Epes Brown (1977) writing on "The Question of 'Mysticism' within native American Traditions" lists "identity" as the criterion, but his discussion only concerns the vision quest, not identity.

If one accepts that the zero experience, being a natural experience, probably takes place in primal cultures, the problem becomes whether such experiences come to be integrated into the religions of the primal cultures. In the following, an argument is presented that they do not, that the developmentalists are correct, not for theological reasons, but rather because of religio-ecological factors (see Hultkrantz 1965).

Shamanism is found in virtually every stage of culture, including contemporary manifestations (Paper 1977b) especially in its healing, divinatory, and exorcist functions. The adaptation to modern culture of traditional shamanistic curing methods is exemplified by the "psychic surgeons" of the Philippines, who were attracting patients from as far as Toronto in the 1970s. The cultures in which shamanism is the predominant aspect of religion, however, tend to be primal and egalitarian. In such cultures, usually the gathering-hunting/fishing, gathering-herding, or horticulture-hunting types, there are no full-time specialists. In the Americas, these are the classic vision-seeking cultures, a phenomenon descriptively termed *democratized shamanism* (Lowie 1934:312).

In vision-seeking cultures, virtually every male and female is to a degree a shaman (defined in Chapter 3). Visions are sought for group survival, to gain access to basic subsistence, gathered plants, and hunted animals, as well as to attain success in raiding, the human cultural concomitant to hunting (Wallos 1919:350ff.). The products of the hunt or raid are distributed among the social unit, the former custom developing as a necessity given the fortuitous nature of hunting and as a means of social bonding, the latter for prestige. Some individuals are seen as having greater power in hunting and warfare and become leaders in these enterprises given their continued visions (Landes 1970:128, 163). Other individuals may become semi-specialist healers, diviners, or sorcerers.

Among native North American cultures with the ordeal-based vision quest and the Meso and South Amerind horticulturalist-hunters who use hallucinogenic substances, circumstances are arranged psychologically, physiologically, and culturally to insure a vision experience. Paul Radin (1914:216) writes that "in the fasting experiences of the Ojibwa, the two most essential elements are the control exercised by the older generation and the formulaic character of what is taught." From childhood a member of such cultures has had expectations of what kind of experience to have, so that, for example, it is not unusual among those of a specific clan in certain cultures to have a vision of the clan totem (Benedict 1923). With the use of hallucinogenic substances or such rituals as "sweat lodge," visions may be communal (R. Underhill 1966; Paper 1990b). In the gathering-hunting cultures, the conceptual system is oriented toward gaining a theriomorphic or other natural guardian spirit, and only such visions meet social expectations and cultural verification.

Hence, should an individual have a zero experience during the vision quest, it is afunctional (but not dysfunctional as it tends to be seen in Western culture) and does not receive cultural and social recognition. Furthermore, the interpretational system is not oriented toward the concept of identification as that concept would negate the relationship between the weak human crying for help and the powerful guardian spirits. Bharati (1976:148) mistakenly cites the Anishnabe phenomenon of "Windigo" as an isolated example of mystic experience in shamanistic culture. However, the experience is not one of attaining union with some ultimate spirit called Windigo, but of the individual being transformed into a monstrous cannibal. The experience, which usually takes place under isolated winter conditions, is related to the horrors of "cabin-fever" among nonnatives under similar conditions: "[The Wiitiko psychosis] usually afflicts males who have spent varying periods alone in the frozen forest in an unsuccessful hunt for food" (Parker 1960).

Nevertheless, an identification may take place in mediumistic cultures. As the medium is repeatedly possessed by the same spirit, he or she may come to identify with the spirit the person often becomes: "One time, a distinguished *santera* [adept in the Santería religion] . . . came to visit . . . I asked, 'What is an *orisha* [Yoroba deity]?' . . . She just said softly, 'I am.' " (Murphy 1988:143). However, such identity does not suggest the zero experience.

Since the zero experience in itself is a powerful experience—one of the criteria for the mystic experience ("deeply felt positive mood") enumerated by Walter N. Phanke (1966) and apparent in Bharati's description of his experiences and my own—such an experience could be a source of power for the shaman. But as it then would not be communicated to others, nor be integrated into the cultural conceptual system (hence, such an experience can and does lead to diagnosis of mental illness in our culture), we cannot, without further evidence, consider it a part of shamanistic cultures.

Therefore, assuming the mystic experience does take place in shamanistic cultures, the experience itself cannot be validated by the culture and, hence, is not an aspect of its religion. In the development of complex cultures, such experiences do become integrated into religion; at least they do for those cultures for which we have sufficient data, for example, the Upanishadic and Buddhist traditions in India, the Daoist and "Neo-Confucian" (see Taylor 1978) traditions in China, and the Jewish, Christian, and Islamic traditions in the West. In this chapter, examples of transitions from shamanistic cultures to ones in which the mystic experience may be interpreted, as well as potential causative factors for the transitions, will be discussed.

From Shamanism to Mysticism in the *Zhuangzi*

As introduced in the preceding chapters, there is evidence for both shamanistic and mediumistic behavior in protohistoric Chinese religion. As discussed in Chapter 4, by the mid-Zhou period, if not before, those usually termed *shamans* in Western-language literature are more probably mediums, and one major study of Zhou shamanism included phenomena more germane to the mystic experience (Thiel 1968).

A number of passages in the *Zhuangzi* refer to the mystical aspects of religion. Indeed, I consider these passages the core of the text, around which the other parts revolve. A. C. Graham (n.d.: 62, 71), whose translations are probably the best, has written, "Much of *Chuang-tzu* [Zhuangzi] is unintelligible at the present state of research." Furthermore,

> Chuang-tzu is a mystical writer, and presents those who like myself are not mystics with the problem that often the choice of Chinese words is determined by a kind of experience which we have never shared.

Having had the experiences described by Bharati, on the contrary, I found those particular passages in the *Zhuangzi* crystal clear, indeed the most lucid in the text. (For an alternative interpretation of the material discussed in this chapter, focusing on philosophy, although not neglecting experience, the reader is recommended to Kohn 1992.)

Transformation to Mysticism

As we have seen (Chapter 3), references to shamanic ascent appear in the earliest strata of the *Zhuangzi* as remnants of an earlier tradition. Although the text is later considered the basis of Daoism, it should be emphasized that aspects of shamanism are but a part of the factors leading to the development of early Daoism and that the transformation of this aspect is again but part of the early Daoist complex (see Girardot 1978). In the second strata of the text, the terminology was utilized metaphorically to refer to individualism in the highly stratified and socially constrained elite culture. Finally, in the latest part of the work, the terminology derived from shamanistic phenomena is used to symbolize the concept of the *xian* as "immortal"; Ying-shih Yü (1964:96) has pointed out that prior to the Qin period, "the idea of 'no death' was only incidentally related to *hsien* [*xian*]."

At the time the earliest strata of the *Zhuangzi* was being written, the fourth century B.C.E., concepts were developing in regard to the nature of the Perfect Man, other than that of shamanic ascent, previously discussed. In Chapter 3, mention was made of Liezi's "flight," considered inferior to "mounting the regularity of Heaven and Earth, riding the changes of the elemental forces [six *qi*, see Paper 1974], to wander in infinity." By itself, this statement is ambiguous and has elicited extensive commentary; it is followed by a concluding explanation that may be a later addition (2/21–22), beginning: "Therefore, it is said, the Perfect Man is without self (*wuji*)" (followed by two other characteristics). Hence, the entire passage could be interpreted as saying that the egoless state, the mystic or zero experience, is superior to shamanic trance flight. Such an interpretation would be tenuous were it not supported by other passages.

Chapter 2 (3/1–3; A. C. Graham 1967:150) begins with a passage describing a person in a trance state: "Nanguo Zichi sat leaning on his armrest, looking up at the sky and breathing serenely, as though his self had lost its opposite." His disciple on asking what was happening received the reply: "Just now, I had lost myself (*wu sang wo*)." Although such a statement could imply a simple reverie, the explanation which immediately follows, as well as other passages, leads to the conclusion that the egoless state is meant. In the first dialogue of Chapter 4 (9/26–27), Kongfuzi explains to his favorite disciple, Yan Hui, what he means by "fasting the mind":

> Unify the will. Do not listen with the ears, listen with your mind; [rather] do not listen with your mind, listen with your essence [or spirit, *qi*]. Hearing stops at the ears; the mind stops at what tallies with it; essence being empty, awaits everything. Only the Dao gathers in emptiness, the fasting of the mind is [this] emptiness.

The relationship between Yan Hui and Kongfuzi is reversed in a brief dialogue in Chapter 6 (19/93–94), where we have the first equation of the egoless state and identification with the absolute. Yan Hui explains to Kongfuzi what he means by "sitting in forgetfulness" (*zuo wang*): "I allow my limbs and body to fall away, expel my intellectual faculties, leave my substance (*xing*), get rid of knowledge and become identical with the Great Universality (*da tung*); this is sitting in forgetfulness."

In an earlier section of the same chapter (17/41), it is related how a person with the talent to become a sage was taught to become a sage. One stage of this process involves becoming as the bright dawn (interpretation based on the Tang dynasty commentary of Cheng Xianying). This concept may be related to the previously mentioned ascent image: "His spirit ascends mounted on light with his bodily form extinguished." (Although this anecdote could be interpreted as concerning longevity, I do not think the earlier sections of the *Zhuangzi* emphasize this concept; rather the person who has "learned the Dao" in a mystic experience, learning the real way of life, loses all concern for it and in that sense, although elderly, has "a complexion like a child.")

The association of experiencing bright light in connection with the mystic experience is common (see Eliade 1965, Deikman 1963). Among many examples, in the writings of Jacob Boehme (*Sex Puncta Mystica* and *Theoscopia* 1958:120,193) we find: "But if [human life] gives itself to a nothing, then it is desireless, and falls into the fire of light" and "the nature of fire; in which fiery nature the eternal One becomes majestic and a light." The experience of dissolving into a bright colorless light often immediately precedes the complete loss of self-identity of the mystic experience.

In the last chapter of the early strata, toward the end of a passage where the ascent motif as metaphor was previously cited—"I'll ride the surreal bird beyond the six directions"—we find (20/10–11), "The Nameless Man said: 'Let your/ Mind roam in vapidity/ Essence unite with the vastness.' " In a following anecdote, which refers to a sage who is probably a mystic, in the sense of one who has had mystic experiences and has allowed his or her life to be influenced by them, Liezi brings a *shenwu* (see Chapter 4) who specializes in prognostication to visit his master. Each time, his master entered a different trance state, leading to the *shenwu* on the fourth occurrence fleeing in terror. Liezi, realizing he had never learned anything, returns home and lives in utmost, undifferentiating simplicity, "united in this way to the end of his life" (20/11–21/31).

In the early strata of the *Zhuangzi*, the references to the mystic experience emphasize the effects of the experience on one's understanding of reality and the corresponding essential falsity of elite life patterns and preoccupations, as well as how to live. Concluding statements of the relationship of this knowledge to governing are written in a different style and have the flavor of having been added at a later date. The references to the mystic experience in the middle of the work also seem to be a later development on these initial statements in that they relate the understanding gained from the experience to the primary intellectual concerns of the period (third century B.C.E.)—governing— or to the growing interest in longevity (Chapters 11–15), or are fully developed statements regarding the experience (Chapter 21). One exception is in Chapter 17 (43/27–28), in which a seemingly earlier saying is quoted: "I have heard it said: 'The Man of Tao is not heard of / Perfect Power is not attained / The Great Man Lacks self.' " (The saying apparently contains a play on words—"power" [*de*] and "attainment" are homophones in Chinese; the statement means "perfect power" comes of itself.)

The above statement is fully explained in a section of Chapter 21 (55/24–56/38) where Kongfuzi receives instruction from Lao Dan. Confucius comes upon Lao Dan who, having bathed and spread his hair to dry, a purification rite preparatory to shamanic trance (M. Chen 1936), is in an ecstatic state seemingly similar to the one referred to in the previously mentioned anecdote in Chapter 2:

> Kongfuzi says, ". . . sir, just before your form and body were as still [following Guo Fan's commentary] as a dead tree; it seemed that you had forgotten things, had left humankind and were standing utterly alone." Lao Dan responded, "My mind was roaming in the beginning of things [the Dao]."

Kongfuzi asks what he means, and Lao Dan responds that the experience is ineffable but he will try to explain it anyway. He does so in the context of Chinese cosmology of the period (see Paper 1974), in the interrelationships of Yin and Yang, Heaven and Earth, and their transformations. To have the experience is to be the Perfect Person. Kongfuzi asks how to attain it. Lao Dan says that, "in the world, the myriad things are one. If you can attain this oneness and become identical with it. . . ." Kongfuzi says much cultivation of the mind must be required. Lao Dan's response is similar to the view of Bharati (1976:65, 175), writing as a mystic:

> The zero-experience comes to those to whom it comes regardless of what they do . . . There is really no predictable link between anything [orthodox practitioners of yoga] or anyone else does and the occurrence or recurrence of the zero-experience.

For Lao Dan says:

> Water flows, not because it does anything, but because it is a natural talent. The power (de) of the Perfect Person [is the same]; he does not cultivate it, and yet he is unable to separate himself from all things. As heaven is naturally high, earth is naturally substantial and the sun and moon are naturally bright, how can it (de) be cultivated?

This understanding of the mystic experience, that it comes not from trying, but rather from ceasing to try, for it, if one has a nature (talent) suited to it, is reiterated in a passage in the last Chapter (33:93/56–57) that has the appearance of being a quotation from a no longer extant older work:

Barrier Keeper Yin said: "Where self is without an abode,/ Things of themselves will manifest their forms [to him]./ His movements, like water;/ His stillness, like a mirror;/ His response, like an echo./ ... / In union with it, he is harmonious;/ [If he tries to] attain it, it will slip away."

This important anecdote has been commented on by Theil (1968:183) as shamanistic ascent related to mystical wandering and by Girardot (1978:38–39) in regard to meditation techniques.

The Transformation of the Mystic Experience

The zero experience can lead to a questioning if not a rejection of social and cultural norms, since it provides a reality other than the reality provided by language and acculturation, except in cultures where the experience has been incorporated into the core ideology. When interpreted, the experience comes to be understood through and related to the culture of the experiencer, but would still lack social value and, hence, not receive reification.

In the early strata of the *Zhuangzi*, those parts that treat the mystic experience indicate that the experience leads to a rejection of the traditional or developing roles of the elite, to the adoption of a rustic (without, one assumes, the burdens of the peasant) existence. This interpretation, being socially afunctional, would have little appeal except to those who had or were inclined toward the experience. For such concepts to survive, and for us to be aware of them two millennia later, they would have had to be integrated into the cultural system and come to be seen as having positive rather than negative value. The history of Buddhism provides a classic model of what one assumes to have been a zero experience becoming with considerable synthesis and transformation the framework of several cultures. To lesser extents, zero experiences have been integrated into Hinduism, Judaism, Christianity, and Islam, as well as the dominant ideology of later China, for the mystic experience came to be accepted as an aspect of 'Neo-Confucianism' (see Taylor 1978:279).

In the development of the *Zhuangzi* we see the same process taking place. In the middle strata, as previously mentioned, most of the sections which refer to the mystic experience do so in the context of third century B.C.E. elite concerns. Hence, the earlier sections came to be interpreted differently than perhaps was the intention of the original author. It is probably because the middle section dealt with these concerns that the *Zhuangzi* survived into the Han period. Similarly, in the late third century C.E., with the Xiang Xiu/Guo Xiang commentary, we have a reinterpretation according to the concerns of that time, a synthesis between "opposing claims of activism and quietism" (Mather 1969).

In Chapter 11, we find a section relating the mystic experience to the developing interest in longevity, an interest which becomes one of the central concerns of Daoism. In a dialogue (27/39) between the Yellow Emperor and a master who lived on Emptiness and Identity (as a place), the Yellow Emperor learns to renounce active governing and turn toward the Dao of Perfection. In this discourse, the master says: "I maintain this unity in order to abide in this harmony; therefore, I have been able to cultivate my body for twelve hundred years and my form has never become feeble."

The mystic experience does have the effect of rendering death meaningless, as stated in the self-report of Alfred, Lord Tennyson:

> Individuality itself seemed to dissolve and fade away into boundless being, and this not a confused state but the clearest, the surest of surest, utterly beyond words—where death was an almost laughable impossibility. (Cited in James 1902:295)

For those reading interpretations of the experience in a culture which values long life, it is quite understandable that the experience came to be understood to actually lengthen life. Hence, in a fifth-century text, the *Santian neijie jing*, we find:

> Thus Laozi ordered all men to meditate on the True, to collect the Tao [Dao], to harden and strengthen their root and origin. Thereby man should reach a state in which he never loses his original source of life and can live forever. (Cited in Kohn 1989a:132)

Henri Maspero (1950:217) has discussed the relationship of mysticism to immortality in the *Zhuangzi*: "Au but final de la vie mystique toaiste, l'Union avec le *Tao* confère au Saint l'immortalité." However, Maspero considers the relationship more important than would contemporary scholarship. For example, Nathan Siven (1978:314) has pointed out that immortality is perhaps overly stressed by modern scholars as the goal of Daoism; union with the Dao and appointment to the celestial hierarchy are other goals.

The zero experience comes to be interpreted as not only having the function of promoting longevity, but more important to the dominant elite concerns of the third century, to bring about truly effective governing. In a dialogue following that previously cited (27/44–28/57), the experience is related to inactive governing (*wei wuwei*) in distinction to normal governing (*zhi*) which inevitably leads to disaster. Cloud Chief, who is followed as a leader in spite of his inclination not to lead, asks a master what to do. The master responds: "As a *xian*, as a *xian*, return [to the source]" (see Chapter 3 for analysis of the term, *xian*). Cloud Chief asks for instruction. The master responds with terminology identical to the previously translated statement of Yan Hui to Confucius in Chapter 6 of the text:

> You only need abide in inactivity (*wuwei*) and things will transform themselves. Allow your mind and body to fall away, spit out your intellectual faculties, forget you are like other things, and [become one with] the Great Unity (*da tung*) vast and deep.

Become thus and each of the myriad things will return to the root without being aware of it.

The term *great unity* later took on the meaning of political unity; currently, it is found in the Guomindang (Nationalist Party) anthem. However, it is clear that the term refers to the mystic experience in the *Zhuangzi* from its context with the segment following (28/65–66), also concerning government: "[Join with] the Great Unity and become selfless."

The following four Chapters (12–15) utilize terminology and concepts derived from the mystic experience in places to discourage and other places to enhance governing the world, becoming a true king. Most of the segments are probably contemporaneous with the editing of the *Daode jing*, a work primarily concerned with the same theme, a subject in and of itself (Lau 1963:43). The point emphasized here is that a philosophical extension of the mystic experience, with perhaps the experience itself lost, has taken place; that is, the mystic experience has been successfully integrated into the emerging elite culture as a novel approach to the dominant concern.

Indeed, with the development of institutional Daoism in the late second century, not only did Laozi (or Lao Dan), the metaphorically named reputed author of the *Daodejing*, become divinized (see Seidel 1969), but even earlier so did one of the terms for the mystic experience, *taiyi*: "The Great One as a personified god has been commonly venerated as an astral deity in the official cult ever since the Han dynasty" (Kohn 1989a:134).

Shamanic flight continues in institutional Daoism as a meditation technique, but in the highly literary Chinese culture, written works can replace guardian spirits: "The scriptures revealed by the gods inform them of the roads of the divinities" (Robinet 1989:163). These ecstatic flights in turn became integrated into the search for longevity: "true immortality is found only after ascent into heaven, a state that may be tasted prematurely in ecstatic excursions to the otherworldly realms above" (Kohn 1989b:199).

From Shaman to Mystic in Anishnabe Religion

Traditional native American cultures are shamanistic. Indeed, it has been argued that these cultures should be taken as the model for ur-shamanism rather than the Siberian cultures from which the word is derived (Paper 1990b). In this section, a twentieth-century native American shaman who became a mystic due to a major transformation in his culture will be described. The causative factors illuminate the possible reasons for the considerably earlier transition in Chinese culture described above.

The Transformation of Culture and Religion

At the time of contact with Europeans, the Anishnabe under discussion were an Algonkian-speaking, gathering-hunting-fishing culture found in the forested (nonarable) areas of the upper Great Lakes. They were composed of groups speaking a number of dialects, including Odawa, Potawatomi, and Ojibwe, the latter also called Salteaux (Anglicized French) and Chippewa (American English), now located in Ontario, Manitoba, Michigan, Minnesota, and Wisconsin. According to differing traditional accounts, they migrated westward over two centuries from a region east of Montreal, reaching the area of lakes Huron and Superior by the seventeenth century.

(The people under discussion call themselves "Anishnabe" in their own language, a term by which most Algonkian-speaking peoples call themselves. However, most publications use the term "Ojibwe," or variant spellings. In the following, "Anishnabe" will be used when a general term is appropriate, and "Ojibwe" when referring to a specific Anishnabe group.)

The relational pattern between native and foreign (European) culture was already established shortly after initial contact. The destruction of traditional native North American gathering-hunting culture, especially for eastern Algonquian-speaking groups, began as early as the late sixteenth century with the European demand for beaver pelts and the native desire for iron. The latter led to a "profound revolution in the economic life of the Atlantic littoral" (Bailey 1969:10), the former to a change from a primarily subsistence economy to one of barter for the necessities of life: from gathering-hunting to trapping.

By the early seventeenth century, liquor and firearms were highly sought after by native peoples; the use of alcohol, along with newly introduced diseases and warfare resulting from competition for trading rights, led to a considerable decimation of the population, and firearms to the destruction of the ecological balance. Further contacts between the Europeans and the natives involved the latter in the military struggles between the French and the English, the American Revolution, and the War of 1811 to 1812.

Land was first alienated from the Anishnabe by purchase in 1764 (in the area of Niagara), and in the 1830s treaties concerning central and near northern Ontario were signed; Manitoulin Island, the locale of later discussion, was signed away by Odawa and Ojibwe in August of 1836 (Patterson 1972:8). Treaties involving the Anishnabe continued to be signed as late as 1923.

Except for a limited amount of horticulture, the Anishnabe did not farm until the institution of reserve life. By 1837, on Manitoulin Island, the largest fresh-water island in North America at the northern end of Lake Huron, the Ojibwe and Odawa were living in fixed settlements administered by the Catholic church, hunting on the now limited land available to them and attempting to raise crops. In that year, a Euroamerican observer reported that:

> for the natural progress of arts and civilization springing from within, and from their own intelligence and resources, we have substituted a sort of civilization from without, foreign to their habits, manners, organization: we are making paupers of them; and this by a kind of terrible necessity. (Jameson 1943 [1837]:251)

Pre-contact Anishnabe lived in bands which perhaps reached a maximum of 150 in the summer, and broke into small family groups for winter survival. Most of the year, people resided in small isolated groups, but the hunter was often completely alone for long periods. The environment was understood as filled with *manitou* (power, spirit) found in all animals, plants, stones, bodies of water, the earth, and sky phenomena, and especially strong in particular objects, persons, and forces. Anishnabe religion, based on developing a relationship between individuals and *manitou*, centered on the vision-quest and the gaining of one or more guardian spirits (see Hallowell 1976).

The Anishnabe vision quest emphasized fasting and isolation; not having a vision could lead to loss of self-esteem and make it difficult if not impossible to function in any socioeconomic role. After the puberty vision quest, further visions could come from repeated quests or dreams. The term *shaman* is frequently used in the literature to designate those who through the quest attained particularly powerful guardian spirits, usually more than one, and whose success in hunting, warfare, curing, and so on, demonstrated their powers. However, in that all persons in the culture required a guardian spirit to function, Lowie's (1934) term, *democratized shamanism*, is far more appropriate.

Around 1680, the Ojibwe established the village of Chequameg on the south shore of Lake Superior which was, according to tradition, the center of the Midéwiwin religion. Hickerson (1962) and Dewdney (1975), contrary to the native perspective, have argued that the Midéwiwin is an early eighteenth-century phenomenon, having developed in reaction to the changing economic and social circumstances that began on the south shore of Lake Superior and spread with the establishment of Anishnabe communities to the west and south. (Except for isolated migrants from the west, the religious modality was not found in eastern Ontario.)

The Midéwiwin is a graded set of revival and curing ceremonials conducted by shaman-priests who are initiated into a graded series of ranks. The religious institution incorporates a systematized mythology, recorded by pictographs on birchbark scrolls. Hickerson (1970:65) considers the institution a nativistic movement which developed after the decline of the Feast of the Dead in response to tribal displacements (the movement westward) "to lend coherence and stability to the new assemblages," that is, the continued development of multi-clan habitation centers. The development of these villages into semipermanent settlements with log structures would have further encouraged institutionalized religion (for description, see Hoffman 1891, Landes 1968). Whether or not Hickerson's interpretation is correct, it should be understood that the noninstitutional elements of the Midéwiwin are of considerable antiquity.

By the early twentieth century, the fear and suspicion of sorcery had begun to place the Midéwiwin in disrepute. Jenness (1935:61) wrote: "As currently used on Parry Island, however, the term midé [members of the Midéwiwin] carries an evil connotation, and is practically synonymous with sorcerer or witch." This attitude is confirmed throughout Landes's book. Combined with the growth of Western education and increased missionary influence, this identification with sorcery led to the decline of the institution. James Stevens wrote in 1972, in retrospect inaccurately, that James "Redsky [or Red Sky] is, however, the last of the Mide masters in the Lake of the Woods area [western Ontario]" (Redsky 1972:21). Redsky, a Presbyterian deacon, had already sold his birchbark scrolls to Selwyn Dewdney for the Glenbow-Alberta Institute, claiming there was no disciple to whom they could be passed (Dewdney 1975:4), although this was at the time of the initial Midéwiwin revitalization.

The practice of sorcery is ubiquitous to Algonkian-speaking cultures in general, but the Ojibwe were notorious among other native American cultures for their use of power. For example, Ruth Landes (1970:45) found that the Kansas Potawatomi, a closely related culture, "feared the Ojibwa shamans more than any others." The earliest observers noted: "It is strange to see how these people agree so well outwardly, and how they hate each other within" (*Jesuit Relations*, 1637; see Hallowell 1955b:141); that is, overt equanimity masked covert aggression carried out through sorcery (Hallowell 1955a). Studies of Ojibwe culture three centuries later continue to note the importance and effects of sorcery on Ojibwe life. Jenness (1936:87) writes

> It is pathetic to observe how universal is this fear of witch-craft among the present inhabitants of Parry Island. Every man suspects his neighbor of practicing the nefarious art to avenge some fancied grievance, and the older and more con-servative the Indian, the more he is held in suspicion.

It is to be noted that the Cree, who inhabit a similar terrain to the northern Ojibwe, do not evidence nearly the same orientation toward sorcery (Rogers 1969).

Landes (1968) in a study based on fieldwork of 1932 to 1935 in Minnesota and western Ontario notes that "good" shamans were less respected than "bad" ones. The deleterious effects of sorcery have been noted by several mid-twentieth century studies (e.g., Rogers 1962). Landes (1968:60) reports that Midéwiwin priests, especially those with high ranks, were feared as sorcerers, using methods that are still feared in the Manitoulin area (without the association with the Midé-wiwin): "Mide sorcerers were said to drop herbal and other 'poisons' into a victim's food, causing ailments that range from partial paralysis to death." W. S. Hoffman (1891:236) at the end of the nineteenth century associated "Bearwalking" with the Midéwiwin, and such association still continues among Ojibwe.

Sorcery, although present in pre-modern Anishnabe culture, may not always have been a negative factor. Landes (1968:59) notes that "a sorcerer was the Ojibwe ideal strong man, defying and holding at bay the terrible forces of existence, manito and human." Furthermore, in the traditional culture, there were checks on evil sorcery, normally directed outward from the group. In the related Potawatomi culture over a century ago, "each camp appointed and maintained a policing shaman to watch other shamans [for the exercise of evil power]" (Landes 1970:126). Rogers (1962:7) notes that each Ojibwe band chose a leader for his "superior religious power" whose role included "the protection of [his] followers from harm [i.e., witchcraft]."

Anishnabe religion, hence, has undergone a number of transitions. Following contact with European civilization, it has moved from a gathering-hunting, shamanistic culture to a fur-trapping, trading culture to semi-permanent and permanent larger settlement patterns and the development of institutionalized shamanism, the Midéwiwin, and, in modern times, at least among the southern Ojibwe, to fixed settlements (reserves). The traditional clan heads and charismatic shaman-leaders have been replaced (at Euroamerican insistence) by elected, politically instead of spiritually based "chiefs." By the beginning of the fourth quarter of the twentieth century, socioeconomic patterns and resources came from without the community through the Christian churches, public schools, and government-supplied monetary payments (welfare, etc.), and native religion almost disappeared, except for unchecked, negatively oriented sorcery, which was directed inward toward members of the group, making almost impossible the continuation of what little social interaction remained.

In the last two decades, there has been a significant revitalization of traditional Anishnabe religion. Indeed, in the last few years, traditional ceremonies, including those of the Midéwiwin, have been held on both Manitoulin and Parry islands, discussed above. On a major reserve of Manitoulin Island, a traditional native healer works with Western physicians. Wasausink (Parry Island Reserve), which had been exclusively Christian for the last half century, has become the center for Midéwiwin ceremonies for eastern Ontario. The shaman, John-Paul, who is discussed later, would have had a very different life in relation to his community had he lived into the late 1980s.

Shaman and Mystic

Transition can be found not only in the larger culture, but also in individual manifestations. A former student of mine, whose mother is Ojibwe, had been "trained" by the shaman John-Paul, until recently considered the last shaman in the Manitoulin area (see the following section). Her training began during the year preceding his death in 1976. Enrolled in an undergraduate course on Chinese religion and aesthetics, I suggested she write a paper presenting an interpretation of the *Chuci* (see Chapter 3). I expected her to concentrate on the earlier poems, depicting shamanic flight; instead, she focused on the later "Yuan You," a poem that concerns the mystic experience rather than shamanic ascent (Hawkes 1959:81; Hightower 1954; Maspero 1950:204).

In the introduction to her paper (M. Johnson 1978), she presented a typology of ascent experiences as imparted to her by John-Paul:

"Flights" serve three purposes:

1. To inspect the physical and emotional well-being of friends, relatives, and other individuals under one's care. A shaman can be a spiritual guardian for people he has met or people he has never physically met but who are of specific interest to him; e.g., future trainees for shamanism. If the shaman cannot physically be in a specific place, then he can still check on a particular individual who may be far away.

2. To seek the advice from the spirit (soul) of one's ancestors or from the spirits of other departed individuals, or to obtain information from them about a particular person or event in one's life.

3. A "flight" to the place where the spirit abides ("Paradise"). One seeks a harmonizing union of pure spirit, the purpose being one of revitalization of spirit and body; i.e., a revitalization of power.

In the third type of flight, the spirit travels westward [traditional direction of the abode of the dead] to "Paradise." The spirit upon arrival meets the Spirit which appears in the form of a brilliant ball of light—sometimes glowing white or with golden hues. Then a harmonizing union of the Spirit and the spiritual essence of the shaman takes place.

The shaman experiences a fulfilled nothingness state; he is not aware of anything—there exists a fulfilled void or holistic emptiness. Then one catches a glimpse of the "earth" below and the spirit must return to physical reality. The descent then takes place and the return is immediate. The shaman comes out of the trance feeling peaceful, full of power, and numb for a short period as the body awakens; there is a great feeling of revitalization.

In regard to *Yuan You*, she wrote the following, which, I conclude, documents, in conception, a transition from shamanic ascent to mystic experience within the author of this commentary:

In comparison with all of the other parts of the *Ch'u Tz'u* [*Chuci*], I was most impressed and excited by *Yüan Yu* [*Yuan You*]. The experience of the poet is very similar to the flight experiences I have had. Therefore, I can relate to it better than the *Li Sao* or *Chiu Ko* [those parts of the *Chuci* considered shamanic]. The poet had a successful flight from my point of view. Flight experiences, especially of the third type, are meant to be successful and one should never embark on a flight journey unless one knows when the time is right. The meeting of the spiritual essence of an individual with the Spirit is meant to be triumphant and a revitalizing experience to renew one's Power to enable one to continue and make everyday living easier for one's self and others.

The poet goes to a Master to learn about the "balance made by unifying essence" (Hawkes 1959). What the Master told the poet is similar to what the shaman near Manitoulin Island said in reference to obtaining Power and the ability to "travel":

Keep your soul from confusion, and it will come natu rally. Unify the essences and control the spirit. . . .

The poet expresses feelings similar to those I experience when I am going into trance (of the third type). One seems to glow with changing colors and the spiritual essence becomes stronger; the body feels like it melts, and the spirit grows light and wants to move (leave on its flight):

My jade-like countenance flushed with radiant color; Purified, my vital essence started to grow stronger; My corporeal parts dissolved to a soft suppleness; and my spirit grew lissome and eager for movement.

The poet later says, "I wanted to leave the world and forget about returning." This is the usual sentiment I feel during flight. One does not want to give up the bodiless freedom—it is not that one does not want to return to the physical world, but one is extremely free as the poet describes in the poem. There is joy, freedom, peace and pure ecstatic happiness.

In couplet 87, the poet begins to reach the climax of the flight. In couplets 88 and 89, he reaches the fulfilled nothingness state, which by my definition, is the whole purpose of the flight. There is no mention of whether he has a spiritual union with the Spirit. However, whether one unifies with the Spirit or reaches the fulfilled nothingness state without the symbolic union (I believe the 'Spirit' is just a symbol for the fulfilled nothingness state) does not matter. The result is the same: the empty void is reached; the flight has served its function.

The Relationship between Shamanism and Mysticism

John-Paul of the Birch Island Reserve (just north of Manitoulin Island) was born in the early part of the twentieth century, the son and grandson of shamans, the latter being the famous nineteenth-century shaman, Shaw-wan-oss-way. He was in his mid-sixties or mid-seventies when he died. His father and grandfather had undergone the vision quest, but he had not.

(I am indebted to Prof. J. E. Newbery of the University of Sudbury and Leona Nawagebow of the Birch Island Reserve for sharing their memories of John-Paul with me. I have been given to understand by others that the character, Clarence Wahsay, in the unfortunate novel *Bearwalk*, by Lynne Sallot and Tom Peltier [1977], who considered himself an apprentice of John-Paul toward the end of the latter's life, is a rather accurate depiction of John-Paul; all else in the novel is fiction.)

In the early part of this century, vision questing was dying out. Landes (1970:183) reports that an informant among the Potawatomi in the mid-thirties told her that the "obligation had waned before 1920, though the practice had lingered." Rogers (1962:D5) reports that in the late fifties among the western Ontario Ojibwe, "informants stated most emphatically that this is no longer practiced and they themselves have never been on an *antapawa mo* [vision quest]."

Even the influence of dreaming had been waning due to the changed ecological circumstances—"I did not follow up my dreams because I lived like a white man" (Landes 1970:195)— although it has far from disappeared. Radin (1936:233) provides examples, from the beginning of the nineteenth to the early twentieth centuries, arguing that

> as the puberty fasting experience lost its social significance, dreams, in general, lost theirs and relapsed into their true significance, that of being more or less symbolic disguises and distortions of personal problems.

John-Paul's "calling" came later in life when, in his twenties, on a boat in the midst of a thunderstorm, a vision was induced by a lightning flash—Ojibwe seers tended to derive their power from the thunder spirit (Jenness 1935:64). He then began to function as a shaman. Hence, he gained his status by all three means of early twentieth-century Ojibwe culture, "by means of dreams, by inheritance through the male line, and through instruction" (Rogers 1962:D5) which, at least in regard to herbs, he must have received from his father or grandfather.

Jenness (1935:60) delineated three kinds of shamans using quite different methods in eastern Ontario: "*Wabeno*: the healer and charm-maker; *Ojiskiu*: the conjurer [shaking-tent]; *Kusabindugeyu*: the seer." John-Paul would fit into the latter category, although he also practiced as an herbalist.

By the time John-Paul had reached middle age, the older members of the community who, during his youth, had sought his services were deceased, and the members of his community who had been brought up in the twentieth century had become oriented towards the dominant culture. Furthermore, the Catholic church, with the only imposing building in the area, and the schools deliberately oriented the people away from the traditional culture. A series of Roman Catholic priests not only denounced John-Paul to their congregation and forbade the people to go to him, but, in a travesty of traditional concepts of interpersonal behavior, went to his home to denounce him to his face. The priest was seen by the members of the reserve as an intermediary with white culture and, hence, highly influential on their subsistence—government payments of divers sorts. It is possible that the fear of shamans as sorcerers also contributed to his isolation. In any case, John-Paul had considerably reduced contact of any type with his community. And the community became alienated as well from the traditional culture. From an autobiographical essay by Wilfrid Pelletier (1973) of a Manitoulin Island reserve, it is clear that until the recent revival of native American religions, he had been ignorant of traditional culture.

In John-Paul's typology of "flight," the third type pertains more to the mystical experience than to shamanism. He further described such a flight as traveling to and merging with God, a ball of light, and, while the first two types of flights are done for others, the third and highest is done for oneself (Johnson, personal communication). In other words, the shamanic ascents of John-Paul, when he had lost his function, became individualistic, were not integrated nor integrable into the cultural matrix, and were conceived in purely personal terms: the union with the ultimate of the mystic experience. Hence, John-Paul illustrates in his own person the transition from shamanic flight to mysticism and the factors behind this transition.

What is yet to be determined is whether the change is in the nature or in the interpretation of the experience. The typology of John-Paul suggests that the trances are different in kind, although the mystic experience may serve as a source of power to enable the shamanic trance flight. Rasmussen (1925:240–41, in Lommel 1967:60) quotes an Inuit shaman:

> Every real shaman has to feel an illumination in his body, in the inside of his head or in his brain, something that gleams like fire, that gives him the power to see with closed eyes into the darkness, into the hidden things or into the fu-

ture, or into the secrets of another man. I felt that I was in
possession of this marvelous ability.

This was the desired ecstatic experience that began this individual's career as a shaman; he then goes on to detail his accu-
mulation of tutelary spirits. The Inuit's experience corroborates
the theory that the mystical experience does take place in shamanistic culture but is not in itself a shamanistic experience,
it having no social function, one of the deterministic criteria according to Hultkrantz (1973) and the factor by which Helmut
Hoffman, discussing Tibetan religion (1967:103), distinguishes the
mystic from the shaman:

> The shaman establishes his connection with the supernatu-
> ral world in trance not for the sake of his personal experi-
> ence (like the mystic or ecstatic of almost all higher religions)
> but for the well being of his group.

Causative Factors for the Transformation

The causal factor leading to John-Paul's transition from shaman
to mystic (and shaman again in the last decade of his life following a re-interest of some youths in traditional culture—a few natives continued to consult him at least as an herbalist throughout
his life) was his loss of social function because of the transformation if not the disintegration of his society. Rogers (1962:E7)
found that

> the Round Lake Community [a group of northern Ojibwa in
> Western Ontario] no longer forms a society in the strict
> meaning of the word. Certain structures necessary for the
> group to operate as an autonomous unit now exist external
> to the community within Canadian society . . . [Furthermore],
> there is no overall authority structure . . . nor is there now
> any religious organization of a single homogeneous nature
> which might unify the group. . . . Economic organization is
> restricted primarily to the household level.

The disintegration is similar, if not more severe, in the Manitoulin
area. Radin (1936:233) points out, "The moment the economic
conditions disintegrated, then the purely personal content of the

dream seized the opportunity afforded and easily regained its old ascendancy."

John-Paul illustrates the inception of the mystical experience within a particular culture, a stage prior to its integration into a culture should such take place. This development followed a series of religio-ecological transformations of Anishnabe culture over the last three centuries in response to contact with European culture, almost ending in the virtual disappearance of a viable culture. Among many examples of the combined effects of social and cultural disintegration in the Manitoulin area was the "suicide epidemic" at Wikwemikong (Ward 1975; Ward and Fox 1977). The transformation of John-Paul from shaman to mystic between approximately 1940 and 1950 is coincident with the near termination of Anishnabe religion at the time.

During the time of Zhuang Zhou, fourth-century B.C.E. Chinese culture was also undergoing profound change, a change as important and immense as that of twentieth-century China. By the third and second centuries B.C.E., many religio-ecological features of the preceding period had disappeared.

This period of Chinese history, the Zhanguo (period of the Warring States), relative to the preceding and following times, is not well known. However, the basic features of the transformation have been clarified with contemporary scholarship. The transformation began at least as early as the sixth century B.C.E., reaching its culmination in the third century B.C.E. with the unification of China under the centralist policies of the Qin state and a mercantile, metropolitan economy. Prior to this period, Chinese culture was quasi-feudal, primarily divided into two classes: an aristocracy composed of literate, professional warrior-ritual specialists with a clan orientation living in an advanced, metal-using culture; and peasants, using stone tools, living a life little changed from that of the late Neolithic period.

In the fourth century, we find "dissemination of iron agricultural implements on a significant scale," and "verified evidence of the use of human, animal and green manure" (P. T. Ho 1975:83); and soybean culture had become widespread, allowing effective crop rotation with millet. The economically self-sufficient manorial system was disappearing, replaced by private ownership of land and state land taxes (Hsü 1965:112) This led to a greater differentiation between classes: those who accumulated land, especially the new, rising merchant class, and the peasants who became hired laborers. The merchant class was an effect of the development of specialized trades and regional economic independence. All of these factors, especially the use of cast iron for agricultural implements, led to considerably increased agricultural efficiency, allowing the growth of large metropolitan manufacturing and mercantile centers at the junction of trade routes, in comparison to the much smaller fortress-administrative center of the preceding period.

Other developments affected the traditional aristocracy. In the fifth century B.C.E., chariot (with aristocrats as warriors) warfare was replaced by the use of infantry (peasant-soldiers), leading to considerably larger armies. In the fourth century, cavalry was adopted from the northern nomadic tribes (Hsü 1965:68–70; incidentally leading to a change in dress style with the adoption of trousers). By this period too, the shift from hereditary officials to those chosen for their qualifications enhanced the increasing social mobility within the culture. All these changes led to considerable intellectual ferment, and many of the new ideas are promoted or attacked in the *Zhuangzi*, whose original author clearly enjoyed intellectual debate.

With the breakup of traditional extended noble families, virtually defined by clan myth and ritual, manorial agriculture on which it was superimposed, and the relationship between these families based on allegiance to the Son of Heaven expressed ritually, a profound transformation of religion is to be expected, although there has been little research on this transformation. As early as the sixth century, we find Kongfuzi concerned about the decline of interest in the traditional elite rites and ritual relationships, and by the late fourth and early third centuries, we find Xunzi promoting ritual for its social utility (see Chapter 2).

It is at the peak of this major transformation of China's cultural ecology, the fourth century B.C.E., that we find in the *Zhuangzi* evidence for another religious transformation, from remnants of an earlier, now virtually unknown type of elite shamanism (see Chapter 3) to the initial, unintegrated stage of mysticism (to be integrated into the cultural milieux in the following century). This transformation was due not only to this aspect of shamanism losing its function, but also to a number of the aristocrats losing theirs.

The author of the early strata of the *Zhuangzi*, from his education, literacy, and concerns, was clearly from an aristocratic background. Yet the few hints of his living conditions indicates a lifestyle only marginally above that of the peasants. Religion of the family is not only ignored, but even opposed in the few passages concerning ritual. The author clearly had no social function; anecdotes about Zhuang Zhou demonstrate a strong disinclination for government service, the elite occupation of the time. Unconnected to the basic elite social unit of the extended family, the larger clan, or the state, the socially afunctional author, prone to ecstatic experience, had zero experiences and discussed them with terminology based on remnants of the earlier *xian* shamanism.

That the *xian* was a shaman who had become transformed at the end of the Zhou period has been previously noted by Edward Schafer (1973:11):

> But the *hsien* [*xian*] had abandoned the helpful social role of the ancient shamans and, like most Taoists, looked only for their own salvation. However, they had not forgotten the archaic techniques of soul projection, and they continued to dream of magic flight to paradises in the sea and air.

However, as per the discussion in the preceding Chapters, I do not agree with Schafer (1977:234) that the decline of shamanism per se within the dominant culture was due to persecution by the elite.

An indication of a shift in the nature of a person's orientation toward ecstatic experience is fortuitous. Both John-Paul and Zhuang Zhou are individual cases of such transformations. Yet the seeming similarity of their experiences indicates the potential for generalization. Thiel (1968:203) has raised the question of how shamanism developed into classical Daoism as found in the *Zhuangzi*. The life of shaman John-Paul, on the opposite side of the globe from China and chronologically distant by nearly two and a half millennia, provides a plausible explanation.

The loss of social function, due to religio-ecological transformations, allows the socially afunctional mystic experience to become more important than functional shamanic trance. The loss of social function also shifts ecstatic religious experience toward the individualistic. In summary, the mystic experience, which apparently occurs in all cultures and potentially to all humans, becomes valued over other ecstatic religious experiences when the culture disintegrates, as in the case of John-Paul due to oppression, or socio-economic developments allow elite individuals the option of an economically unproductive and individualistic existence, as in the case of Zhuang Zhou.

6   the mystic experience in chinese religion II: expression

Over a quarter century ago, I showed a calligrapher in Taiwan a tiny tianhuang seal I had just acquired cut with the expression "baiyun xin" (white cloud heart/mind). That incident blossomed into a continued friendship and this study, which is an imperfect translation of my intuition of my friend's intuition of the import of those words.

Functional religious ecstacy among the aristocracy and the common people was discussed in Chapter 4. In Chapter 5, the initial integration of the mystic experience into elite Chinese religion was analyzed. Yet to be investigated is the further integration of the mystic experience in traditional elite and semi-elite cultures. The subject is moot for the common people, because, as discussed in Chapter 5, while mystic experiences undoubtedly occur among ordinary Chinese people, they are unlikely to be in a socioeconomic circumstance that would allow for the valuing of nonfunctional ecstacy. In any case, as the literary and elite traditions were coterminous, we cannot expect anything to be recorded of these publicly unspectacular experiences for the non-elite, in contrast to the many recorded stories of magicians and other wonder workers (see DeWoskin 1983).

The introduction of Buddhism and the development of institutional Daoism enhanced the interest of the Chinese elite in meditation and related practices. There have been recent major studies of Daoist spiritual practices, especially by Livia Kohn. However, these practices were not necessarily oriented toward attaining the mystic experience (see Robinet 1979 and Kohn 1992 for studies including those that are). The focus of this chapter will be limited to the mystic experience in its relationship to the avocations of the elite. It will be argued that the mystic experience was a major stimulus to the primary pastimes of the traditional elite: aesthetic activity. As well, aesthetic expression was the solution to a problem found in all cultures: how to express the ineffable mystic experience.

The relationship of aesthetics and religion in China, in part, is no different from that of other traditional civilizations—art serves as an adjunct to religion and morality. Music, as has often been pointed out (e.g., Monroe 1965:21ff.), was considered by Kongfuzi and his followers to affect the emotions and, accordingly, should be controlled for the good of society. As elsewhere, art served to decorate temples, enhance ritual, provide objects for worship, and so on. The relationship in China is unique because aesthetic activity itself became an alternative mode of religious behavior for the traditional elite.

Aesthetics and the *Wenren*

Theoretically and, more often than not, in practice, the traditional Chinese elite were males (only males were eligible to take the civil-service examinations, the only recognized and legitimate means for obtaining elite status, socially acceptable wealth, and political power) who were highly accomplished in *wen*, in all its multiple meanings: the corpus of received literature, the creation of literature, writing as an art, clan and state rituals, and so on, all the constituents of being "civilized" from the standpoint of the dominant class. There were four theoretical occupations (two root: scholar-official and farmer; and two branch: artisan and merchant) but only two officially recognized classes: scholar-officials and all others (excepting the imperial family who were above all such distinctions). In actuality, merchants vied with the scholar-officials for power and status.

A millennium and a half of power struggles (among scholar-officials, the military, merchants, court eunuchs, and the hereditary aristocracy) were ultimately won by the scholars, who wore distinctive garb and had a special legal status, with the full development of the civil-service system by the eleventh century. Merchants were co-opted into the system by being allowed to purchase civil-service ranks at a price which reduced their economic power. Recent scholarship has expanded this view to include a somewhat differently educated middle class of middling-wealthy merchants, professionals (physicians, etc.), and government clerks, who were often oriented toward Daoism and formed poetry and calligraphy circles.

The *wenren* (*wen*-person) or literati, the traditional elite, stood between two opposite ideals: *ren* and *ziran*. (*Li* [ritual/propriety] is more commonly opposed to *ziran*, as will be discussed later in this chapter.) *Ren* (etymology: man and two), usually translated "benevolence," means the ultimate in social responsibility. *Ren* was the ideal of the *rujia* (usually but incorrectly translated as "Confucianism" and *ru* alone as "scholar"), the dominant ideology of state and clan religion combined, as interpreted by Kongfuzi and those who nominally followed him. *Ziran* (literally: "of itself," "spontaneity") expresses both the ideal of nature (as opposed to human artifice) and individuality or personal freedom. *Ziran* is one, if not the basic, tenet of *daojia* (usually translated as "Daoism" but nonetheless distinct from *daojiao*: Daoist religious institutions per se, albeit the two are considerably interrelated).

A *wenren* could express his individuality in many ways, including modes of living, but usually did so as a *wenren*, that is with his brush, the basic *wen* implement of poetry, calligraphy, and painting. It must be understood that in China in comparison to the West, individuality was and is suppressed by the dominant ideology and circumstances. A person is brought up to be a member of a unit, the family, and among the elite, the clan and state as well (nowadays until recently party and people). Hence individuality, although less common, is considered more noteworthy.

Where a *wenren* could be found between the two polar ideals of *ren* and *ziran* depended on both circumstances and personal inclinations, but rarely would be exclusively one or the other. I will illustrate the range with several twentieth-century examples, all of the last generations to reflect the traditional culture.

Mao Zedong (Mao Tse-tung) hardly requires an introduction. Although of peasant background, Mao received a traditional education (against his father's will). Even when attending normal school (1913–18), he received training in classical prose, a skill which he continued to maintain (Snow 1961:143). Throughout his life, he practiced calligraphy and wrote poetry in the classical style. Although it is unlikely he would have used the term to describe himself, he was a *wenren*. In inclination and occupation, he fully maintained the dominant elite ideal, service to others (*ren*): "party" and "people" replacing "clan" and "state" as objects of service.

Among Mao's published poems, one is exceptional in regard to the sentiments expressed. The following translation is overly literal in order to indicate the parallel structure of the middle lines (for other translations, see Barnstone and Ko 1972, Ch'en 1965, Schram 1966, and *Mao* 1976):

Ascending Mount Lu

Single mountain peak floats beside Great River [Yangtze];
Briskly ascend four hundred verdant switchbacks.
Coldly look toward ocean, see world—
Warm wind blowing rain from sky to river.
Clouds hang over Nine Tributaries, yellow crane hovers;
Waves descend toward Three Wu, white mist rises.
Magistrate Tao not know what place gone—
Perhaps at Peach Blossom Spring ploughing a field?

The poem is in the Tang (seventh to tenth centuries) eight-line regulated verse form, a highly structured poetic genre, little of which can be indicated in translation. In this genre, the poem is divided into two quatrains with the import of the entire poem in the last couplet. The first quatrain provides the setting; the second, the meaning. The fifth and sixth lines oppose rising to descending.

The "yellow crane" here has two closely related meanings, each well known through a number of poems, including those of China's most famous poet, Li Bo (701–762). In one (see Yip 1976:323), Li Bo mentions a Yellow Crane Tower by the Yangtze, a name derived from its primary meaning as a familiar of the *xian* (see Chapter 3). This sense of "yellow crane" is found in another poem by Li Bo (Yip 1976:362). In turn, Li Bo's use of the term derives from the poetry of Ruan Ji (210–63—see below). The Yellow Crane Tower was built to commemorate the place where, according to legend, a person attained *xian*hood, flying off on a yellow crane. Mao referred to the tower in an early (1927) poem, "Tower of the Yellow Crane" (Barnstone and Ko 1972:37).

"White mist" has been a variant of "white cloud," a symbol of shamanic ascent, since it is first found in the *Zhuangzi* (see Chapter 3). From the time of the *Chuci*, it has come to serve as a poetic (or visual in painting) metaphor for a euphoric state, ranging from the mystic experience to the simple ecstasy of freedom. Although the two lines could be read somewhat differently, its meaning is certain when we realize that Bao Zhao (421–465), one of China's most important medieval poets, wrote a poem with the same title which contains the following lines (Yip 1976:199):

> We will mount the road of feathered men
> And merge forever with smoke and mist.

By using Bao Zhao's title, Mao is clearly referring to the older poem, especially the two lines on which he writes a variation.

"Magistrate Tao" refers to the famous poet, Tao Qian (Yuanming, 365–427), who is the traditional epitome of a Daoist poet, an individual who rejects the dominant social ideals to live a life of wine, rusticity, nature, and mystic experience. His home was a village at the south foot of Mount Lu. The key word here is *magistrate*, because it is unusual to refer to him in that manner. Tao only held that position once for a brief period, and he gave up the position and refused to hold others. "Peach Blossom Spring" is the title of his well-known allegory which describes the social ideal of the *Zhuangzi*: an isolated egalitarian village where food, shelter, and leisure time are in sufficiency but not excess.

I have discussed the meaning of the poem in some detail, because scholars have gone to great lengths to find exclusively political meaning in the poem (e.g., Schram 1966). The poem was written on 1 July 1959 when Mao was sixty-five. He had to a degree retired, giving up (or forced to give up) chairmanship of the government half a year previously (while retaining chairmanship of the party) following growing dissatisfaction with his "Great Leap Forward." In August, a plenum of the Central Committee was to be held at Mount Lu, where Mao maintained his summer retreat, reversing many of his policies. Also, serious difficulties were brewing with the Soviets, leading to the rupture soon to follow.

In his poem, Mao is expressing a longing for freedom; freedom from responsibility, from cares, from office. He does so through the traditional mode, through a literary expression of the Daoist ideal. For Mao, Daoism (as a set of *daojia* concepts, not a *daojiao* system of doctrines) meant an alternative to the dominant ideology. This Daoism was understood as an aesthetic sensibility expressed through poetry and painting, as well as a mode of living (retirement). Wolfgang Bauer (1976:411–18) has related Mao's famous Yangtze swims, interpreting swimming as a variation of the flying metaphor, to the association of Daoism with "the idea of renewal, mobility and revolution."

Many further examples of this pattern of ideologically orienting oneself toward Daoism only when in political retirement could be provided, one being Sima Guang (1009–86), twice prime minister and a major historian. Politically conservative, when temporarily forced out of office by his radical political opponent, he built himself a complex garden and wrote an essay on it (a recognized masterpiece of prose style) in which he rejected *rujia* values and lauded Daoist ones:

> My ears, eyes, lungs and bowels are all my own personal possessions—I utterly follow my will, am utterly unbounded in scope . . . what pleasure can be greater than this! (From the *Duloyuan ji* [Record of the garden for solitary enjoyment])

Near the opposite end of the scale and living a generation after Mao Zedong is a calligrapher and connoisseur, now around seventy-five, who is known only to a small circle of like-minded friends. He is from an educated Henan farming family. His grandfather studied for but failed the civil-service examinations; his father maintained an interest in calligraphy and painting. Until drought and locusts reduced the family to poverty and his education became sporadic, he was sent to both a modern school and a traditional one. With the Japanese approaching while in secondary school, he joined the army. Following the war, he studied Chinese literature at a university for a short time before returning to the military, in part, for the opportunity to travel. Taking leave for an excursion to the newly liberated Taiwan, he found the entire Nationalist army soon following him.

He retired in 1960 as a major in the quartermaster corps and quickly spent his terminal pay on books, inks, and brushes. Separated from his family, and with no money, no profession, and only an interest in calligraphy, painting, enjoying the company of friends, and traveling in the mountains to collect unusual stones (see Chapter 7), he opened a tiny shop to sell his library and meet like-minded persons. When the books were gone, he continued as a calligrapher and a seal artist (a type of calligraphy), collector of stones, and creator of tray landscapes (miniature gardens), making a modest living by buying and selling the odd piece of art or antique among his friends.

In this case, a Daoist mode of life—a life exclusively devoted to the enjoyment of nature, friends, and artistic activity—is due entirely to circumstances. Cut off from the family cult (as of 1979, he had not seen any member of his family since 1947) although he maintains a small shrine—and with little opportunity to serve the state, which he had done in his youth within the modern context of "nationalism" and "patriotism" by joining the army—he is that rare Chinese phenomenon, an individual. Given a different world (I asked him what his plans were before the Japanese invasion), he would have continued his education and become a college teacher, a *rujia* occupation. Although he is not a teacher or a government official, he still considers himself a *wenren* in retirement, expressing *wen* through aesthetic expressions.

In another autobiographical sketch I collected, a Chan Buddhist scholar-monk from a distinguished Henan family oriented toward Buddhism (his grandfather had been a general during the Qing dynasty) had taken his vows after retiring from the army in Taiwan with the rank of lieutenant colonel (with no remaining family connections and his adopted son married). Before joining the army after the Japanese military invasion in 1937, he had decided to spend "twenty years serving the state and twenty years attending to his own religious needs." It is an interesting solution to the existential problem of the elite appearing as early as the third century: the "opposing claims of activism and quietism" (Mather 1969:169).

This pattern is again not unique. It has been especially prevalent after the collapse of dynasties when *wenren* who could or would not serve the state lived as recluses (i.e., did not hold office) or monks (after the introduction of monasteries): "The renunciation of the official life . . . is the keystone of Chinese eremitism . . . which distinguishes it from the connotations of the word in other civilizations" (Mote 1960:204). These individuals often devoted themselves to poetry, painting, and other aesthetic pastimes. A number of examples will be cited in the following section.

History of Aesthetic Expressions

For over a millennium, poetry, calligraphy, and painting have been considered by the elite as the Three Incomparables (*sanjue*, see Sullivan 1974). (Prose is not discussed because essays and memorials to the throne more commonly were on *rujia* themes, and writing fiction was not considered a proper *wenren* avocation.) Together with music of the *qin*, they comprise the traditional Chinese aesthetic activities. In the following, I will present a brief history of each, focusing on their relationship to religion.

Poetry

As discussed in Chapter 3, the earliest extant Chinese poem (excluding the *Shi*) is "Li sao" by Qu Yuan (fourth century B.C.E.) in the *Chuci*. It is a long description of a shamanic flight written by the author after he had retired or been dismissed from office. The poem both established a poetic style and provided a terminology (based on a past form of shamanism) for later poems (first century B.C.E.) also contained in the collection. Some of these poems, written in a period when Daoist thought had spread among the intelligentsia, emphasized the mystic experience (see also Chapter 5):

> When I looked, my startled eyes saw nothing;
> When I listened, no sound met my amazed ear.
> Transcending Inaction, I came to Purity,
> And entered the neighborhood of the Great Beginning.
>   (Last lines of "Yuan you" in Hawkes 1959:87)

Other poems simply emphasized freedom, a concept that continued more than just the language of shamanistic experience:

Far and away my thoughts aspire,
Enjoying the freedom of the floating clouds.
>   (From "Pei hui feng" in "Jiu zhang," in Hawkes 1959:78)

Just grant me my worthless body and let me go away,
To set my wandering spirit soaring amidst the clouds.
>   (From "Jiu pien" in Hawkes 1959:99)

With the collapse, two centuries later, of the Han dynasty went the *rujia* synthesis as well. A failure of one reform movement by the *fangshi* (court exorcists/priests) may have led to the formation of institutionalized Daoism (Kaltenmark 1979). The *ru*ists, many of whom were slaughtered by their political opponents, the court eunuchs, moved first toward the earlier discredited Legalist (*fajia*) concepts and then toward *xuanxue* ("abstruse learning," often misleadingly translated as Neo-Daoism), all the while expressing their Daoist inclinations in poetry (Balázs 1950:55). These tendencies reached their culmination in the third century, when we find the first maturing of Chinese poetry.

The two greatest poets of the period were Cao Zhi (192–232), the son of Cao Cao (founder of the Wei dynasty, also a notable poet) and Ruan Ji. The former was greatly interested in Daoism, a Daoism that by this time emphasized the gaining of longevity in order to join the company of flying *xian*, and wrote poems on this theme. The latter not only turned pentameter verse into a major poetic mode, but his poems were highly influential on the great Tang (seventh to tenth century) poets.

Ruan Ji is a fascinating figure in legend and history. From both standpoints, he is "a forerunner of a new kind of hermit, a religious recluse" (Holzman 1976:23). A military official caught in a complex political situation, much of his poetry is a carefully hidden commentary on his times. He is remembered, however, for drinking and is the first of the famed drinking—hence, unconventional and individualistic—poets.

Drinking alcohol had a number of functions in regard to aesthetics. First, alcoholism, whether real or feigned, could be used as an excuse to avoid the normal political life of the educated. Second, the excuse of being drunk, here symbolic rather than actual, allowed for the dropping of complex precedence and rituals among the educated (who were with few exceptions hi-

erarchically ranked officials or "retired" officials) enabling them
to relax at literary and artistic gatherings. Third, it was used to
gain ecstatic states to facilitate spontaneous artistic creations (see
Chapter 4 for other uses of alcohol in regard to ecstatic states).

Ruan is also remembered as a recluse oriented toward nature, again setting a legendary pattern: "He would climb upon
the heights to look down upon the mountains and rivers for days
on end, forgetting to return home" (*Jinshu* 49, Holzman 1976:234).
Among many subjects, his poems refer to *xian*:

> Let us ride on the clouds and summon Song and Chao [two *xian*]
> And breathe in and out forever!
>
> (Holzman 1976:234)

Ruan Ji's poems also allude to the mystic experience:

> At last I am able to forget my difficulties:
> But will I know how silently to leave my self behind?
>
> (Holzman 1976:169)

> Isn't it better to leave behind the things of this world
> And mount in brightness, swirling with the wind?
>
> (Holzman 1976:182)

It is generally accepted that the most important poets between the third century (some would say since Qu Yuan) and the
Tang period are Tao Qian (365–427) and Xie Lingyun (385–433).
Each became an archetype, both of poetic genres and of lifestyles:
Tao, the epitome of the Daoist, drunken recluse, was later exem-
plified in Li Bo; and Xie, the Buddho-Daoist landscape poet,
caught between official life and retirement, was later exemplified
in Wang Wei (701–761). (Li Bo and Wang Wei together with Du
Fu [712–770] are the three great lights of Chinese poetry's
"Golden Age.")

Often a third poet, Bao Zhao, is included, who accords well
with the following pattern, both in regard to the use of wine and
of nature mysticism; e.g., the last lines of his previously mentioned "Ascend Mount Lu":

> Among the steep precipices, traces of Transformation.
> Upon the peaks, the lasting spirit.
> To follow this delight in mountain's natures
> And deep love for long excursions

We will mount forever upon the road of feathered men
And merge forever with smoke and mist.

(Yip 1976:199)

We have little hard data on the life of Tao Qian. The traditional biographies are apocryphal and dwell on his legendary aspects. However, they do agree with his autobiographical essay—"I have lived alone in my poor house, drinking wine and writing poetry" (Hightower 1970:58)—and his poetry. Rejecting office, the only source of wealth available to a member of his class, and lacking a large inheritance, he lived as a farmer. Tao took pleasure, perhaps even focused his life, on drinking and writing poetry, and he came to represent for subsequent generations the alternative lifestyle to the dominant imperatives, which were to serve family, clan, and state. His image is that of the semi-recluse having like-minded companions (Tao was reputedly a friend of Huiyuan—see below) and living a simple life close to nature (interpreted in various ways).

For Tao, wine was perhaps not so much an escape from reality (it was certainly used as an excuse to avoid offers of government positions) but a means to another reality (altered state of consciousness), and poetry was the means of expressing it. The fifth poem of the series "Twenty Poems after Drinking Wine" is often cited as a classic example of the mystic experience achieved through nature and expressed via poetry (C. Y. Chang 1963:190–91):

> I built my hut beside a traveled road
> Yet hear no noise of passing carts and horses.
> You would like to know how it is done?
> With the mind detached, one's place becomes remote.
> Picking chrysanthemums by the eastern hedge
> I catch sight of distant South Mountain [Mount Lu]:
> The mountain air is lovely as the sun sets
> And flocks of flying birds return together.
> In these things there is a fundamental truth
> I would like to tell, but there are no words.

(modifying Hightower 1970:30)

(Contrary to my own interpretation, Hightower argues that the poem is concerned with the search for longevity, but he earlier [p. 6] points out that this search was not of particular importance to Tao Qian. Also, on visiting Tao's home at the foot of Mount

Lu, I found that no hills can be seen to the south; hence, the reference in line six must be to Mount Lu.)

We have considerably more data documenting the life of Xie Lingyun (see Frodsham 1967). Scion of one of the two most powerful families of medieval China, Xie's paternal great-uncle, Xie An (320–385), was a major statesman and a frequent companion of the foremost Chinese calligrapher, Wang Xizhi (321–378—see below). Xie's mother was the niece of the calligrapher Wang Xianzhi (344–388—see below). As a child, Xie was temporarily adopted into the family of a follower of the Way of the Heavenly Master (Tianshidao)—a major institutional Daoist sect in which calligraphy was of considerable importance—who resided in the scenic area of Hangzhou. Xie's father died young, so Xie inherited the title, vast estate, and wealth of his grandfather, an important general.

As a young man, Xie visited the Buddhist center at Mount Lu (the same mountain referred to in the poems of Mao, Tao, and Bao) that had been founded by an essential figure in the history of Chinese Buddhism, Huiyuan (334–416). He there joined a group of lay followers that included the calligrapher and painter Cong Bing (375–443—see below). Later in life, Xie was to write several important Buddhist treatises, one of which presaged the later Southern Chan focus on instantaneous enlightenment. Yet throughout his life, he maintained his family's interest in institutional Daoism and the search for longevity.

Well known as a poet, a leader of society, and politically important as head of a major branch of the Xie clan, Lingyun was caught in a change of dynasties which severely compromised his sense of *rujia* loyalty. He accepted offices but retired several times, was twice exiled, and was finally executed.

As a poet, he considered himself the follower of Cao Zhi. Later generations considered him, not quite accurately, the founder of landscape poetry. "Landscape" is the common translation for *shanshui* (literally: mountains and streams), but *shanshui* connotes far more than our word landscape implies. It arises from several sources: Chinese nature sacrifices which have been made to particular mountains and bodies of water as far back as we have historical records (see Chapter 8), the combination of Buddhism and Taoism that took place in southern China in the fourth and fifth centuries, and the fabulous scenery of places such as Hangzhou and Guizhou, which became the centers for major developments in painting as well:

> Landscape was not just a *symbol* for the Tao [Dao]—the term was in this period as much a Buddhist as a Taoist expression—it is the Tao itself. This is brought out very clearly by a passage in Sun Ch'o's [ca. 300–380, protégée of Wang Xizhi] "Fu of My Wanderings on Mount T'ien T'ai":
> When [the Dao] dissolves it becomes rivers;
> When it coagulates it becomes mountains.
> So the contemplation of landscape is the contemplation of Reality itself. It brings on that state of mystical detachment which could either be described in Taoist terms . . . or as the trance of visualizing the Buddha, *buddhānusmrti-samādhi*.
> (Frodsham 1967:100)

The linkage of mountains and water to express nature, particularly in the religious sense, is not uniquely Chinese. For example, the highland Maya in Mesoamerica recognize paired public shrines: "the low shrine, or 'water place,' and the high shrine, or 'mountain place'" (Tedlock 1982:54).

Xie not only contemplated mountains, but also hiked in them (he is reputed to have invented a climbing boot with reversible studs), an activity which Frodsham (1967:65) considers "almost a devotional practice, bringing him into contact with the 'Body of the *Dharma*' itself." Certainly it was in the mountains and in their ascension that Xie achieved the experience expressed in his poem "I Follow the Jinzhu Torrent, Cross the Peak and Go along by the River." Following the description of ascent of a mountain alongside a stream and allusions to the "Li sao" (common in his poetry), he concludes:

> When I look at all this, the world of men disappears,
> In a flash of enlightenment everything falls from me.
> (Frodsham 1967:147)

Calligraphy

As with most early civilizations, writing was a characteristic of Shang culture. Less typical was a major use: the means for communicating with supernatural powers. Toward the end of the Shang period, the questions and later the responses to divination were written on the scapulae and plastrons used in pyroscapulamancy. By the Zhou period at least, petitions to the spirits were offered in written form, a practice that continues to the present. When, in the late first millennium B.C.E., the warrior-priest clansmen who comprised the elite became semi-military protobureaucrats, they remained ritual specialists. However, writing (*wen*) then took precedence over military skills (*wu*). Jonathan Chaves (1977:200) has articulated the relationship between religion and calligraphy in China:

> The fact [remains] that Chinese writing originated in an environment of magic, perhaps even of shamanism, and that these roots were never entirely forgotten. During the late Han and Six Dynasties periods, when calligraphy was transformed into the medium of aesthetic expression we are familiar with . . . there began the long-lived tradition of describing calligraphy in terms of nature imagery. But this very nature imagery is the link, I believe, between archaic conceptions of writing as magic and later attempts to characterize the inner power of this remarkable art form.

With improvements in brush (known as early as the Shang period) and ink and the development of paper (see Tsien 1962), the style of writing became more fluid, allowing many minor variations, hence it became more personal. By the first century C.E., examples of particular individuals' writings were collected, and by the late second century, major pieces of calligraphy (engraved on stone) were signed. Mention of calligraphy at this time becomes more frequent in the histories, and by the end of the Han dynasty, Zhang Zhi is exclusively remembered as a calligrapher (Ledderose 1979:30–31). However, calligraphy as an aesthetic mode actually begins in the fourth century.

In the early fourth century, the brief unification of China under the Jin dynasty collapsed, and the north was conquered by non-Chinese. There was an exodus of the elite to the south of the Yangtze River, an area that had been considered a frontier, where different cultural traditions had been maintained throughout the Han dynasty. In the period following this exodus, we find further developments in institutional Daoism and its development into a common factor of elite culture (Hisayaki 1979). We also find the development of gentry Buddhism, closely connected to Daoism and the great families (Zürcher 1959).

It is a father and son of the second of the two most powerful families in the south during the medieval era whom Chinese tradition considers the progenitors of calligraphic aesthetics. Although the accuracy of this tradition is questionable, it is certain that the Taizong emperor of the Tang dynasty (reigned 626–649) and his appointed advisor, Chu Suiliang, are responsible for basing the aesthetic standards on purported examples of the Wangs' calligraphy (Ledderose 1979:24–28). Both Wang Xizhi and his youngest son, Wang Xianzhi, were followers of the "Way of the Celestial Master." The two medieval critics responsible for propagating the tradition of the Wangs, Yang Xian (370–442) and Dao Hongjing (456–536), were also important in the development of institutional Daoism. Institutional Daoism reinforced the very early tradition of writing for communication with spirits and introduced aspects of calligraphic style as essential features of their sacred manuscripts and spiritual petitions (Chen Yinko 1983).

The fourth century witnessed the development of Mao Shan Daoism (Strickmann 1979) and the use by its visionary founder, Yang Xi (b. 330), of automatic writing (writing in trance). Among the scripts used was *caoshu* (a free, rapid, fluid style) which the Wangs preferred. Stylistic connections have been noted between Wang Xianzhi and Yang Xi (Ledderose 1977), and the former's calligraphy was later noted for its spontaneity. Both Xie An and Xie Lingyun were noted calligraphers and associated with institutional Daoism. The origin of the classic tradition of calligraphy was more a fourth-century phenomenon than solely that of the two Wangs.

The southern tradition of calligraphy was brought north with the unification of China under the Sui emperors (at the end of the sixth century), who were especially interested in calligraphy. The second emperor of the succeeding Tang dynasty showed particular favor to the calligraphy of the two Wangs, which became established as the traditional standard.

172 . THE SPIRITS ARE DRUNK

The Northern Song dynasty (960–1126), which followed the chaos resulting from the collapse of the Tang, was in many respects a reverse of the expansionist, cosmopolitan spirit of the preceding era. In intellectual endeavors it was a period of a comprehensive search for the past, of the creation of encyclopedias, and, in the arts, of the development of connoisseurship: not only the collecting and enjoying of archeological artifacts, crafts of the past and present, rare books, and particularly calligraphy and painting of the past, but of grading and evaluating them and determining standards for the present. It was an activity in part due to the fact that the Northern Song emperors did not maintain the Sui and Tang concepts of all-inclusive imperial collections, which, in turn, allowed the creation of private collections that were more accessible to the scholar-artists. The most influential of these connoisseurs, perhaps in his own time, certainly to future eras, was Mi Fu (1052–1107).

Through his critical works and in his own calligraphy, Mi Fu reinforced the tradition of basing the standard on the two Wangs.

> [His] theory of calligraphy is characterized by dialectical contrast: on the one hand, he emphasized an art historical approach and thus fostered the intellectualization of calligraphy; on the other, he declared such unintellectual qualities as tranquility and naturalness to be the highest artistic values. (Ledderose 1979:48)

The term translated as "tranquility" (*pingdan*, "calm and easy") was also a value applied at this time to poetry: "In writing poetry, there is no past or present;/ The only thing is to be calm and easy" (Mei Yaochen [1002–1060] in Yoshikawa 1967:39). Chaves (1976:114ff.) translates the term as "even and bland." The same term ("blandness" below) and naturalness were applied by Mi Fu to painting: "Tung Yüan [Dong Yuan] has much blandness and naturalness" (Bush 1971:72).

Hence, calligraphy, in which all the elite, the scholar-officials, were adept to some degree, could also serve as a complementary but opposite activity to those of the official realm—the spontaneity (*ziran*) of Daoist thought and, since the Tang, Chan Buddhism, as opposed to the ritual order (*li*) of official life:

In studying calligraphy one has to observe well the handling of the brush; that is to say, the brush has to be held with ease, and the palm should curve spontaneously. The movements should come swiftly with a natural perfection and emerge unintentionally. (Mi Fu in Ledderose 1979:58)

The influence of Mi Fu on calligraphy (and painting) was reinforced by the foremost theorists and practitioners of succeeding eras: Zhao Mengfu (1254–1322) of the Yuan dynasty and Dong Qichang (1555–1636) of the Ming (see below).

The extremes of spontaneity to which calligraphy could be carried in Chan Buddhism is exemplified by the "Mad *caoshu*" of the Monk Huaisu; for example, as described in the poem attributed to Li Bo:

> The Master high on wine, sits in his rope-chair
> in an instant he has covered thousands of sheets:
> the room is filled with whirlwinds and driving
> rains, falling flowers and flying snowflakes!
> He stands, goes over to the wall, with a single sweep
> he brushes a line of words as big as dippers!
> We hear the voices of gods and demons.
>
> (Chaves 1977:212)

Painting

Poetry and calligraphy were the "stock in trade" of the elite; only certain aspects of each furnished an alternative to official activity and concepts. James Liu (1966:63ff.) enumerates four critical approaches to poetry of which my treatment concerns two (poetry as self-expression and as contemplation) and excludes two (poetry as moral instruction and social comment and as literary exercise). Painting only became an important elite activity later and remained an avocation.

Prior to the Yuan period, with few exceptions, painters were professionals who were considered craftsmen by the scholar-officials, even if they were of the Imperial Academy. Hence, they were not considered members of the elite's own self-defined class. With the full development of the civil-service system, class distinctions were based on success in literary examinations that were in turn based on *rujia* texts. However, at times office was not held as it was unhealthy due to despotic emperors, unnecessary because of economic stability, difficult because of an excess of examination graduates, or unpopular because of loyalty conflicts due to a change of dynasty. Many of the elite, already experts with the brush, then took up painting as an activity suitable to retirement. At least theoretically, they were amateur painters. The preferred subjects were the landscape (*shanshui*) and bamboo, which was treated as intermediary between calligraphy and painting.

Previously mentioned as an associate of Xie Lingyun at the Buddhist retreat in the vicinity of Mount Lu was Cong Bing. Also a participant in intellectual circles, a noted calligrapher, and author of Buddhist treatises, he never held office (Zürcher 1959:1:218–219). However, he painted. Although we do not know what his paintings were like, we do have a prefatory essay to one of them. In it he points out the religious dimension of landscape: "Where the concern is with mountains (*shan*) and rivers (*shui*), [the fact is that,] while having the existent as their basic stuff, yet they tend toward the numinal realm" (Hurvitz 1970:148).

Cong writes that the action of painting can serve as an alternative to institutional Daoism and *rujia* (the allusion of "the stone gate"):

> I was ashamed that, unable to concentrate my vital vapors and thus to give pleasure in my body, I was trampling on the traditions of the stone gate. Thereupon I drew images and spread colors [over them], forming this cloud-covered range. (Hurvitz 1970:151)

Landscape poetry and painting expressed the Dao not only to the artist but to the viewer as well. Along with gardens, tray landscapes, and distinctive rocks (see next chapter), they served to stimulate the Daoist aspect of the literati's mind, when by the Song period, most lived in an urban environment. The reverse is also true; the mountains stimulated the painter:

> At the beginning of the Ming period, when he [Wang Li (b.1322)] was about fifty, he climbed the summit of Hua-shan, the towering mountain of Shensi Province that drew pilgrims both as a Taoist holy place and for its awesome

scenery. The experience was apparently overwhelming, transforming his life and his painting style. . . . When asked later who his teacher had been, he replied: "My teacher is my mind; its teachers are my eyes; their teacher is Hua-shan. That's all." (J. Cahill 1978:5–6)

A scholar who is a Chan monk, Mingfu (1976), has argued that landscape painting from its inception has been intimately related to meditation. For example, Cong Bing's painting developed from meditational practices. By the seventeenth century, Chan monks used landscape painting as both activity and object in their religious teaching.

Guo Xi (1020–1090), a major landscape painter of the Northern Song Academy, begins his "Essay on Landscape Painting" with a discussion of their purpose:

> Why does a virtuous man take delight in landscapes? . . . The din of the dusty world and the locked-in-ness of human habitations are what human nature habitually abhors; while, on the contrary, haze, mist and the haunting spirit of the mountains are what human nature seeks, and yet can rarely find. . . . [But] in the face of such duties [rujia virtues] the benevolent man cannot seclude himself and shun the world. . . . Having no access to the landscapes, the lover of forest and stream, the friend of mist and haze, enjoys them in his dreams. How delightful to have a landscape painted by a skilled hand! Without leaving the room, at once, he finds himself among the streams and ravines. . . . Does not such a scene satisfy his mind and captivate his heart? (Sakanashi 1935:32–33)

Guo Xi was a professional painter who stressed representation rather than expression. A contemporary, Su Shi (Dong-po, 1037–1101), together with several friends, anticipated the development of the wenren painting concept (J. Cahill 1960:129), in which the goals were reversed: painting expresses the painter, not the subject, to lead to a communication of minds. In seeking past models, Su preferred the work of Wang Wei, the Tang literati poet-painter (oriented toward Chan Buddhism) to the most noted professional painter of that day. It was the start of an elite theory that valued the products of their own class, turning painting into an amateur activity. As a literati avocation with the concomitant valuing of amateur qualities over professional skill, painting was closely related to calligraphy: "The more painting emphasized inner experience and resembled calligraphy, the more it devalued representational context in favor of the purely aesthetic" (Fong 1976:91).

Su Shi was a friend of Mi Fu, and the two were later listed among the "Four Masters" of Song calligraphy. Su Shi was one of the major Chinese poets of all time, an important official (when not in political exile) who was leader of the conservative faction in Song politics and an amateur painter. His paintings were apparently created spontaneously after attaining an alcoholic trance. Mi Fu wrote of him:

> When I first saw him, he was slightly drunk and said: "Could you paste this paper on the wall? It is Kuan-yin paper." Then he rose and made two bamboos, a bare tree, and a strange rock. (Bush 1971:9)

Another painter described Su Shi's tendency at literary gatherings to fall asleep after several cups of wine, then awaken and rapidly paint (Lin 1947:277); in Su Shi's own words:

> When my empty bowels receive wine, angular strokes come forth,
> And my heart's criss-crossing give birth to bamboo and rock.
> What is about to be produced in abundance cannot be contained:
> It erupts on your snow-white wall.
>
> (Bush 1971:35).

Su Shi explicitly relates trance to artistic activity in a poem on the painting of his close friend Wen Tung:

> When Yü-k'e [Wen Tung] paints bamboo
> He sees bamboo, not himself.
> Not only is he unaware of himself
> Trance-like he leaves his body.
> Body and soul once merged
> Endless freshness flows.
> Since Chuang [Zhuangzi] is no longer here
> Who else can know such absorption.
>
> (Stanly-Baker 1977:14)

By the Song period, given the nature of the examination system and a heightened interest in revitalizing the *rujia* tradition, the intelligentsia were primarily oriented toward *rujia*. However, in their leisure time and during periods of retirement, they tended to focus on institutional and philosophical Daoism and Chan Buddhism and expressed this interest, often at social gatherings, in poetry, calligraphy, and painting. Su Shi was involved with both Daoism and Buddhism, and his two "Red Cliff Odes" (see Birch 1965:1:381–82) are among the finest expressions of Daoist thought (and his writing of them considered among the finest examples of calligraphy). A contemporary, Huang Tingjian (1045–1105), another major poet, explicitly related painting to the techniques of Chan:

> At first I could not appreciate painting, but then by practicing meditation (*ch'an*), I came to understand the efficacy of effortlessness, and by studying *Tao* I realized that perfect Tao is simple. (Bush 1971:49)

Following the Mongol conquest of China (thirteenth century), many literati would not (or could not, as the case may be) serve the foreign Yuan reign. As hermits (in the Chinese sense), they focused their lives on calligraphy and painting. In reaction to the professional court painters of the preceding Southern Song period, the term *wenren hua* (literati painting) came into use, and this concept was further developed, ironically, by one who did accept office (after ten years of Mongol reign), Zhao Mengfu. He sought his models in the tradition of Su Shi and Mi Fu, who had sought theirs in Wang Wei. By example, Zhao was highly influential on the calligraphy and painting of his own as well as succeeding eras. Although he left little writing on aesthetic theory, other major Yuan dynasty painters left poems reflecting the Northern Song literati views. Wu Zhen (1280–1354) wrote, "When I begin to paint I am not conscious of myself / And am completely unaware of the brush in my hand" (Bush 1971:132). Ni Zan (1301–1374) wrote,

> By the eastern sea there is a sick man,
> Who calls himself "mistaken" and "extreme."
> When he paints walls and sketches on silk and paper,
> Isn't it an overflow of his madness?
>
> (Bush 1971:134)

This pattern was again repeated with the collapse of the succeeding Ming dynasty and the return of foreign rule by the Manchus in the mid-seventeenth century. A number of the elite became Chan monks or "mad" hermits, and these "Individualist Painters" produced brilliantly innovative works based on the now historic Yuan models. The major figure was Taoji (Shitao, 1641–c.1720), whose treatise on painting is of major interest and relates to the theme of this study (see Chou 1977).

Due to a number of political factors—Ming imperial despotism, reliance on eunuchs, regional quota system for civil servants—there developed, especially in Jiangnan, that locus of culture, wealth, and scenery that has continually been the center of the arts since the fourth century, a class of "retired scholars":

> [Their] affluence, either inherited or acquired during their period of service, enabled them to spend their leisure in elegant and aesthetic ways: building gardens and libraries, collecting books and works of art, exchanging invitations to literary banquets, practicing calligraphy and painting. (J. Cahill 1978:60)

Another class also developed, the "scholar-official manque":

> His position in society is anomalous, since his education has not been put to the normal use: he is learned and talented without possessing either wealth or rank. Typically, in China, such an artist [true also of poets] cultivates in his life and art an attitude of eccentricity, or at least evidences a degree of emancipation from the rules and conventions to which others, whose roles are better defined are bound. (J. Cahill 1978:99)

An official for most of his life, reaching the office of president of the Board of Rites, Dong Qichang codified the theory of the *wenren hua*, was considered the greatest calligrapher since Zhao Mengfu, and was a noted poet. He was highly influenced by the Ming revival of Chan Buddhism and the development of Wang Yangming "Neo-Confucianism," which stressed meditation and incorporated the mystic experience. At the end of his life in 1636, Dong had his family dress him in Daoist garb and said:

Although I have occupied some of the highest positions in the government, I never belonged there. I belong to the "clouds and the waters," as you can see from my appearance and manner. (N. Wu 1962:293)

The primary purpose of Dong's theory of art was to distinguish between literati painters (amateurs who painted by intuition—see fig. 12) from professionals (who painted by design—see fig. 13). The literati sought "spiritual harmony," "a lofty and ecstatic aesthetic state, the most abstract of poetic essences" (Ho Wai-kam 1976:127). Dong utilized the distinction between Northern and Southern Chan Buddhism (the latter stressing sudden enlightenment, a concept discussed earlier by Xie Lingyun) to distinguish between professional and literati painters:

When painting was approached with such a subjective, transcendent attitude, the creative process itself, and not the end product, became first in importance. Art was a form of self-realization; and since brush and ink were the most direct and effective means for self-expression, they were accorded primacy over other formal pictorial elements such as composition. (Ho Wai-kam 1976:122)

Dong's aesthetic theories determined the standard for both "individualist" (see fig. 14) and court artists into the twentieth century.

Music

Ideally, in every *wenren*'s study not only were there the necessary implements for *sanjue* activities, preferably antique, but also an antique sword and *qin*. The former symbolized the original meaning of *shi*, the term for scholar-official, a knight, that is, a hereditary professional warrior. As well, many literati practiced *wushu*, the martial arts, as a set of exercises promoting mental and physical health and longevity. Furthermore, some familiarity with weapons was useful, as, since the Song dynasty, high civilian officials were sometimes given military commands.

FIGURE 12. Landscape by Zhang Jin, done in 1642—colored ink on paper (50 x 32cm). Zhang Jin is a relatively obscure painter who was from the same town as Dong Qichang and studied under his most famous student, Wang Shimin. The painting reflects a competent rather than brilliant example of the developed orthodox literati landscape painting. Author's collection.

FIGURE 13. Landscape by Qian Weicheng (1720–1772)—black ink
on silk (64 x 37 cm.). Interesting attempt by professional painter to
paint as a literati. Qian was a member of the Imperial (Painting)
Academy, but, in the inscription, pleads for his painting to be
understood as a literati painting, and he signs it without his court
title. Although, the composition and atmosphere of the painting
reflect literati aesthetics, the structures are far too detailed and
precise for a literati painting. Author's collection.

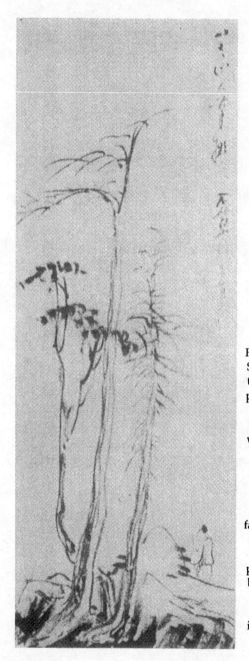

FIGURE 14. Landscape by Sheng Zhang (active early twentieth century); ink on paper (80 x 28 cm.). Zheng was a supporter of Sun Zhongshan (Sun Yat-sen) who was forced to flee his native Canton for Hong Kong. An excellent example of a landscape reduced to the essentials: rock, vegetation, and a faceless literati figure. Both mountains and water are implied rather than portrayed. The terse, fluid brushwork represents the nineteenth-century Cantonese interest in the individualist literati style. Author's collection.

The *qin*, however, was understood as a complement to the *sanjue*, the one literati aesthetic pursuit not directly connected to the brush. For the *qin* was a musical instrument almost exclusively played by the elite; its small sound box does not put forth a volume sufficient for concerts. The simple structure of the *qin*—seven (originally five) fretless strings on a long box of thick wood—indicates its development in the archaic past. At least by the mid-Zhou period, it was played by the elite; for example, by Kongfuzi. Yet its very simplicity renders it difficult to play. Most of the technique lies in the many different vibrato effects given by the left fingers, while the right fingernails strike the strings in different ways.

At least by the Han period, playing the *qin* had religious connotations. According to the *Huainanzi* (second century B.C.E.), the *qin* developed "to make man return to his divine origin, to restrain his low passions, and make him revert to his heavenly nature" (van Gulik 1940:40). Many *qin* compositions were based on passages from the *Zhuangzi*; for example, "Liezi riding the wind." Xi Kang, a friend of Ruan Ji discussed above and one of the apocryphal "Seven Sages of the Bamboo Grove," wrote a famous *fu* (prose-poem) on the *qin* (see van Gulik 1941). Famous painters such as Ni Zan were known for playing the instrument, and painters frequently portrayed literati followed by a servant carrying a *qin* while strolling in nature, in case the mood to play should arise.

Qin music was equated with landscape painting. In the famous piece, *Yuge* (Song of the Fisherman)—the fisherman together with the woodcutter are ubiquitous symbols of the ideal *daojia* existence—the description of the last part is "Lofty mountains [*shan*], eternal streams [*shui*]." Playing the *qin* was understood as a means for gaining and expressing the mystic experience through *ziran*. Toward the end of a sixteenth-century essay on the *qin* we find:

> When one's self is naturally aloof and earnest, then one shall correspond to the Mystery [*xuan*] of the Way [Dao], and one's soul shall melt together with the Way. Therefore it is said that successfully executing music is not caused by the hands, but by the heart, that music is not produced by notes, but by the

Way. When one does not strive to express music in tones,
but lets it come naturally, then one may experience the Harmony of Heaven and Earth, then one may be in communion with the virtue of the Universal Spirit. (van Gulik
1940:78)

Aesthetics and Religion

There is nothing original in any of the preceding statements; to
a traditionally educated Chinese, what has been discussed above
is matter of fact. The point of this chapter is to illustrate how aesthetic expression in traditional China may be understood from a
Western perspective, for 'aesthetics' and 'religion' are Western
concepts.

Harold Osborne (1968:67) has pointed to language itself as
a major source of the difficulties in applying Western aesthetic
concepts to China:

> The language and the concepts of Chinese [aesthetics] dif-
> fer from those which we use and some considerable effort
> may be needed to bring them into connection with the
> art from which they are derived and to grasp what they
> are about in terms of categories with which we are more
> familiar.

Like the word *religion*, the word *aesthetics* has no Chinese
equivelent. The modern translation is *meixue* (literally: the study
of the beautiful). *Mei* (etymology: a man with a head adornment
in the form of a ram's horns; Karlgren 1957:151) like *bellus* means
"beautiful" in the sense of "pretty"; but *mei* is not a value in traditional Chinese aesthetics. Rather, the major value is *ziran*, a term
that includes in its meanings "nature," "spontaneity/originality,"
and "self-expression/self-indulgence." However, as *meixue* is
understood to refer to the appreciation of art, including Chinese
art, it is not as problematic as the word *religion*, as discussed in
Chapter 1.

When we examine the history of the primary modes of elite
aesthetic expression, from their origin to the establishment of
their basic standards over the span of two millennium, we find

considerable commonality. All major personalities were involved with aspects leading to the development of Daoism or later Daoist-influenced institutional and/or philosophical developments: from Qu Yuan and a poorly understood institutionalized shamanism; to the Daoism of the later *Chuci* poems; to the *xuanxue* of Ruan Ji and Xi Kang; to the institutional Daoism and gentry Buddhism of the medieval founders of calligraphic art, landscape poetry, and painting; to Daoist philosophy and institutions as a complement to the *rujia* of official life for the literati of the Song and thereafter; to the Chan Buddhism and Wang Yangming "Neo-Confucianism" of the Ming theorists and practitioners. In all instances, it is the experience of aesthetic creation and of intuitive understanding of that experience by others that is emphasized.

It is to be further noted that virtually all of the persons discussed had been brought up in or had lived in a relatively small part of China, Jiangnan ("Yangtze River South," including Hangzhou and Suzhou), whose original traditions were different from those of the North, the home of the *rujia* tradition. (Even in the Han period, Chu had different religious traditions from the North, and Wu, which was not part of the early Han politically or culturally, was the origin of many of the *fangshi*.) This area, which formed the locus of the emerging Buddho-Daoist traditions from the fourth century on, developed into a rich rice- and silk-producing region, the economic heartland of China. Linked by extensive canal transportation networks to the various Chinese capitals (during its long history), Jiangnan was the home of many wealthy literati and merchants. They built a number of large, complex *shanshui* gardens which housed the literati artists they patronized. Jiangnan was the favored area of residence for literati who gained sufficient wealth in government service to allow for early retirement to artistic pursuits. The aesthetic traditions that developed there spread throughout the rest of China.

Although this chapter has not focused on the terms and concepts of art criticism, a number have been noted in passing as deriving from the *Zhuangzi* or Chan Buddhism. Susan Bush has argued that such references are quite understandable since the Taoist classics were the only ancient stories that could be related to artistic creativity. In themselves, these Taoist references need not indicate more than an imaginative interest in such literature. (Bush 1971:48)

However, as has been indicated in this chapter, the use of such terms does not occur, either in theory or practice, in isolation from both philosophical and institutional Daoist values. This is not to deny that terms relating to trance flight or the mystic experience in much earlier periods become clichés in latter periods. On the other hand, their becoming stylized expressions does not mean they are entirely devoid of the original religious content.

When a functional approach to religion is applied to China, the nature of aesthetic experience is clarified. Aesthetic activity is the means by which the *wenren* as *wenren* (i.e., with brush and ink) experience as well as express their experiences as individuals, a heady value given the rigidly conformist and nonself-assertive nature of most of their lives and their occupations. For with few exceptions, the elite continually functioned in highly ritualized dual hierarchies, that of clan and state. Aesthetic experience is usually based on contemplation or trance experience of nature (not necessarily direct), which in itself is the Dao. Aesthetic experience, then, is the experience of the Daoist (*daojia* and *daojiao* or Chan as a later phase of Daoism) component of the *wenren* gestalt (the dominant *rujia* aspect experienced primarily through state and family rituals); that is, aesthetic activity serves as an alternative, complementary mode of religious behavior for the traditional elite.

The above conclusion is a generalization; indeed, a generalization concerning stereotypes. Typically, Chinese biographies reveal legends and the idealized attitudes toward aesthetics. A *wenren* who engages in the Daoist-derived genres of poetry, calligraphy, painting, or music does not necessarily see himself engaged in a Daoist or romantic activity. Should he become famous, others posthumously may see him in that light. Should he act the eccentric, it may be for a multitude of reasons: it is expected of him, it is a way of avoiding political recrimination, or it may enhance the value of his product. However, varying degrees of religiosity are brought by different individuals to every religious phenomenon. For example, from my experience in contemporary Chan monasteries in Taiwan, I found that the majority of monks became so for the most mundane of reasons, and their devotional activities in the monastery may have meant no more to them than bookkeeping to a clerk who is not particularly fond of keeping figures. My point concerns the derivation of the primary modes of aesthetic activity and the relationship of experience to the dominant modes of religiosity.

This chapter has focused on aesthetic experience rather than the art object, the usual subject for Western aesthetic consideration, because it is this aspect of aesthetics which elicits comparison with the West. Calligraphy and painting were evaluated on quite different criteria than other objects of *wenren* aesthetic appreciation, such as archaic jades and ceramics. The former were appreciated by persons of the same class and training as the artists, while the latter were considered products of craftsmen, nonelite not worthy of consideration as persons; hence, the latter are purely objects. All the major aestheticians, as previously mentioned, were themselves considered major artists, and artists do not judge works of art by fellow artists from the standpoint of "art objects" alone. Paintings and calligraphy were accordingly evaluated and appreciated in two ways: from the standpoint of authenticity, including considerations of previous ownership, that is, intellectual aspects; and, relevant to the theme of this chapter, as a mechanism for creating an experience in the viewer corresponding to the experience of the artist, that is, the emotional component.

Since Chinese poetry, calligraphy, and painting are often created in a social setting, they verge on performance. My most memorable parties in Taiwan were those when someone decided to write or paint, and I observed the contemporary artists discussed in the next section paint in the midst of groups of admirers.

Because the viewer as a *wenren* was also a master of the brush, in viewing the work, he was automatically aware of the process of creation and concentrated on the brushwork in the order of its application to the paper or silk. Furthermore, respected

pieces of *wenren* painting and calligraphy were not hung on walls
as in the West, but unrolled for viewing at approximately the
same distance as brushed by the artist, often in a similar social
milieu as when created. Hence, in being continually recreated,
the works continued as event. It was the viewer's concentration
on technique—brushwork—that enabled the "mind-to-mind"
communication to take place.

Contemporary China

With the passing of a decade and a half since the end of the Cultural Revolution in China, one can observe a flourishing of traditional religious practices and an expansion of artistic pursuits.
These two activities have coincided in ways unexpected in a
Marxist-Leninist society, long before the recent shift in economic
orientation, and further indicate that Chinese communism is primarily an indigenous phenomenon.

Following the massive destruction of temples and temple
statuary during the Cultural Revolution, artisans and artists have
been employed in the reconstruction of the major historical
temples and monasteries, both as cultural treasures and as attrac-
tions for tourism. The sculpture faculties at the major academies
of art have been engaged not only in creating Western-style sculp-
tures for public parks, but in recreating temple images.

In the last decade, there has not only been a considerable
growth of domestic tourism, but increasingly these travelers are
approaching the famous temples as pilgrims. At the temples, de-
votion and offerings are presented to the images. This is probably an unexpected development, but in effect it does mean that
state-paid artists, including the most reputable sculptors, are creating images for devotional purposes.

Although contemporary China is nominally egalitarian, I
was surprised to find the literati mode of artistic pursuit still
present. In 1983, when I first traveled in the Jiangnan region, still
a locus for extensive internal tourism where so many of the activities discussed took place, I found a revival of the "Three
Incomparables." Not only was I informed of this by contemporary calligraphers in Hangzhou, but I found the calligraphy and

painting supply shops thronged by young adults. I was given to understand that young factory workers are studying calligraphy at night (surely a more interesting way to spend an evening than the frequent political awareness meetings of the Cultural Revolution), and the activity is being introduced into the elementary schools. These activities are encouraged by the government as they are considered particularly appropriate for "raising the spiritual aspect of the culture" (*tigao jingshen wenming*). Many of the Suzhou gardens that were the residences for literati artists have been refurbished and are popular recreation (in its literal sense) sites for both local residents and tourists from all over China.

In 1986, I returned to Jiangnan as the guest of the Zhejiang Academy of Fine Arts in Hangzhou, China's premier college for the traditional fine arts. There I found an expansion of the activities I first observed in 1983. For example, exhibitions of laborers' painting and calligraphy displayed exuberant versions of traditional styles. While most of the teachers and artists I met would be professional artists, according to the traditional categories, I unexpectedly found artists who have maintained the *wenren* tradition. The focus of this section will be on two individuals who, in their lives and art, provide evidence that the religio-aesthetic (Pilgrim 1977) tradition of the traditional literati is still a vital force.

Mo Daoren

During my trip in 1986, I finally had the opportunity to visit Mount Lu, the geographic focal point of much of the discussion of this chapter and, at the south base of the mountain, the home of Tao Qian. There I found that different from Mount Tai (see Chapter 8), the locale had been shorn of its Chinese religious associations. Christian missionaries had taken over the lush, flat expanse of the mountaintop in the late nineteenth century as a summer resort and replaced all the temples and monasteries with churches. Eventually Mount Lu became the summer residence for first Chiang K'ai-shek and then Mao Zedong. It is now primarily a resort and sanitarium. While struggling with this culture shock on my first day there, I met the first Daoist monk I encountered in contemporary China who embodied the charisma of the legendary adepts.

Mo Daoren (The "Ink Daoist") is both the studio name and the religious name of Sun Mingrei. He is a monk of the Quanzhen order of Daoism, the northern school of Daoism headquartered at the Baiyun Guan (White Cloud Monastery) in Beijing. His own monastery is the Louguantai in Xian, Shanxi Province, the home province of the founder of the order, Wang Chongyang (1112–1170). The Quanzhen order is known for asceticism and is the Daoist response to the influence of Chan Buddhism (Saso 1978:52).

Mo Daoren leads a strict Quanzhen monastic life; for example, when he is away from his monastery, he will only eat food he prepares himself. However, his primary interest is painting. Although Mo Daoren's interest in Daoist monasticism is serious and thorough, the life of a Daoist recluse was also an option open to the traditional elite as a means of avoiding office or political turmoil.

Mo Daoren specializes in plum blossoms and also paints pine boughs, but interestingly in the style of plum blossoms. The prunus, blossoming plum, is a well-established symbol of rejuvenation, flowering as it does at the end of winter, often before the last of the snow has melted. It is a favorite poetic subject and reflects his own life-style:

> The flowering plum in the grove is like a recluse,
> Full of the spirit of open space, free from the spirit of the worldly
>   dust.

> (By Yang Wanli in Frankel 1953:106)

The pine is the common symbol of longevity, a primary *daojiao* value.

The most famous early painter of plum blossoms is Wang Mian (1287–1359), who lived the archetypical life of a Yuan dynasty artist—the literati recluse. Mo Daoren's painting style is reminiscent of Wang Mian, not in technique, but in regard to a line of poetry on a plum blossom painting by Wang in the Palace Museum in Beijing: "Are in full bloom with flowers like traces of pale ink" (J. Cahill 1976:159). For although Mo Daoren paints the branches with a large, worn, ink-laden brush in bold, black strokes, the blossoms are often painted with pale, watered inks or paints. Another Yuan dynasty painter, Wu Taisu, painted flowering plum and pine branches against a flat wash. This is a technique Mo Daoren also often utilizes in a modified version. His pine and prunus boughs are sometimes painted in the midst of snow or waves. Hence, Mo Daoren's aesthetics, following as it does Yuan dynasty hermit painters, directly reflects his eremitic lifestyle.

Physically tiny, Mo Daoren manifests a calm but vivid presence that is the epitome of the legendary Taoist adept. In contrast to his size, Mo's paintings tend to be huge in both height and in appearance: a pine bough flashes across a roiling seascape in a painting much taller than the viewer. His composition and brushwork are unique and exude an energy that cannot be contained by ink and paper. His plum blossoms represent the emerging force of life itself.

Mo Daoren is a frequent visitor to Mount Lu, and it is there that he prefers to paint. When at Mount Lu, he resides as a guest of the local art association. A highly respected visitor, even though he is not local, he has been appointed (1986) to be the priest of Xianren Dong (Cave of the *xian*) when it is returned from its present commercial use as a photographers' backdrop (a Cultural Revolution ploy to prevent religious activities from taking place). This site is the only Daoist "temple" left on Mount Lu since its take-over by Christian missionaries in the late nineteenth century. Therefore, Mo's vocation is that of priest, and painting is his avocation, following the traditional elite mode.

Hong Shiqing

Born in Fujian province in 1929 and educated at the Shanghai and Zhejiang academies of art, Hong is a faculty member of the Zhejiang Academy of Fine Art in Hangzhou, one of the two national art institutes in China. There he teaches Western printmaking and commercial design. Outside of China, among overseas Chinese in Singapore, he is known for his Chinese painting. Hence, although a professional artist, his Chinese painting is an avocation and approaches the traditional literati model. It was not unusual for professional painters, particularly court painters, to paint in the literati mode as an avocation and to value these paintings over their professional ones (see fig. 13, for example).

While still a teenager, his seal calligraphy impressed Qi Baishi, with whom he studied along with Huang Binghong, Pan Tianshou, and Liu Haishu. During a 1986 trip to China, I travelled as an official guest of various regional art academies and met and saw the works of those considered to be the finest Chinese painters and seal calligraphers. From my three decades' experience with Chinese art, none seemed to me comparable to Hong's combination of vitality, virtuosity, technical skill, originality, and spontaneity.

However, in China, very few are aware of his Chinese paintings and seal calligraphy. Although he lives in Hangzhou, he is not a member of the famous Xiling Seal Cutting Society (see following chapter). I was introduced to him outside of my official introductions. He was not as poorly treated as most artists and teachers during the Cultural Revolution, and he attributes this to the fact that few at the Academy were aware that he did other than Western art.

He does not specialize in either Western or Chinese art. The former, although original, is ultimately derivative, but his Chinese paintings, in various styles, are all unique creations. His landscapes and flower paintings evidence an exuberance that cannot readily be compared to those of previous artists. His bamboos are reminiscent of Xu Wei (1521–1593) in their free brushwork, and his animals remind one of the work of Zhu Da (?1625–1705) in their individualistic, anthropomorphized, "what-the-hell" expressions, but both are otherwise his own style. He has mastered not only brush techniques but also the finger and palm style of painting. His seal calligraphy is closer to the aesthetics of the Eight Eccentrics of Yangzhou (eighteenth-century) than that of any other seal calligrapher in contemporary China of whom I am aware.

Aside from his traditional modes of artistic creativity, Hong has spent more than ten summers creating rock images of fantastic sea creatures on the cliffs and rocks along the coast of an uninhabited island off the Zhejiang coast. Commissioned by a fishing commune at a very high fee, he refused to accept any funds except to pay the skilled rock cutters who assist him. As with his paintings, he quickly brushes the designs on the rocks; he then assists the workers in cutting the lines into the stone. He has to date nearly completed the planned one hundred figures, ranging in size from a half meter to seven meters in length. Eventually, the island will be turned into a park.

His creations follow the natural markings and crevices of the rock face, and the subjects relate to the seashore location. In his own words, "Working with rock is equivalent to the 'splashed ink' technique in painting—one's creation must respond to the given" (my translation of a personal communication). He considers this work "Great Earth art" and "a living form of art." He "utilizes spontaneity [ziran] to beautify nature [ziran]." 'Unity' is a concept foremost in his thoughts: "My artistic creations must become a single entity with great nature/spontaneity [ziran]," and "The artistic creation must achieve complete harmony and unity with the natural [ziran] scenery." Hong understands his rock art to be "essentially the same as seal calligraphy" (see next chapter).

Thus, Hong's remarks are replete with (unsolicited) Daoist and Chan sentiments and references, as well as terminology relevant to the mystic experience. The "splashed ink" technique is particularly associated with the Chan painters of the Southern Song, such as, Mu Qi and Liang Kai. Ziran, in expressing both the ideal of nature (as opposed to human artifice) and individuality or personal freedom, is one of the basic tenets of daojia. Unity is a key term in understanding the mystic experience described in the Zhuangzi (see preceding chapter).

Conclusions

Although both Mo Daoren and Hong Shiqing are highly skilled in traditional Chinese brushwork, both work within traditional Chinese genres as amateurs: Mo Daoren is professionally a Taoist priest, and Hong Shiqing is a professor of Western art. The traditional art of neither is officially appreciated, but they are both recognized among Chinese outside China. This is a situation preferred by both, since official recognition would lead to a professionalism neither desires. Professional status, as in the past, would mean that one is subject to producing art on demand and would inhibit artistic freedom which is of crucial importance to both. Here, artistic freedom is to be understood as spontaneous (*ziran*) creation, mirroring the continuous creation within the Dao. Hong writes that "the attainment of freedom within limits is the greatness of art."

Accordingly, both are within the long religio-aesthetic tradition of literati art stretching at least as far back as Su Shi and Mi Fu of the Song dynasty, Zhao Mengfu and the "Four Masters" of the Yuan dynasty, and Shen Zhou and Wen Zhengming of the Ming dynasty. Certainly the two would fit within the Southern (i.e., literati) artistic category of Dong Qichang.

The art of Hong and Mo Daoren evidences the major Daoist value, spontaneity and nature, in both method and subject. Each is able to capture the *qi* (vitality/inner essence) of the Dao with only brush and ink; their brushwork crackles with energy. Hong's brushwork takes one to the reality within reality; Mo Daoren's brush leads beyond surface appearances to the eternal flux that is the only truth.

Since Mao Zedong's talk at the Yenan Forum in 1942, it has been understood in China that art is to serve the people; this is still a fundamental attitude. That art exemplifying Daoist aesthetics can be understood to serve socialist purposes is an intriguing development. The government has realized that the loss of traditional cultural values (i.e., religious values in Geertz's terms), including aesthetic ones, has led to a serious loss of civility, the primary Chinese value. The government therefore encourages the pursuit of the arts both for workers and for specialists (artists), through government-sponsored professional and amateur artist associations, as well as a limited return to traditional religious practices, and provides limited support of religious specialists.

Mo Daoren, when he planned to take over Mount Lu's Daoist shrine, hoped to found an art school there. Hong understands his purpose in creating art to "lead people to return to nature [*ziran*], to love and care for nature." Thus, the tradition of Daoist individualism is in accord with the moderately liberalized communism of contemporary China. Indeed, a reawakened awareness of nature cannot but help to alleviate the problems of massive pollution and ecological disasters engendered by recent economic growth.

7 the fundament of religio-aesthetic expression: stones and seals

"Dreaming of Stones" (meng-shi)—*Cut by my friend Zhao Keli on*
dengguangtung *as his personal seal*

In the preceding chapter, it was argued that the doing of aesthetics and the primary subject of aesthetic activity, *shanshui* (mountains and streams, the Dao), were fundamentally religious in
nature. The first aspect revolved around the expression of the mystic and other ecstatic religious experiences, and the second symbolized the essence of reality, the Dao, in its created, material
aspect, Earth. In this chapter, it will be argued that the ground and
tools of aesthetic activity also are replete with religious import.

For example, the first quarter of Xi Kang's "Prose-poem on
the *Qin*" (see Chapter 6) concerns the nature of the material from
which it is made. Of importance is that the trees from which the
wood comes grow "on the lofty ridges of steep mountains":

> Rich soil ensures them great age, their tapering stems rise high
>   into the sky.
> They are saturated with the pure harmony of Heaven and Earth,
>   they inhale the beneficent splendor of sun and moon.
> (van Gulik 1941:52)

The poem continues with a rich depiction of the mountain scenery, the meaning of mountains, and their effects on humans who
enter them. In other words, not only does the music of the *qin*
reflect *shanshui*, but so does the very material, the wood, of the
instrument itself:

> The spiritual haze that hovers over these *mountains* mingles with
> the clouds, and from their mysterious founts *streams* gush forth.
> (van Gulik 1941:53; emphasis added)

197

However, because of the focus on the brush in the vocation and avocation of the traditional elite, the tools and medium relating to its use are of especial importance. Among the enduring aspects of Chinese aesthetics are the emphasis on the written word and the tools for creating writing, as well as the love of stones as the natural object par excellence. When these are combined, one encounters the height of Chinese religio-aesthetic sensibility.

As discussed in the preceding chapter, because a high degree of literacy became the entree to political power and because of the use of writing since the beginning of Chinese civilization to communicate with spiritual powers, as well as the permanence of an archaic, partial pictographic system, calligraphy became in China the highest form of artistic expression. Those Chinese thinkers who rejected the striving for social order with concomitant political structure as the highest good, found instead meaning in an undiscriminating acceptance of the natural world. Stones, each unique and eternal, with an utterly natural beauty, became symbolic of this orientation. When the Chinese literati began to cut their own seals in the late thirteenth century, necessitating the use of soft stones to replace hard jade and metal, a new art form, utilizing styles of calligraphy both archaic and untrammeled, slowly began, not reaching its fruition until the eighteenth and nineteenth centuries. Hence, seal calligraphy is perhaps China's most recent traditional art form. And, because the calligraphy expresses a person's name, favorite appellations, or expressions, it is a highly personalized art form.

While the calligraphic aspects of seals are accessible outside of China as imprinted on paintings and specimens of calligraphy and in the many books of collected impressions, the stones themselves are rarely seen. This chapter is an introduction to the history and religio-aesthetics of the material on which the calligraphy of seals is engraved. It is intended to serve as an example of how religion permeates all aspects of Chinese aesthetics, including connoisseurship.

A History of Seals in China

Seals have apparently been used in China since as far back as we can trace its civilization and writing system. Three bronze seals in the Palace Collection Museum in Taiwan are generally accepted as artifacts from tombs at Anyang, the last Shang capital—although they were not verifiably excavated—and would be from between the fourteenth and the eleventh centuries B.C.E. A number of late Zhou texts indicate the widespread use of official seals, and bronze seals have been excavated at various Warring States (fifth to third centuries) sites. Jade, along with bronze, the substance used for royal regalia and religious ritual artifacts, was also used for seals by that time.

Qin Shi Huangdi, the first Chinese emperor (reigned 221–209), had a number of jade seals made for official use, one of which he wore on his person as a symbol of imperial authority (see David 1971:242–47). This particular seal was also worn by the first Han emperor (reigned 206–195) and continued as the sign of imperial succession until it was lost at the end of the Han dynasty and a new one had to be made.

Seals in China then had a similar use as seals in the West. First, they served as symbols of political authority. By the Han period, officials possessed seals which distinguished their rank by material (jade, gold, and silver-plated bronze, and bronze), the design of the grip, and the colors of the cord strung through a hole in the grip. By this time, private seals of jade, bronze, and wood were also prevalent among the upper class. Because the seals of the elite were often interred with their corpse, numerous Han seals have been excavated.

A second use was that from which our English term derives: to seal or secure. Documents written in Zhou and Han times on vertical bamboo or wooden slips were rolled up, and the knot of the binding cord could be sealed with clay or clay mixed with glue on which the seal was impressed. Prestigious documents written on silk were placed in boxes and sealed with glue-like substances colored with purple dye or gold powder.

With the increasing use of paper in the Six Dynasties period (220–589), following its invention in the Han, seals were used for printing on paper, to authenticate documents and letters, using red or black water-soluble ink; the red came to be preferred to distinguish the seal imprints from the black ink used in writing and because of the auspicious aspect of the color red, the color of life in Chinese culture. It was also at this time that the red character seals cut in relief came into greater use, most Han seals having been cut in intaglio for sealing use, which with ink presents characters the color of the imprinted material in red relief. In the Tang period (619–907), honey was added to the water-based red ink, and by the Song dynasty (960–1279), a paste of oil, vermilion powder, and binder substance (moxa fibers preferred) had been developed, which is still used.

By the fourth century, the complex system of ranked official seals had died out and seals passed into ordinary use. Besides being engraved with formal names or office titles, seals were cut with literary expressions, informal names, and so on. With the end of the government office for casting bronze seals, jade became the more popular material among the wealthy. Seals also came to be made from ivory and horn, certain woods and bamboo, and semiprecious materials, such as crystal and agate. They were usually cut by artisans as a minor craft and, with the development of "Neo-Confucianism" in the twelfth century, those scholars who did cut seals were urged to refrain from what was then considered a frivolous hobby, although there was a government official to manufacture imperial seals.

However, one of the major factors behind the later development of seal art was the heightened antiquarian and literary interests of the elite in the Song period. Along with an interest in proto-archaeology, books of collected seal impressions from the Han period were published and served to renew interest in that style of calligraphy. The decline in the quality of seal calligraphy since the termination of the Han office for seals was reversed. Also, with the development of a printing industry, the number of government and personal libraries increased and the custom developed of using a library seal to mark books. From this, it was but a short step to the application of seals to paintings and calligraphy by collectors, perhaps begun by Mi Fu (see Chapter 6), the Northern Song dynasty artist and connoisseur, and the emperor he served, Huizong (reigned 1101–1126), necessitating a heightened calligraphic quality for seals to suit the quality of the collected work.

It is during the following Yuan dynasty (1279–1368) that we find those developments which ultimately led to the birth of seal art in the sixteenth century. As discussed in the preceding chapter, many literati refused to serve the new Mongol emperor in an official capacity or were not trusted by the foreign regime, and in forced or self-imposed early retirement devoted themselves to such pursuits as painting or literature. As Hangzhou, the Southern Song capital and cultural center, and its traditions had been destroyed, innovation was inevitable.

At this time, the tradition of the literati amateur painter became the accepted mode, and his calligraphic brushwork, the aesthetic standard. These painters began the custom of placing the imprint of seals after their signature. This custom derived from a scholarly, literary taste that would eventually demand a seal calligraphy equal in quality to the calligraphy written on the painting. The seal imprints increasingly became an aspect of the aesthetics of the work as a whole. The phenomena of the artist cutting his own seal starts perhaps with a literati who had served the Mongols in a high capacity, Zhao Mengfu (see Chapter 6), the founder of the new literati painting style, who may have used ivory or stone. Rather than the Han seal style, he cut his seal in *xiaozhuan* (small seal script).

But it was not until the late Ming period that a heightened interest in the images from seals of Han times led to the modern art of seal cutting. By this time, a movement founded by Shen Zhou (1427–1509) and continued by his student, Wen Zhengming (1470–1559), led to Suzhou becoming the aesthetic center of China. Wen Zhengming, who occasionally wrote in *xiaozhuan* (e.g., Ecke 1971:pl.50), the script in which he cut his seals, encouraged his son Peng (1498–1573) in the study of Han seals. Peng and his friend Ho Zhen, both of whom held official positions, are the founders of seal cutting, for others as well as oneself, as a literati avocation in distinction to the cutting and drilling of seals by professional craftsmen. The art of seal cutting reached further heights in the late eighteenth century, when several calligraphic "schools" were founded, and continues into the twentieth century.

The cutting of seals by the literati determined the need for a new substance from which seals could be cut. The scholar-artists used a long, chisel-like knife similar in size to the brush and called the "iron brush." The material had to be sufficiently soft to be cut freely, hard enough to leave many impressions without showing wear, regular in texture to allow for continuous smooth cuts, and finally, of aesthetic interest, for seals are an important member of the scholar's writing implements, all of which were carefully selected for a gentile beauty and, ideally, antiquarian flavor.

Metal and jade, the traditional materials, were, respectively, usually cast or drilled. When cut, they require either multiple strokes, negating the religio-aesthetic concern with *ziran* (spontaneity), or an unusually strong hand, not often found among the literati. The frequently used ivory and horn came to be considered too vulgar, too lacking in character, and too hard for the best movement of the cutting tool. Certain woods from tree roots had the proper flavor, but their fibers were too irregular for a smooth cut, and they wore out in time. Other less frequently used materials such as porcelain and crystal were similarly far too hard to be suitable. Only certain kinds of stone met all the requirements.

(For more detailed studies of seals, see Yen 1962 and Yeh 1940. The books on seal cutting in the *Meishu congshu* [eighteen titles] have been collected in *Juan* 1973. For illustrations of seal imprints with photographs of the seals for the Six Dynasties, Sui, Tang, and Song periods, see Lo 1963. An extensive selection of seals from later periods is available in Contag and Wang 1940; however, the brief introductory essay by Contag, "The Chinese Seal," is incorrect on a number of points.)

Religio-Aesthetics of Stones

In a late Ming text on connoisseurship (Zhang 17th cent.), of the items discussed as suitable for collecting, more than half reflect an exclusive literati interest, being paintings, calligraphy, books, and the material for their creation. In ninth place of nineteen, we find listed unusual stones, not to be identified with precious and semi-precious stones which are lower on the list. Here we have an aesthetic interest which first develops in China and remains unique to East Asia.

First on the list of collectibles is jade, which in China was always distinguished from stone. Jade, specifically nephrite, was identified as a hard, fine-grained mineral, translucent when cut thin, cold to the touch, sounding a musical tone when struck and smooth when polished. It was considered particularly suitable for interment with corpses. Only ancient jades, usually from tombs and preferably Han or earlier, were considered desirable. Antiquity was an essential aspect of this aesthetic.

Second on the list are the early bronzes discussed in Chapters 3 and 4, of similar antiquarian interest. The next three items are all literati productions: calligraphy, paintings, and ink-squeeze reproductions of early calligraphy carved into stone. Ceramics, especially of the Song period, follows. Seventh on the list are seals from the Qin and Han periods, of interest exclusively for their antique calligraphy. Eighth and ninth are inkstones and stones.

Of all the appurtenances for writing, it is the palette on which the ink is ground and prepared, rather than the brush, ink, silk, or paper, that is most valued. While a few of these palettes are made of pottery, the majority are of stone or stone-like compressed earth. Among others of his time, the Song calligrapher, collector, critic, and petrophile Mi Fu, who once paid obeisance to a rock, wrote a rhapsodic handbook on ink stones (*Yenshi* in van Gulik 1938). Mi Fu, whose mania for stones enhanced their popularity, saw in the inkstone a total religio-aesthetic experience, the combination of nature in its purity and uniqueness serving the creation of writing, the ultimate human-made art.

The interest of the Chinese in semiprecious stones as items of tribute can be traced as far back in literature as the fifth century B.C.E., but interest in stones as primarily aesthetic objects developed slowly, alongside the interest in landscape painting (see Chapter 6). For the love of stones for their own sake, as Edward Schafer (1961:3) so well put it, lay precisely in "their microcosmic mimicry of mountain landscapes."

Mountains early came to symbolize in China untrammeled nature for a combination of obvious reasons: their closeness to Heaven and its spirit realm, where the female Earth, shrouded in mist, merges with male cosmic potency; the mystery of inaccessible heights, ravines, and caves; and more simply, that in intensively cultivated China, only the upper slopes of mountains remained in their original state. Hence, mountains came to be associated with Daoism (both *daojia* and *daojiao*), and later Buddhism, both as symbolic and as realistic places of refuge from the mundane world. As analyzed in Chapter 3, the term for the successful Daoist adept, *xian*, is an ideograph composed of the pictographs for human and mountain; the mountain-shaped bronze censors of the Han are one of many early indications of this link.

Landscape gardens were a feature of Chinese palaces by the end of the Zhou period and came to be a small-scale representation of the entire world in the imperial Han parks. Following the Han period, miniature garden mountains were constructed from rocks. By the early Tang, a single unique rock stood for a mountain and became the focal point of the garden (see fig. 15). At this time too, the art of the desktop tray landscape composed simply of a rock, dwarfed trees, or a combination of the two arose. Small individual rocks were mounted on carved wooden pedestals as objets d'art, similar to the treatment of antique bronzes and ceramics (see fig. 16). Slices of rock whose veins resembled mountain ranges, being natural landscapes, were set into furniture, framed as pictures, or made into desk screens. A bowl with small stones under water to enhance their appearance would become a common feature of the literati's study. (For a comprehensive study, see Hay 1985.)

The famed Tang poet Bo Juyi and Mi Fu's contemporary Su Shi wrote poems in praise of particular rocks. The latter considered his favorite stones as valuable as the most sought after paintings from the previous Tang dynasty. Rocks were laboriously transported thousands of miles for the gardens of high officials, and the petromaniac emperor Hui Zong of the Song dynasty enfeoffed a particularly fine specimen. Books on the connoisseurship of stones were published. Even earlier, seminal landscape painters such as Guo Xi and Li Cheng did paintings on the theme of stones.

The term *stone* came to be part of the *hao*, the artistic informal name, of a number of literati. Among many examples, Shen Zhou, quoting the mid-Zhou text, the *Zuozhuan* (Prince Ai, eleventh year), called himself Shitian, "Field of Stones"; and the individualist seventeenth-century painter-monks Daoji and Kuncan called themselves, respectively, Shitao ("Wind among Stones"),

FIGURE 15. Largest rock transported for a garden in China. Caught up in the turmoil of the Taiping Movement (see Chapter 9), the rock was never placed in a garden and now sits in a Suzhou schoolyard.

FIGURE 16. Rock mounted on a wooden stand as an object d'art
for a desk or table. Collection of Zhou Monan.

and Shichi-heshang ("The Monk of Stone Gorge") and Shidaoren
("The Stone Taoist").

Why stones? The opening statement on the purpose of landscape painting by Guo Xi in his *Essay on Landscape Painting*, ex-
cerpted in the preceding chapter, fits stones as well. As with
landscape painting, to focus one's attention on a stone is to place
one's mind within ultimate reality, the natural realm of creation.

One cannot only see in particular stones landscapes, mountain ranges, or the universe itself, but stone is the very substance

of the cosmos. A miniature mountain range is just that, a miniature mountain range. And stone, different from dwarf trees and other plants, is relatively eternal, never dying, never changing. Yet the stone presents continual change; no two facets of even the same stone are the same. The swirling lines of stone striations portray the one eternal truth, the constant change of the universe; the eroded lines and holes, the power of water, of the weak and yielding on the strong and dominant, of change on permanency. Touch a stone and, as frames the novel *Honglou meng* (Dream of the Red Chamber), originally entitled "Story of a Stone," one touches the mythocosmic building block, the very stuff and substance of the world.

The Chinese in their use of stones did not strive for a natural, in the sense of normal, appearance. In Japan, where the Tang and Song interest in landscape gardens was accepted with Chinese art in general, due perhaps to the continual orientation of Shinto toward quiet naturalness and simplicity, the stones used in tea ceremony, Zen meditation, and ornamental gardens have an archetypal mundane appearance. Due to Daoist ideology, the Chinese, on the other hand, prefer stones that are unique, appearing bizarre and fantastic in shape, color, or markings.

The stone symbolizes not the world as we see it, but the creative energy of which the world is composed; not the world in which we live, but the craggy reaches beyond the habitations of men to which our spirits yearn. Caught up in the affairs of clan and government, our eye can align on a twisted, swirling stone and we are transported to the fringes of civilization, where with the Tang poet Han Shan (Cold Mountain), we can sit among white clouds. Seal stones, when they came to be used, were chosen in part, for their warm intimacy and ability to transport us to the realm of *xian*, to the "isle of the immortals."

Seal Stones

In the late Ming period, a stone seal dating to the beginning of the Tang period (623), had been found (Zhu 1778:7/17B–18A). By the Song period, stones were used for private seals, but were not a favored material (Schafer 1961:78,99). The predominance of stone for the cutting of seals clearly is due to the literati beginning to cut their own seals, a phenomenon that began in the Yuan which became increasingly popular from late Ming times to the present.

With the use of stone, the shapes of seals changed radically. The early seals of bronze, jade, and wood were of low height, commonly with a grip on top and a hole for a cord bored through it, although a variety of other shapes were used. The grip designs were often of animals or a plain semicylindrical knob. Tang and Song official seals had a peg-shaped handle. Stone seals became taller to allow the beauty of the stone to be seen, to serve as a medium for calligraphy along the sides and, at times, even the top, and for easy purchase in applying the seal to paper. As the height of the stone obviated the necessity for a grip, the upper part when carved was done exclusively for ornamental purposes and usually composes the upper third of the seal. Occasionally, almost the entire seal will be carved into a human or an animal figure. A hole was rarely bored through the grip as the wearing of seals had long passed out of fashion, and soft stones are too fragile for such use. Beginning in the eighteenth century, some seals were carved with a continuous landscape in shallow relief around their sides, utilizing the natural striations of the stone.

With the increasing use of seals, matched pairs were often cut from the same stone. One would contain a pen or artistic name cut for red characters, while the second was cut with the formal name using white characters. There were also sets of three, a third matching stone cut rectangular or oblong to half the width of the others with a literary expression to be used at the beginning of calligraphy.

Between the sixteenth and eighteenth centuries, one finds an increasing love for the stone itself and a lessening of the amount of side cutting (always direct and usually in nonarchaic characters) on the seal (see fig. 17) so as not to obscure the beauty of the stone. In the second half of the nineteenth century, the aesthetic focus on *ziran* was accentuated. This led to a tendency to use the stone in its natural nugget shape, with perhaps the most subtle carving along the sides of scenes or flowers according to the natural veins and striations of the stone (see fig. 18). The imprint will then not have the common square, rectangular, round,

FIGURE 17. Round, multicolored, eighteenth century *shoushan* seal—
upper part carved, with side-cut calligraphy. Collection of Yu Deho.

or oblong shape but will be free-form. A similar phenomenon can
be seen in a number of late eighteenth- and nineteenth-century
jade carvings, where the nugget shape and brown skin of mut-
ton-fat nephrite become an integral part of the design.

FIGURE 18. Seal of *baifurung* in natural, nugget shape, faintly carved on surface. Carving is of a fisherman, who, along with the woodcutter, symbolized the Daoist ideal of rustic simplicity. Author's collection.

Because seal stones are soft and fragile, few old ones remain. Connoisseurship in seals is a relatively modern phenomena; seal stones were not considered collectibles when such taste was set in the Ming period since they were just coming into use. Also, because good stones are rare, many of the old ones are recut so as to be reused and cannot be dated from the names found on them. Indeed, the best stones may have been recut a number of times. Furthermore, collections are private and not readily accessible.

Although there are a number of different kinds of stones from many parts of China used for seals, only three are considered highly desirable in that they meet the dual requirements of beauty and being easy to cut. All are named for the districts in which they are found: *qingtian* and *changhua* from Zhejiang Province and *shoushan* from Fujian Province.

Qingtian was the first of the three used and was so popular in the seventeenth century that the source is said to have been exhausted. According to tradition, the famous Yuan painter of flowering plum, Wang Mian (1335–1407), was the first scholar-artist to cut his seals from *qingtian* stone (Dai 1973). The beauty of good *qingtian* stones lies in their similarity to old jade. Valued pieces of *qingtian* have the coloring, veining, and slight translucency of mutton fat, pale green, or dark brown nephrite. Although in appearance jade and *qingtian* stone are similar, the two are quite different in feel. Jade is hard and cold to the touch, *qingtian* and the other seal stones, absorbing body moisture and oil, feel soft, warm, and intimate.

The *qingtian* stone considered best, indeed that stone considered most excellent of all for seals, is of a different sort. Called *dong* stone, it is sometimes classified separately from *qingtian*. "Dong" means translucent to the point of near transparency; the word is used in terms for ice and gelatin. Being soft and smooth, lacking suspended particles, grain, and striations, it is very easy to cut (see fig. 19); it accepts ink readily, and its transparency provides a haunting beauty, suggesting the mysterious unreality of mundane existence. The most valued of the *qingtian* stones are called *dengguangdong* (lamp-flame *dong*); second best are *yunaodong* (fish-brain *dong*); and third best, "yellow-colored *dong*."

Changhua stone is the rarest of the three, being found only deep in a mountainous area. The most valued *changhua* called *jixue* (chicken-blood) possess a startling beauty in their vibrant, brilliant red, the color of fresh blood, of the essence of life. *Changhua* stones range from predominant red, to red on a white or translucent background, the reds ranging from bright to dark in hue, to predominant white. The less valuable stones are of a dark color with red spots or pure white. *Changhua* stones, although rare and beautiful, are difficult to cut. The stone is soft but contains tiny nodules of harder material. It is found in an area rich in iron, and the minute flecks of iron and other minerals in the stone can impede and deflect the movement of the knife.

Shoushan stones became popular as *qingtian* stones were becoming scarce. At first stones were used which contained many colors or approximated those of *qingtian*, but as different stones became available, certain of the *shoushan* stones became the most

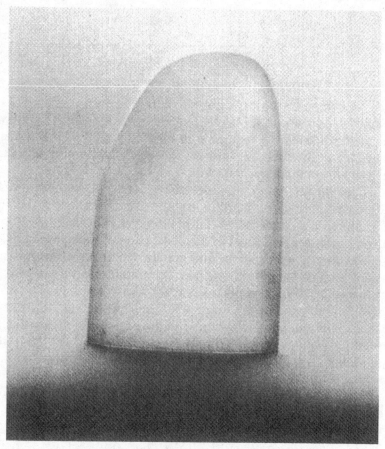

FIGURE 19. Seal of translucent *dengguangung*.
Collection of Zeng Shaojien.

treasured of all. Because these stones are the last of the three to be used for seals, more historical data is available on them (see Gao 1968, Mao 1968).

Shoushan is about twenty miles north of Fuzhou in a mountainous area. Below Furung Peak, about three miles from the district seat of Shoushan, a pit containing white jade-like and multi-colored stones was discovered during the Song dynasty. For a reason which has not been ascertained, removing stones from this pit was made illegal, and the local magistrate closed it with a boulder. Of course, stones still found their way out, but since they could not be openly displayed, the descriptions and names for the various types of stones used at this early date are far from clear. In the last years of the Ming dynasty, *shoushan* stones came to be used by the arbiters of taste for decorative purposes; very few of these stones were cut into seals.

A monk at this time from a local Shoushan monastery cut seals from small stones he found in a stream bed, and his may be the earliest ones. In 1668, a young literatus traveled to Shoushan to collect stones and brought a great many to the capital, Beijing, where he made his fortune selling the best for an equal weight of gold. (The price for the best is now equivalent to several times the price of gold per unit weight.) At that time, the finest stones were displayed on pedestals and tables, and only the poorest were cut into seals. Within a hundred years, with the increasing interest in seal stones, the situation became reversed; the natural pockets of stones were depleted, and the better stones were cut into seal-sized pieces.

From the late eighteenth century to today, those *shoushan* stones most appreciated for seals are semitranslucent medium yellow, white, or red. They supposedly come from pits in a field and have the word *tian* (field) in their name. Second quality seals, darker and less translucent, are called *furung*, after the nearby mountain in whose caves they are said to be found.

The best stones are called *tianhuang* (field-yellow) and are a warm, luscious, glowing medium yellow. Next in order is *bai* (white) *tian*, and third and less common is *hung* (red) *tian*. More rarely yet one finds *tianhuang* with streaks of red in it and *baitianhuang*, a half white, half yellow stone. The less desirable yellows range from pale lemon to chestnut brown, all called *huangfurung*. The lesser quality whites have a more solid and creamy appearance and are called *baifurung*. *Shoushan* stones are also found in greys, the darker, more translucent, called "ox horn *dong*." Those with clear areas called *bing* (ice) are the most appreciated. The majority of *shoushan* stones are of variegated colors, the less translucent, the less desirable.

Of *shoushan* stones, the poet Mei Jing (1623–1697) wrote in a poem entitled, "Shoushan Seal" (see Chapter 8 for more on the creatrix Nüwa):

Is it true that Nu Wa, while mending the sky
Pried loose these precious stones, the cream of heaven?
Thunder and storm came like the rising of dragons;
Then the earth split, and lo!
    out poured the glittering gems.

(Lai 1976:5)

What is the relationship between seal calligraphy and the seal stone? There are a number of seal calligraphy styles, but all, without exception, are either directly or indirectly derived from styles used prior to the determination of the modern standard script in the third century B.C.E. In other words, all are written in archaic script, some styles reflecting the earliest written signs on divination scapulae and plastrons and sacrificial vessels from the protohistoric period. Yet, simultaneously, seal calligraphy encompasses the most free and most expressive writing styles, the epitome of *ziran* in calligraphic aesthetics.

Following the Chinese tendency to enumerate aesthetic characteristics, the qualities of seal cutting have long been spelled out. One work lists "Six Laws," "Six Essentials," and "Six Merits" (Yeh 1940:19).

The first of the Laws is that "there should be a liveliness of manner in the way the seal is cut." The second of the Essentials is that "the surface cut must be given an appearance of primitiveness and clumsiness and yet there must also be a liveliness of manner." The Merits are "elegance in a clumsiness," "strength in delicate lines," "rhythm in empty space," "reasonableness in unreasonableness," and "softness in roughness."

The medium for seal calligraphy parallels the aesthetics of seal calligraphy. Seal stones are old as the most ancient substance, alive in their vibrancy, and primitive in their utter naturalness; they are elegant in appearance and strong but delicate; their markings are one with cosmic rhythm; they are natural yet artificial; they are stone yet soft and fragile. Perhaps no other substance so suits the art of which it is the medium.

When a *wenren* caps his calligraphy or painting by impressing a red-ink-laden sealstone on the silk or paper, he is engaging in a sacred act. In his hand he holds a beautiful and vibrant piece of the cosmos, a fragment of solidified cosmic energy that responds to the warmth of his hand and attunes its resonance to his own energy. On this stone, his individualistic, personal name used only on poetry, painting, and calligraphy, the name that he gave himself to express his sense of his own meaning, has been engraved by himself or a calligrapher he greatly admires with the iron brush. This name has been cut into the stone in the most creative, the most individualistic of all forms of calligraphy. As the seal prints his name on his creative work with red ink, the color of life, so the stone brings the harmonizing energy of the cosmic flux to imbue his completed work with the touch of the primordial Dao.

The seal is a unique natural artifact, both in substance—no two stones are exactly alike—and in creative expression—an artistic rendering of an artist's name so unique that it will be utilized to authenticate his calligraphy or painting. In the highly conformist realm of Chinese culture, each artistic seal has a unique, individual existence. The private seal radiates *daojia* nonconformity as the official seal bonds the *wenren* to his office and symbolizes *rujia* responsibility.

Contemporary China

Little has changed in over three thousand years of formal seal use in China. Government documents and private contracts are all authenticated by impressions from the appropriate seal. Indeed, the uses continually expand. For example, a couple often obtains a matched pair of seals with a design that bridges the two for signing the marriage contract, a custom mentioned at least as early as Shen Fu's (1983) remarkable eighteenth-century biography of his wife. Modern developments include the adoption of plastic seals for ordinary use and computer controlled drills for cutting them, but seals for ordinary use in pre-modern times were not cut by calligraphers nor made from fine stones.

As discussed in Chapter 6, there has been a resurgence in the traditional arts in China, particularly painting and calligraphy. This has both engendered a need for artistic seals by the artists and an interest in practicing seal calligraphy. In Hangzhou, still the center for the traditional arts, art supply shops carry seal stones and seal ink of greatly differing quality and price, along with "iron brushes" and other needs for seal calligraphy. In the last decade, there have been a number of new Chinese publications on seal cutting and impressions of seals.

In Hangzhou, too, the Xi Ling Seal Society, founded toward the end of the last dynasty, is again functioning. Creative and talented seal calligraphers can be found both in Taiwan and mainland China. The movement toward originality and individualism begun with Wen Peng and Ho Zhen in the Ming period, expanding with the Eight Eccentrics of Yangzhou in the late eighteenth century, and flourishing in the nineteenth century, still continues. For example, Liu Jang, the professor of seal calligraphy at the Zhejiang Academy of Fine Arts and vice-president of the Xi Ling Seal Society (in 1986) has created new directions in writing *jiaguwen*, the archaic script. Whether this religio-aesthetic tradition will continue to be understood as it was in the past remains a question. Certainly in the case of Hong Shiqing, discussed in the preceding chapter, there has been no change in the meaning of seal stones and seal calligraphy.

8   female spirits and spirituality
    in chinese religion

The Son of Heaven [King] is to the Queen as the sun is to the moon, as
yang is to yin; in their being essential to each other [in the performance
of rituals], their sovereignty is accomplished.

—*Liji:* "Hunyi"

As discussed in Chapter 1, the Western understanding of Chinese religion derives from the first reports of Matteo Ricci, a Jesuit missionary, four centuries ago. Brilliant as he was in coming to terms with an alien culture, he was still a product of his own culture, and he perceived Chinese religion through sixteenth-century European cultural filters. Ricci's and his colleagues' biases led to fundamental misperceptions that became a virtual dogma in Western studies unchanged to this day. Of these errors, perhaps the most important are the concept of "Three Religions," the assumption that the elite were utterly rational and dismissed nonrational behavior, and the belief in the supremacy of a masculine deity.

The first two errors have been analyzed in preceding chapters. In regard to the third error, contrary to the established Western understanding of Chinese religion based on the imposition of Eurocentric perspectives, this chapter will argue that although China has a patriarchal social system, its religious system considers male and female spirits of equal importance and power. Nonetheless, there has been a significant devolution of female ritual roles over the last several millennia.

In the last decade, studies have appeared on specific Chinese female deities (e.g., J. M. Boltz 1986; S. Cahill 1984, 1986 and i.p.; D. Paul 1985; J. L. Watson 1985). This study is a more general analysis of the broader issue already noted by P. Steven Sangren (1983:4):

217

Female deities occupy prominent positions in the Chinese religious pantheon and in Chinese ritual. Hence, it is somewhat surprising that the cultural significance of female gender in the realm of divinities has received so little attention from students of Chinese religion.

This chapter is divided into five parts; the first will focus on the understanding of Earth. The second part will depict particular temples or sacred sites that demonstrate the failure of varying attempts to patriarchalize female spirits. The third part will describe a family with matrifocal rituals that are counter to the patriarchal norm. The fourth part will discuss female religious roles in the context of Chinese male-female dualism. The last part will introduce the relationship between cosmology and values when approached from a Chinese perspective rather than a Western one.

Earth

Earth as a numinous entity is not a single concept. She is part of both a major cosmogonic concept and the major paired cosmological deity whose worship was reserved to the emperor and his consort. Lesser mortals offered sacrifice to Earth in a number of different aspects.

Earth as a deity or spiritual force has several appellations in Chinese. In the cosmological male-female pair of Heaven and Earth (*tiandi*), the term *di* is used; the compound is understood as the equivalent of our term, *nature* (Eno 1990:293). For the spirit of the land and the fecundity of the soil, there is the term *she*. When the earth is personified as a deity, the compound Sovereign Earth (*houtu*) is used, as well as the popular *Houtu niangniang* (Mama Earth). The compound *tudishi* (Spirit of the Place) is found in common parlance, along with the couple, *tudigung tudipo* (Grandfather and Grandmother Land). To a limited extent, all of these terms are interchangeable. *Di*, *she*, and *houtu* are general terms; *tudishi*, as well as *tudigung* and *tudipo*, however, are utilized when specific places or pieces of land are intended.

Tiandi

Matteo Ricci as an Italian Jesuit reflects a similar cultural background to the French Jesuits who missionized New France from
the late sixteenth century. That background included the understanding that female subservience to the male was part of God's
plan and the mark of a civilized society. Le Jeune, a Jesuit who
missionized among the Montagnais-Naskapi in the early seventeenth century, understood women having "great power" in that
culture to be a mark of the native Americans' savagery. He strove
to civilize them by introducing into the egalitarian society means
for enforcing male authority over women: "I told him that he was
the master, and that in France women do not rule their husbands"
(Jesuit *Relations*, cited in Leacock 1978:249).

These attitudes of the Jesuit male monastic order toward
women continue into the present. Father Paul Steinmetz, S.J., has
relatively recently expressed this medieval view using a mistaken
historical "fact": "It was not the general practice for women to
smoke in pre-contact days . . . helps us to appreciate the sacra-
mental nature of the Sacred Pipe by way of contrast" (Steinmetz
1984:30; for the counter position, see Paper 1988:37–38). In other
words, he assumes an inverse ratio between sacredness and female participation. This attitude in and of itself has blinded Western observers of native American religions to the major and
crucial participation of women in religious practice and ideology
(see Paper 1990c, 1994). One of the reasons that the Jesuits wrote
glowing accounts of China as a model civilization apparently was
their perception of China as totally patriarchal, in religion as well
as in social structure.

Ricci, in a letter dated to 1609, wrote that the Chinese "wor-
ship only heaven and earth and the master of both" (Gernet
1985:25). The Chinese objected to the creation of a monotheistic
Master of the dualistic male Heaven and female Earth (*tiandi*).
In a work dated to 1639, a Chinese critic of Christianity and
Ricci's interpretation wrote: "The mode of action [the Dao] of
Heaven and Earth can be summed up in a word. It is not double.
How could it be controlled by the Master of Heaven, Yesu?"
(Gernet 1985:205).

The same critic noted that the Jesuits particularly objected to the Chinese sacrificing to a female deity:

> Confucius and Zilu always associate Heaven and Earth together . . . these Western monsters disrupt the ideas of our Confucianism [rujia] on the subject of Heaven and the Sovereign on High [shangdi]. That is why they are absolutely set against speaking of prayers to the spirits of the Earth. (Gernet 1985:199)

W. E. Soothill, in the most influential English-language work on Chinese religion referred to in Chapter 1, seems to have accepted the concept of ur-monotheism, the universal acceptance of a single, male supreme deity in all early human cultures, promulgated by Schmidt (1912). Soothill (1913:146) argued that the concept of Heaven was originally a monotheistic deity in China, "[but] as time passes, 'Heaven' underwent a change by the addition of the word Earth. . . . Here, then, is an apparent *descent* from the earlier supreme monotheism" (emphasis added).

Subsequently, there has been a tendency in Western writing to only consider Heaven, half of the pair of Heaven and Earth, a deity. Most major translators only capitalize the "H" in Heaven and not the "E" in Earth. Even contemporary works written from a feminist perspective have unintentionally continued this essentially misogynist practice (e.g., Kelleher 1987). For many Westerners, it is inconceivable that civilized people could consider a female deity worthy of the respect due to a male deity.

In the standard Chinese religious cosmology, humans receive their material form (xing) from the conjunction of Heaven and Earth and their life-force (qi) from the conjunction of yang and yin. Since the late Zhou period (fourth century B.C.E.), yin and yang have stood for all complementary oppositional forces, including, respectively, female and male. At least by the same time, for example, as found in the Xunzi, Heaven and Earth represent, respectively, male and female, otherwise nonanthropomorphic, creative deities.

The first hexagram of the Yi, the oldest Chinese text, is associated with Heaven, and the second, with Earth, in the later additions to the text. There are indications in the older part of the text that this may have been the original understanding: the interpretations of the lines for the first hexagram focus on the ascending *long* (dragon), a male symbol (see Chapter 3), and the interpretation of the lines for the second hexagram mention "square" and the "yellow below," both symbols for the female Earth.

Heaven and Earth are equal complementary deities, and the emperor sacrificed to both. These sacrifices can be traced back to the beginning of Chinese civilization when "the highest of the Shang sacrificial rites . . . was offered to Yue, the 'Peak' and 'He' the river as well as to the four quadrants (Allan 1991:78). Indeed, only the emperor could sacrifice to *tian* (Heaven) and *di* (Earth), all others could only sacrifice to the lesser deities of *tu* (Soil) (Wechsler 1985:108). The emperor also sacrificed to the productive energy of Earth at the Altar to Soil and Grain (*shejitan*), which as Chavannes (1910b:511) has pointed out, served as the female complement to the patrilineal ancestral temple.

When Beijing was constructed to be the capital of the Ming dynasty in the early fifteenth century, the Altar to Soil and Grain and the Great (Imperial Clan) Temple flanked the entrance passage on the south side of the Imperial Palace. This design followed the injunctions of the classic ritual texts that the Altar to Soil and Grain should be on the right (facing south) and the Ancestral Temple on the left (*Zhouli*: "Qunxiaocong"; *Liji*: "Yi"). Both are inside the Forbidden City. The Altar to Heaven (and Earth—the early Ming emperors did not separate sacrifices to them), at a moderate distance, was south of the inner-city wall.

The three locations for imperial sacrifice form a triangle, representing the triad of Heaven, Humans, and Earth; the first two are of immediate human awareness, the last is more distant. This pattern can be traced back to the earliest historical narratives (ca. 1000 B.C.E.), when the Duke of Zhou, on establishing a new city, sacrificed to Heaven (or Heaven and Earth) outside the city and to the Soil inside the city (*Shu*: "Shaogao").

In 1530, the complex was made more elaborate. A separate Altar to Earth was built north of the city wall and altars to the Sun (male) and the Moon (female) to the east and west. Directly to the west of the Altar to Heaven was built the Altar to the First

Agriculturist where the emperor performed his annual ritual plowing. (There was later added a complementary altar to the silkworm where the empress made offerings.) Directly south of this last complex were altars to heavenly (Winds, Clouds, Rain, and Thunder) and earthly (Five Sacred Mountains, Four Seas, etc.) spirits. The more elaborate complex, in its placement of altars, continued the

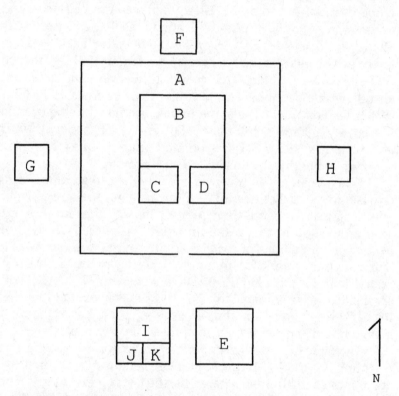

FIGURE 20. Imperial Altars in Beijing (not to scale)
(F=female, M=male):

A. Primary city wall   B. Forbidden City (Imperial Palace)
C. Altar to Soil & Grain [F]   D. Grand (Ancestral) Temple [M]
E. Altar to Heaven [M]   F. Altar to Earth [F]
G. Altar to Moon [F]   H. Altar to Sun [M]
I. Altars to First Agriculturist (Shennung) [M] and First Sericulturist [F]
J. Altar to Earthly Spirits [F]   K. Altar to Sky Spirits [M]

complementary equality of male and female spirits (see fig. 20). (For a detailed description of early twentieth- century Beijing, see Arlington and Lewisohn 1935; for a history of Beijing's sacred sites, see Meyer 1991.)

Ricci came into contact with this placement of official altars when he became part of the imperial government in Beijing. His inability to understand complementary female-male spirituality and his reading of the Chinese patriarchal social structure into spiritual understanding is not due to ignorance; Ricci was a highly intelligent person. Rather, as with his monastic colleagues in the Americas, Ricci's misogynist cultural blinkers blinded him to the obvious.

The influence of this Western viewpoint is evident in present-day Beijing where the Altar to Heaven has kept its name and is part of the standard foreign tourist itinerary, but the Altar to Soil and Grain was changed, first to Central Park and then to Zhongshan [Sun Yat-sen] Park in the early twentieth century and is not normally visited by foreigners. The altar has not been demolished and is still there for those who realize the change is but in name. The Altar to Earth has more recently been refurbished, due to the increase of internal over foreign tourism. Because, as a locus for spiritual energy, it was the preferred spot for *qigung* masters to practice at dawn, it is now (1992) not opened until eight o'clock in the morning. The nominal reason is to prevent deterioration of the altar; the more likely reason is to prevent spiritual use of the altar.

Houtu

In southeastern Chinese grave architecture, there is a shrine to Houtu by the side of the grave to which offerings are also made during the Qingming festival. The practice itself is found throughout China; Zhu Xi's *Family Rituals* describes it in the twelfth century (Ebrey 1991:176). When the deity is represented by an image rather than the written name, the figure is of an elderly male, which replaced a female image in the seventh century (Zong and Liu 1986:193). This replacement figure is of Gou Lung, understood since at least the middle of the first millennium B.C.E.

as the son of Gung Gung, the minister of agriculture under the mythic emperor Yao (*Zuozhuan*: "Jao Kung," 29th year). During the Han dynasty, the emperor offered a parallel sacrifice to Houtu when he sacrificed to Heaven, indicating that Houtu was then understood as a female deity (Bodde 1975:191). This linkage to a male figure would seem to contradict the perception of Earth as a female deity. In the past, I used it as an example of the patriarchalization of Chinese religion.

A process of euhemerization linked all deities with mythic or historical personages. Sarah Allan (1979:3) has objected to this concept, pointing out that "gods have always been considered dead men [or women]; there was no 'long time' ago when spirits different from men inhabited this world." However, this is not necessarily the case in regard to cosmic principles and nature itself.

In many parts of the world, female figurines have been found in upper Paleolithic and Neolithic contexts, often interpreted as representations of the Earth Mother (for Europe, see Gimbutas 1989; for native America, see Paper 1990c). A similar figure has recently been found in Manchuria, at the Dongshanzui site, Kazuo, Liaoning Province (S. Wu 1988:pls.4, 5), that have identical characteristics to such figures elsewhere. Whether or not this pottery figurine represents the Earth cannot, of course, be determined.

As officials, deities were necessarily male. (For the role of Tudigung as official, see Wolf 1974.) However, this patriarchalization seems not to have affected either the theoretical understanding of complementary opposition or common understanding. In the popular mind, the deity is known as the Sovereign Earth Mother (Houtu Niangniang). (*Niangniang* is difficult to translate; it is formally used for an older woman who is a mother, but informally within the family it means "mama.") At least by the beginning of the Common Era, according to the *Hanshu* (History of the Han, *juan* 22), she was officially termed the Sovereign Earth Mother of Happiness (Houtu Fuao). In field shrines and on the household altars of many farming homes, the deity as Spirit of the Place is represented by a couple: the male being Tudigung (Grandfather Land), and the female, Tudipo (Grandmother Land).

A hypothetical explanation of this divergence in regard to the gender of the deity can be made on a functional basis. The Chinese underworld as the realm of the dead came to be understood on the model of the Chinese court, replete with officials, passports, seals, and so on. Hence, in connection with the dead, Houtu is male. However, as soil from which the grain comes and which nourishes human life, Houtu is the Earth Mother (Lü and Liu 1986:193). Symbolizing the joining of the female and the male energies essential to germination and growth in particular fields, Houtu is represented as a divine couple. Therefore, aside from her role as the abode of the corpse, which became a realm of male officialdom, Houtu is essentially female.

The Location of the Goddess

There are a number of major female deities in Chinese religion; their names and functions vary from region to region. The major female deity in southeastern coastal China is Mazu (Ma-tsu). In Taiwan, Mazu has become the preeminent deity. Reducing her story as it is now understood to its bare essentials, she is an unmarried female who, nearly a thousand years ago, with spiritual powers saved her brothers from drowning. (For the possible origin of Mazu, see Eberhard [1968:402–403]; for her historical evolution, see J. L. Watson [1985].)

In this regard, Mazu fits the pattern of Chinese deities who frequently are ghosts become beneficent. Unmarried females are particularly prone to becoming ghosts rather than ancestral spirits, because, not being a part of any patrilineal-patrilocal family, they have no one to sacrifice to them (Harrell 1986). Such ghosts are considered dangerous, but on possessing individuals may demonstrate helpfulness, to the community or to those who seek them, and become considered a deity.

Mazu became the patron deity of seafarers. Eventually, her prestige developed to the degree that the Ming emperor, Chengzu (early fifteenth century) gave her the title of Holy Mother of Heaven Above (Tianshang Shengmu); a century later, she further gained the title of the Empress of Heaven (Tianhou). Her image wears archaic imperial regalia. Given her titles, one would assume her to be a sky rather than a sea deity. The construction of a modern temple in the suburbs of the southern Taiwan port city of Kaohsiung indicates rather that she functions as the Earth deity herself.

Chinese temples traditionally are one-story affairs, although the roofs may be multilayered. Modern ferroconcrete construction allows for an inexpensive vertical structure. The Lungch'eng Kuan in Feng-shan, Kaohsiung County, completed in 1986, has an unusual two-storied main hall. The lower hall has a horizontal display of five life-sized images; the upper hall has a two-layered display of five images per layer. In total, there is a massive display of fifteen deities ranged in three layers (see fig. 21).

The upper layer, which cannot be directly approached, centers on the Jade Emperor, the supreme celestial deity, with Shakyamuni and Guanyin (Kuan-yin) at the ends of the row. The middle layer, directly on the second floor, centers on Kongfuzi and includes Laozi. The lower layer on the main floor, from which the other layers cannot be seen, centers on the Holy Mother of Heaven Above and includes local protector deities and the Goddess of Childbirth (also known as the First Princess of Purple and Azure Clouds—see below). On asking one of the temple caretakers regarding the obvious interpretation, he confirmed that the layout of the deities in three levels indeed was intended to indicate, in physical ascending order, Earth, Humans, and Heaven.

The Western cultural tendency, of course, is to equate physical location with worthiness: the higher the location, the greater the power; the lower the location, the more mundane. The great Western spirits reside in the sky, not on earth. In Chinese culture, on the contrary, Heaven and Earth are equally essential to life. Here, the location of the Goddess has a very different import from the common Western interpretation.

Therefore, regardless of her title and original specific function as protector of seafarers, Mazu has become the Earth Mother. In other words, her title, Holy Mother of Heaven Above, indicates rank and regard, not location. It seems that in the Chinese religious mind, any powerful female deity, excepting the Buddhist Guanyin, is essentially an earth deity. This may be a universal human tendency; it has been argued that the Virgin Mary took on the role of the suppressed pre-Christian European earth-

Guanyin	Goddess of the North Star (Daoist equivalent of Guanyin)	Pure August Emperor on High (Daoist supreme sky deity)	God of the Southern Stars	Shakyamuni
Eastern Kitchen Emperor	Holy Emperor Guan (God of Martial Qualities)	Kongfuzi (Confucius)	Taishanglao (Laozi)	Shennung (God of Agriculture)
Zhusheng Niangniang (Mother of Generations*)	Daifu Yuanshuai (Protecting spirit)	Holy Mother of Heaven Above (Mazu)	Qingshui Zushi (Local Fujian protecting spirit)	Duke of Walls and Moats

* equivalent to First Princess of Purple and Azure Clouds (Mount Tai Mother)

FIGURE 21: Vertical and Horizontal Placement of Deities, Lung-ch'eng Temple, Feng-shan, Kaohsiung County, Taiwan

grain deity (Berger 1985). Mazu as Earth is immediately approachable, different from the distant Heaven (an attitude also found in native American agrarian culture; e.g. Allen 1988:152). No matter how Earth is locally understood, she is also the deity of fertility, nurture, and sustenance—to her we owe our existence.

The Failure of Patriarchalization

The increasing patriarchal nature of Chinese society and culture led to attempts to patriarchalize deities. Nevertheless, the major Chinese deities outside, of course, of ancestral spirits and the state sacrificial complex, including the temples to Kongfuzi and other scholars, from the standpoint of general veneration were and remain female such as, Nüwa, Xiwangmu (The Queen Mother of the West, see S. Cahill, i.p.), Bixia Yuanjun, Mazu, and Guanyin.

Bixia Yuanjun

In Western scholarship, it is generally assumed that mountains are male and waters are female, and that interpretation has been unconsciously applied to China. In my own earlier publications, I fell into the same fallacy. In China, on the contrary, mountain and water spirits are female, both being attributes of the Earth. I learned of my own error on examining the associations of the altars to the earth and sky spirits in Beijing described above.

There are five sacred mountains (excluding the four Buddhist ones), the foremost of which is Mount Tai, the Eastern Mountain. Sacrifices by rulers, including the mythic culture-heroes, on Mount Tai are mentioned in China's earliest writings (see Weschler 1985:170–84). The sacrality of this mountain continues even in contemporary China under a Communist ideology: the embalmed body of Mao Zedong lies on a block of granite from Mount Tai (Wakeman 1988:255).

Mount Tai has remained throughout history the major Chinese pilgrimage site. According to the local press, on May Day, 1986, more than sixty thousand ascended the mountain. From my own observations, it seemed that at least half of those making the ascent did so as pilgrims making offerings at the many temples along the route.

The main temple to the God of Mount Tai is at the foot of the mountain; it is one of the three largest in China (the other two are the temples to Kongfuzi in his nearby birthplace and in the Imperial Palace in Beijing). The image of the deity inside is indubitably male. Of the many temples along the route to the summit, there are temples to the Grandmother and to the Mother of the God of Mount Tai, as well as to Guanyin.

On the summit, however, the largest and most popular temple complex is to the First Princess of Purple and Azure Clouds (Bixia Yuanjun). She is assumed to be the daughter of the Mountain, although technically she may be his granddaughter (for details see Chavannes 1910b, Werner 1961:373–75). She is also called the Mount Tai Mother (Taishan niang-niang) and the Jade Maiden (Yunu). The latter name refers to an alternate myth in which she was sent as a fairy by the Yellow Emperor, the mythic first emperor (Zong and Liu 1986:325). She is considered particularly potent in regard to pregnancy and childbirth.

Next to her temple was a smaller one to the God of Mount Tai, already beginning to collapse in the early twentieth century, while the temple to the Princess was being kept in good repair (Baker 1925: 102ff.). By 1942, the remains had been cleared away (as per photographs in Morrison 1987). Today, there is but a clear space where the temple once stood. Without old guidebooks, one would have no awareness of the former existence of a temple to the God of Mount Tai on the summit.

The last temple constructed on the summit, indeed surrounding the highest rock, was built in the late Ming period. It is dedicated to the Jade Emperor, the supreme Daoist celestial deity associated with the sacred mountain to the west, Mount Tai being the sacred mountain of the east. Many of the pilgrims do not visit this temple. Those I asked expressed to me an intuitive feeling that it did not belong there.

Although the deity of Mount Tai is officially male, the Chinese people know their mountains are female. The God of Mount Tai may be worshipped at the foot of the mountain, but on the summit, the goal of the pilgrim, regardless of her relationship to the official deity of the mountain, the Goddess prevails. Nonetheless, it is male children for which the female pilgrims are praying; the importance of female spirits does not negate the patrilineal thrust of Chinese religion.

Nüwa

Near the beginning of the lunar year there is a month-long Renzu (Ancestors of Humans) Festival at the Taihao (Fuxi) Mausoleum in Huaiyang, Honan Province. "Ancestors of Humans" refers to the paired deities, the male Fuxi and the female Nüwa. Prior to the destruction of the Cultural Revolution, among the many temples at the Taihao complex, there were several to Fuxi and one to Nüwa. Recently, three have been rebuilt, two to Fuxi but none to Nüwa.

Before the Han period, the two deities had independent myths. Among her achievements, Nüwa brought the yellow earth together, created humans, and patched the vault of the heavens with five-colored stones (see poem in the preceding chapter). As the Supreme Matchmaker, she presides over marriages. Fuxi is one of the three Sage Emperors or culture heroes, inventing the fishing net and creating the Eight Trigrams. Brother and sister, in Han myths, they married after a deluge to continue the human species. They are portrayed with human upper bodies and intertwined serpent lower bodies. Among the Chinese, there is still some discomfort with their incestuous relationship.

At present, the Renzu Festival draws tens of thousands of pilgrims daily from nearby provinces. Most are women, and many stay for the full month. They go to pay reverence to their ultimate ancestors and to pray for children. Among the many customs specific to the festivals are songs to Nüwa that women learn in dreams; fertility dances that are passed on matrilineally; clay figures, some with symbolic vulva; and a stone Zisui Yao (Pit for Descendants) that undoubtedly represents Nüwa's vagina, which people touch to gain children.

Although the temple to Nüwa has yet to be rebuilt, "its former site is crowded with people praying for children; the walls have been blackened by the smoke of burning incense." Yang Lihui (personal correspondence), a doctoral candidate in the Chinese Department of Beijing Normal University, who provided the above data on the Renzu Festival, concludes:

> Though Fuxi is the apparent dominant deity of the Renzu Festival, the main customs all relate to Nüwa and show a strong tendency for worship of the pudenda and reproductive power. On the other hand, the festival accords in timing with the Shangsi Festival of the last thousand years. In the *Liji*: "Yuehling" and *Zhouli*: "Meishi" of the Classics, a Gathering in the Second Month of Spring is described, when offerings were made to the Supreme Matchmaker and otherwise illicit erotic behavior between males and females were tolerated. This may have been the origin of the Renzu Festival, where the primary worship is directed toward the great Mother goddess and Supreme Matchmaker.

As at Taishan, the patriarchal aspect of Chinese culture over time may have merged Nüwa with Fuxi and made the male deity officially dominant, but the people know to whom offerings are due. Women especially understand who really created humans and to whom they should pray for children, albeit primarily sons.

Guanyin

It is well known that the Indian male Bodhisattva Avalokiteśvara, retranslated into Chinese as Guanyin in the Tang period, became a female deity, although precisely when and how this transformation took place is unclear. Her story dates back to the Tang period, but the best-known version dates to the Song (Dudbridge 1978). Chün-fang Yü (1990), based on the work of Valerie Hansen (1990), suggests that Guanyin, as we have come to know her, arose in the Song at a time when ordinary men and women were being apotheosized into deities after death. Prior to the twelfth to thirteenth centuries, this process of deification was primarily linked to heroes among the elite. Guanyin appears to have gained widespread popularity at the same general time as the First Princess of Purple and Azure Clouds and Mazu discussed above.

Like Mazu, Guanyin is an unmarried female; indeed, one who refused to marry. Most likely, she was a popular deity acquired by Buddhism to balance the important female deities of Daoism, particularly, the Queen Mother of the West. Guanyin in turn was probably the stimulus for the supreme deity, the Eternal Mother of the late Ming sectarian movements (see Naquin 1976, Overmyer 1976), although the two may originally been separate deities who rose simultaneously (C. Yü 1990:84).

Guanyin is by far the most popular deity in all of China. She is worshipped by those who otherwise have no direct relationship with Buddhism. Her special qualities are diverse. She is worshipped by those desiring children, and she is the patron of merchants. She is commonly known through her role in the popular novel *Journey to the West* (Xiyouji). (For major incidents, see Yu 1977–1983:1:184–97,268–78,360–66;2:11–16.) Her image is omnipresent; for example, if an image is placed on or above the family altar, it is usually hers.

Not all temples dedicated to her are Buddhist. In Buddhist monasteries and Daoist temples, she is often an image off to the side. However, in major monasteries in central China, her image has a more central location; (e.g., at Lingyinshi in Hangzhou and Xiyuanshi in Suzhou). In these monasteries' large Buddha halls, the major images, usually centered on Shakyamuni, are backed by a high screen to increase their presence. On the backs of the screens, facing the rear doors, is an image of Guanyin at least as tall as that of the Buddha. She is surrounded by attending figures, and before her is a full complement of paraphernalia for worship, such as braziers, candelabra, and kneeling pads. Prip-Møller (1937:48) noted this architectural feature in the early twentieth century:

As a rule the main altar in the Ta Tian [Great Hall] is screened from behind by a high partition, erected at some distance from the rear wall and extending to the right and left for the full length of the altar. Behind this wall another altar is usually found, facing in the opposite direction. The deity in whose honor it is erected may vary with varying conditions, among which may also be the question of the school to which the monastery belongs or has belonged.

The image most commonly found here is in central China that of the goddess of mercy, KUAN YIN. Usually she is represented as the central figure of a giant relief, which covers the whole screen wall and stretches from the altar to the roof construction.

This region suffered extensive damage during the wars of the Taiping movement in the mid-nineteenth century (see Chapter 9). The above mentioned monasteries were reconstructed in the early twentieth century. The antiquity of the paralleling of the image of Guanyin with the Buddha, literally back to back, remains a question. However, there is no question that, at least in the Jiangnan region, even in Buddhist monasteries the female deity has achieved status equal in the popular mind to that of the male Buddha.

The Variability of Patriarchality

Marcel Granet (1930) posited an early Chinese matrilineal and matrilocal culture, but the argument based on the etymology of the term for surname and analysis of early texts is far from conclusive. Contemporary Chinese historians must follow the Engels-Lenin understanding of Morgan's theory of prehistoric matriarchal human culture. However, few Western anthropologists now assume that early cultures were unaware of the role of the male in human reproduction, since there is clear evidence that they were aware of the role of the male in other mammals' reproduction. It is generally accepted that for at least the last four millennia, a patrilineal, patrilocal, and patriarchal structure for Chinese society was absolute. In actuality, the process took at least several thousand years, as females gradually lost their ritual equality with males (see below).

Theoretically, in the predominant religious practice, the role of the female is to prepare the sacrificial meal to be offered to her husband's ancestors. In practice, at least in Taiwan, women seem to also carry out the offering to the dead of her husband's family, except in clan temples. Furthermore, the patriarchal structure itself appears to be open to some variation.

In 1986, my wife and I traveled to Liaoning Province for her first visit to her maternal relatives in nearly forty years. There we came across a ritual situation quite different from the norm. (For the usual role of females in Chinese family and clan ritual, see Ahern 1973:116–31.)

During Qingming, the spring festival for cleaning and sacrificing at the grave, my wife's aunts, uncle, and their children sacrificed at their mother's tomb (their father was too old to reach the site). One of the aunts traveled from a city a full day's journey by rail. When my wife arrived, although Qingming had passed a month earlier, a sacrifice was again felt necessary at the tomb, with my wife representing her mother. On the journey back from the tomb, I asked the women if they sacrificed at the tomb of their husbands' parents; the response was negative. The reason provided was that either their husband's family home was too distant or their husband was not interested; however, it seemed that their priorities were essentially matrilineal.

These women had strong personalities and appeared to dominate their husbands, a common feature in Chinese domestic life. They also held professional or government positions and were members of the party (professional women in China use their natal surnames). Their deceased mother also seems to have had a strong personality; the offerings included her favorite cigarettes and strong liquor. While one cannot generalize from a single example, it seemed that it is possible in Chinese society for rituals to be carried on matrilineally rather than patrilineally as is the norm. Whether this is due to the changing socioeconomic status of the female in modern times, as is happening in Taiwan, was a question worth exploring.

In 1992, we again visited my wife's family and were able to gather a biography of her grandmother (see Paper and Paper, 1994b). In attempting to understand the 1986 observation, consideration was first given to the possibility that as the family was

Manchurian, Manchurian customs had predominated over Han Chinese ones. Manchurian culture has, or at least had, matrifocal aspects. For example, often the eldest daughter did not marry but became the family shaman, a religious function learned from her mother (see Wu Bingan 1989). Manchurian women, on the whole, took stronger social and political roles than did Han Chinese women. One need but think of Zu Xi at the end of the Qing (or Manchu) dynasty. However, after investigation it was clear that not only was the subject not technically Manchurian, but her mother had been culturally Han Chinese. Moreover, that there was an attempt to bind her feet was conclusive in this regard, since Manchurian women, to distinguish themselves from Chinese, did not do so. (Instead, they wore shoes on a small platform, approximating the size of a bound foot.)

A second possibility was that the changed socioeconomic status of women led to matrifocal rituals. It seems that matrifocal sacrifices are no longer considered uncommon, but it is not possible to know if this was also the case prior to the twentieth century. One daughter's husband explained that the current practice was due both to the (theoretical) equality of males and females under communism and to the one-child policy.

Hence, it was important to determine the ritual activities of the subject of these matrifocal sacrifices, since she had not only lived most of her life before the success of the Chinese Communist party, but her childhood had taken place prior to the 1911 Revolution. Although information on her religious practices was sparse, there was no doubt that she had offered sacrifices to her mother, but not to her father nor to her husband's parents after the late 1940s. She was a very self-sufficient woman and passed on her own feminist ideology to her daughters (see Paper and Paper 1994b). The matrifocal ritual focus she engaged in has been continued by her daughters and grandaughters, proving that Chinese patrilineality is not absolute.

Although the subject of this study was unusual, surely she was not unique. The husbands of the daughters all, save one, seem to accept the situation with equanimity. All five surviving children, including a daughter who resides in Taiwan, three grandchildren (and one of their spouses, myself), including one who resides in Canada, several great-grandchildren, and the spouse of one of the daughters, who took a very active role, were at the Qingming sacrifice at the subject's gravesite in 1992. All offered lit cigarettes, wine, and food to her; all toasted her with *baijiu* ("white lightening").

Furthermore, the normal pattern of female support of the normative patrifocal and patrilineal family sacrifices need not, in and of itself, indicate female subjugation. As summarized in the next section, in the early period of Chinese civilization, well into the first millennium of the current era, women had roles equal to males in rituals, albeit they were patrilineal, given the elite socioreligious structure.

While with a group of female *lingji* (light possession trance mediums) in Taiwan (1992), in one medium's home, one of the women noted that on the family altar the name plaque had only the name of the husband's family (the home is patrifocal, the normative pattern, being the residence of the husband's mother as well). It is far more common for both the wife's and the husband's family names to be on the plaque. The medium responded simply that when she sacrifices to her natal family, she goes to her parents' house, which is nearby. Her attitude clearly indicated that she did not feel left out of the religious system.

The woman is certainly not dominated by her husband, who is not particularly happy with his wife's activity as a medium, since it takes her away from home for periods of over a week and is a drain on the family income. Nor does he believe in what she is doing. He responded when asked about her activity, "She is my wife." In other words, he felt he had no choice but to accept whatever she does.

The traditional term for a Chinese wife is *tai-tai* (literally: "great-great," meaning "the great one"). The term is meant literally. It is a common assumption in China that husbands are *pa tai-tai*, "afraid of their wives." This does not indicate that Chinese males are "henpecked," although being so is far from uncommon. It does signify that a Chinese wife expects to and does dominate many features of family life, particularly economic aspects.

In traditional elite families, women dominated the interior home of the family and controlled the family finances. In peasant families, women and men both farmed. A pervasive image, when traveling through the countryside, is of couples working together in the fields. Chinese wives rarely fit the Western stereotype of them. Indeed, in Taiwan, Chinese males dream of having a Japanese rather than a Chinese wife because of the non-Japanese stereotype of the Japanese female.

All of the above is not meant to imply that traditionally females were not subordinate to males as discussed in the literature in general. This analysis is intended to indicate that one cannot assume that any theoretical socioreligious system is absolute, nor that a patriarchal sociopolitical order ipso facto means that females are powerless. Cultures are highly complex, and the gross oversimplification that frequently occurs in Western writings on China (and other cultures, for that matter) can be highly misleading.

Female and Male Religious Roles and Ideology

Dualism is fundamental to Chinese ideology. Not only is cosmology understood from the dynamic interaction of complementary, gendered opposites, but the ideology as a whole is similarly divided. Government and religion were coterminous; in theory, at least, balance between male and female roles was considered essential in early Chinese culture. In Chapter 3, reference was made to dual sacrifices of a king and a queen, with appropriate symbols on the ritual vessels. In the ritual texts of the Classics, this dualism is frequently explicit.

In these texts, King and Queen share ritual roles in sacrifice; as in the quotation beginning this chapter, their interrelationship modeled the cosmic one (see Legge 1885:2:240–41,433–34). The funeral rites of a queen were equivalent to those of a king (Legge 1885:329), and this is born out by archeology at least until the turn of the era (the early Han period).

Aristocratic females served as incorporators of the dead (see Chapter 4) for their husbands' grandmothers and presided at the mourning rites for their husbands' mothers (Legge 1885:2:75). (Males in turn formally mourned at the death of their wives' parents.) In the *Zhouli*, female *wu* (mediums) are listed among the major government officials (see Biot 1851:2:104), a female non-governmental role which continues to the present in southern China (see Potter 1974). Indeed, in one southern Chinese community, "it is women, and only women, who communicate with the dead through a professional spirit medium, who is invariably female" (E. Johnson 1988:158). Nevertheless, by the later Han period, female ritual and governmental roles were weakening. There were sporadic resurgences of female power, perhaps the last being the Emperor Wu, a woman, of the Tang dynasty.

The *rujia* (Confucian) tradition, with its focus on filial piety within a patrilineal situation, emphasizes the masculine. Based on this ideology, the state religion tended to patriarchalize female spirits. However, the dominant elite ideology, the *rujia* tradition, was complemented by an opposing ideology, and *daojia* ideology focused on the female aspects of the cosmos. This is apparent in the *Daode jing*, one of the two primary *daojia* texts; for example, chapter 6:

> The spirit of the valley never dies.
> This is called the mysterious [dark] female.
> The gateway [vagina] of the mysterious female
> Is called the root of heaven and earth.
>
> (Lau 1963:62)

Among the literati, the traditional elite, the activity complementary to functioning as a government official was the avocation of aesthetic pursuits (see Chapter 6). The iconographic focus of this activity was *shanshui* (literally mountains and water, or "landscape") in both painting and poetry. As previously discussed, both mountains and water are aspects of the female Earth. Hence, the predominant symbol complex in Chinese religio-aesthetics focuses on the female.

In popular thinking, this understanding of the world as the conjunction of female and male spiritual forces is commonplace and pervasive. For example, in the major manifestation of Chinese Christianity, the mid-nineteenth-century Taiping movement, God was understood as a divine family: the concept of God the Father necessitated the concept of the Mother. Hong Xiuquan as Younger Brother of Christ, the Sun, and the emperor was matched by his wife as the sister-in-law of Jesus, the Moon, and the empress (see following chapter). In a contiguous culture, according to the theology of the contemporary Unification Church, a Korean version of Christianity, Jesus was a failed messiah because he died before he married. The true messiah is a marital couple; Moon Sun-myung's wife is called the "Holy Mother," a term used in the Korean origin myth (Paper 1986).

Chinese culture and religion have undergone several thousand years of continuous development. Over this long course of time, many changes have taken place. Given a religion based on patrilineal ancestral sacrifice and a patriarchal social system since at least the late Neolithic period (see Chapter 2), the status of women continually deteriorated, leading to the situation expressed in the first two lines of a third-century poem by Fu Xuan (see Paper 1989a):

> How sad it is to be a woman!
> Nothing on earth is held so cheap.
>
> (Waley 1918:65)

By the same time, with the adoption of surnames and concomitant patrilineal ancestral sacrifice by the peasantry, the lower status of females would have been pervasive throughout the population.

The development of "Neo-Confucianism" a thousand years ago accelerated the deterioration of women's status. At some point in time, female physiology was understood to deem women ritually impure (see Ahern 1975), an attitude that continues in contemporary China (Potter and Potter 1990:260) but certainly did not yet exist when the classical ritual texts were written. Footbinding literally hobbled elite women to keep them from social intercourse outside the family (Levy 1967), although within the family compound women reigned. By the seventeenth century, nonfamily religious roles were taken from nonelite women, who were no longer allowed to act as shamans and mediums (Huang 1984:609). However, with the passing of the imperial government in 1911 and the recent collapse in Taiwan of the Guomindang dictatorship which rigidly adhered to Neo-Confucian morality, women are again assuming their traditional extrafamily religious roles as mediums (see Chapter 4).

Nevertheless, despite many transitions, the complementary dualism of Heaven and Earth never seems to have been successfully challenged; all movement toward the total patriarchalization of religious ideology ultimately failed. This is reflected in all the social components of Chinese society. (There is an increasing understanding of the complexity of Chinese social structure and religion, e.g., Weller [1987], and Jochim [1988] added the concept of gender to a structural analysis of Chinese religion and society.) An androcentric perception of the sociopolitical realm seems not to have determined cultural ideology as a whole. Indeed there seems to be an "indisputable but not so very paradoxical reversal of certain gender-related values when these are transferred from society to the cosmos" (Black 1986:190). In the examples provided above one can see in the oldest continuous civilization in human experience the continuation of what may be the oldest religious concept.

The inability of Ricci and other Westerners to understand the numinous aspect of the Earth as the cosmic Mother is a failure not only in cross-cultural understanding but also in recognizing human nature and the human situation. However, European monastic misogyny need not be continued in the study of Chinese religion. It is hoped that much needed further studies in the female aspects of Chinese religion will become a major research interest.

Comparative Cosmology and Values

The essentials of Chinese cosmology as discussed above are not unique. They can be found not only in native American cultures (Paper 1987a) but also in other East Asian cultures, Polynesia, sub-Saharan Africa, and indeed most of the cultures of the world. It was also common in pre-Christian Europe and the ancient Near East. In essence, it is a cosmos delineated by six directions outward from a ritual center, whether fixed or portable. The six directions consist of four horizontal directions, usually based on the sun's path and its perpendicular, and two vertical directions: above and below. The latter symbolize the cosmogonic forces, consisting of the female earth and male day sky.

Historians of religions agree on a male sky concept for virtually all cultures, but tend to link the concept of a female earth with horticulture (Pettazoni 1956). Such analyses ignore two factors in so-called hunting cultures: that major food resources come from plant gathering by women, and that the earth is the source of the hunted animals, who are also usually understood to be female spirits. The ability to give birth and to nurture biologically distinguishes all female mammals, including humans, from male mammals and is accorded cosmic significance in most cultures. Even cultures with limited plant gathering, such as the far northern Inuit, have a similar cosmogonic understanding. Being a maritime people, the sea fulfills the role of earth for terrestrial peoples, and it is Sedna, the Sea Mother, who controls the hunted animals. Hence, the understanding of the earth (and the sea) as female is virtually a cultural constant regardless of socioeconomic complexity.

In all cultures with the above-described cosmology, there are fundamental differences with Western cultures. Post-classical Western cosmology consists of a single direction, the zenith; astronomy and cosmology are equated. From this perspective, the nadir, the earth, is understood as an insignificant aspect of the zenith. The primary cultural difference between these two cosmologies is one of theology. Only the Western religions are monotheistic; their rituals are ideologically oriented exclusively toward the zenith. (Judaism and Islam ritually face the direction of assumed primary contact with the zenith—Jerusalem and Mecca, but it is the zenith that is the focus of worship.) This factor has a number of ramifications, particularly if the values of monotheistic theologies are not assumed superior to those of polytheistic cultures. The following is an exercise in comparative religion, deliberately disregarding traditional Western values.

First, monotheistic (or semimonotheistic) traditions which are also dualistic interpret the opposition to be antagonistic rather than complimentary. This antithetical opposition is generally understood to be that between good and evil. Neither native American nor East Asian traditions, prior to influence from the West, had a concept of evil, other than recognizing the human tendency toward selfishness, which in these intrinsically communal societies was the epitome of antisocial behavior. The concept of evil requires the separation of humans from the rest of nature, since the ability to choose evil becomes the distinguishing characteristic of humans in Western ideology.

In polytheistic religions, deities tend to be neither good nor evil. Rather the gods are morally neutral, although some may be capricious and a few may be dangerous, reflecting the nature of life, but virtually none are ipso facto evil. Humans may elicit the aid of the neutral spirits to help or harm other humans. In polytheistic religions, there are a sufficient number of deities to reflect all the varieties of the human personality and potential.

Some native American religions had two culture heroes, symbolizing complementary opposition in regard to their helping or hindering human life; it is uncertain as to whether these myths are precontact. In most traditions, these two aspects of life were symbolized by a single culture hero with a complex personality. In any case, culture heroes rarely if ever functioned as divinities in their relationships with humans, as did other spirits. Also, some cultures understood cannibalistic spirits to semipossess humans. Among the northern Cree, such a person might be executed at the request of his or her relatives, while Northwest Coast cultures transformed that potentiality through an elaborate ritual. In Chinese culture, there is a concept of dangerous wandering spirits, but on possessing humans, they may become beneficent deities.

A second ramification of monotheism is that there can be but one gender for deity, which is male in the Western traditions. Although some of the major rituals may distantly derive from gender complementary deities, such as the Eucharist from female grain and male wine deities, this has no effect on Christian ritual or theology. The only mythic and ritual roles for the female are secondary, for example, as the mother of and intercessor with deity. The Western mystic traditions do recognize a female aspect of deity—the Shechinah in Judaism and Sophia in Christian Gnosticism—but these concepts only affect or affected a minority of the respective populations and assume a male practitioner.

In contrast, polytheistic religions tend toward an equality between female and male divinities. Indeed, in many primal cultures such as those of aboriginal North America, males and females have different complementary socioeconomic roles and religious rituals and may relate themselves to different deities. The ethnographic data is often misleading in these regards, as ethnologists almost always focus on male understanding and roles, reinforcing the Western orientation toward male rituals and male deities (see Paper 1994). In cultures with class differentiation, beginning with a professional warrior elite, the patriarchal social order need not, as in China, negate a complementary female-male cosmological order.

A third ramification of monotheism is the locus of deity. If there is but one deity, there can be but one location of deity, which is the sky in Western religions. Western cosmology is hemispheric rather than spherical as in polytheistic cultures, and only the sky is understood to be sacred. The normative cross-cultural understanding is that the sky's gender is male and the earth, female. In the West, when the earth is considered at all, it becomes the locus of evil: Heaven is located in the sky; Hell is located in the earth. Accordingly, Mary, a fertility symbol in her role as mother of Christ, is not located in the earth; rather she ascends to the sky. The logical implication of earth being both female and evil is that females, if not ipso facto evil, are the source of evil. This understanding of the nature of females is one of the essential premises for the Christian concept of original sin.

Rather than the dualistic concept of Heaven and Hell, both native American and Chinese cultures, prior to Western influence, understood the realm of the dead to be the same for all. Many native American religions locate the realm of the dead to the west, the direction of the setting sun, whose path is equated with life. (The Western concept of Hell did influence the native American concept of an afterlife, see Hultkrantz 1980.) In China, the multisoul theory, common to cultures with shamanistic practices, led to an understanding of the locus of the dead being simultaneously both in the earth and in the sky. In China, the Buddhist concept of multiple heavens and hells as temporary abodes evolved into the Pure Land, the Western Paradise, associated with female deities.

All cultures, from the normal ethnocentric perspective, assume their ideology to be the best, although not necessarily the only correct one as in the West. Western cultures value monotheism as vastly superior to polytheism. However, monotheism, from a comparative perspective, has certain inherent drawbacks. Monotheism tends toward positive-negative dualism, which in turn has pragmatic effects. For one, only part, if any, of the environment is considered sacred. For another, only one gender is considered godlike. Contemporary feminist responses to a patriarchal theology often replace it with a matriarchal one; neither monotheistic theology accepts the totality and potentiality of human existence as do polytheistic religions.

9 christianity from the perspective of chinese religion

At the time I ascended into Heaven, I met in Heaven God the Heavenly
Father, Mom the Heavenly Mother, as well as the Great Elder Brother
Christ and the Heavenly Elder Sister–in–Law.
　　　　　—Hong Xiuqian commenting on Mark 12:35–37

Chapter 1 introduced problems in the comparative study of
religion engendered by the natural human tendency toward
ethnocentrism. As delineated in the last chapter, the Western understanding of monotheism as the mark of a good or acceptable
culture has skewed our understanding of many religious traditions, including those of East Asia, Africa, and native America.
At the end of the last chapter, the implications in reversing this
value were explored. Reversals of ethnocentric values may lead
to further new understandings. For example, how would a poly-
theist understand Christianity? In the contemporary, common
Chinese view, at least in Taiwan, Catholicism and Protestantism
are not understood to be variants of a single religious tradition.
Instead, they are assumed to be two entirely different religions.
The former is considered polytheistic, emphasizing a female deity, Mary, and the latter, monotheistic.

From the late sixteenth century, Christian missionaries introduced Chinese culture and religion to the West as discussed
in Chapter 1. But their primary task was to introduce a Western
religion, Christianity, to China. (Many centuries earlier, Moslems
and Jews entered China and became assimilated into the Chinese
cultural matrix.) Eventually the presence of Christian missionaries created an interest, at times subliminal, in Christianity. As
analysis of the sinification of Buddhism helps us to understand
the primary cultural themes of China, so too the sinification of

245

Christianity over the last century and a half can assist in identifying the central themes and concerns of Chinese religion.

Although the history of Christianity in China is considerably shorter than that of Buddhism, there are comparable aspects. In China, their introduction took place during periods of stability and initially had negligible effects, but both had considerable impact in later periods of political chaos. Buddhism had virtually no effect until the weakening of the Han dynasty in the late second century, when movements indirectly influenced by Buddhism nearly succeeded in overthrowing the government (Michaud 1958:80; Wright 1960:245). In that the residence of Nestorian Christians in Tang China and the travel of a few Christian missionaries to China during the Mongol period produced no lasting effects, Christianity could be said to have been introduced in the late sixteenth century. However, Christianity again disappeared in China when the decision of the papacy in regard to the Rites Controversy went counter to the views of a strong emperor. It was only when the last dynasty weakened and Christianity was introduced under the umbrella of Western arms following China's defeat in the Opium Wars that Christianity had a major effect on China, particularly with the Taiping movement, an effect almost identical to Buddhism's first impact nearly two millenia previous. In both cases, the Chinese understanding of the respective foreign ideologies was quite different from that of the missionaries who brought the doctrines to China.

A comparison of the understanding of the Christian scriptures by Hong Xiuquan, the Taiping's founder, with a contemporary Chinese understanding indicates virtually identical interpretations and suggests a Chinese theological predilection. Although two examples are hardly definitive, as they accord with Chinese religious understanding in general, they do suggest a Chinese theological predilection and indicate a normative Chinese understanding of Christian scriptures. The Taiping movement, moreover, cannot be dismissed as a minor aberration, as Western scholars often do. The movement spread over all of central China and might have succeeded in taking over the entire country had not Western armies supported the tottering Manchu regime.

Hong Xiuquan

Since the formation of the first Chinese empire over two millennia ago, there have been three major heterodox, communal revolutionary movements instigated by foreign ideas. The first was the Yellow Turban movement of the second century, probably inspired in part by awareness of Buddhism. The second, the Taiping movement of the nineteenth century, whose name coincides with the name of the first movement's major text, was inspired by Christianity. The last, the Chinese Communist party of the twentieth century, was inspired by Marxist–Leninism. The first two movements swept over much of China before being destroyed by the existing dynasty, which in each case subsequently collapsed after several decades. The last movement ultimately succeeded in unifying and establishing control over China.

Each movement's understanding of the foreign inspiring ideas was partial at best. Buddhism was still a religion of foreign traders in the second century, and Indian ideas were not fully understood in China for another several hundred years when a few Chinese became experts in Sanskrit. Neither Stalin nor Kruschev thought Mao Zedong understood Marxist–Leninism. The understanding of Christianity by the founder of the Taiping movement, Hong Xiuquan, is the subject of this section.

Biography

Hong Xiuquan (1814–1864) was brought up in a southern Chinese farming family but studied for the civil service examinations. Although he passed the preliminary examination, he repeatedly failed the first examination, as did all but a small percentage of those who sat for it.

Following one of these failures in 1837, Hong became seriously ill and in delirium had a vision that was subsequently to form the basis of the Taiping movement. (For details and a history of the movement, see any of the following: Michael 1966, Teng 1971, Jen 1973, Clarke and Gregory 1982.) After his last failed attempt at the examinations in 1843, a cousin called his attention to a book he had been given seven years previous in

Canton but to which he had paid little attention. This book, the *Quanshi liangyan* (English title: *Good Words to Admonish the Age: Being Nine Miscellaneous Christian Tracts*) provided Hong with an ideological basis for understanding his earlier vision.

> Consequently, in the words of one of his followers, He exhorted everyone to worship God and cultivate virtue, saying that people willing to worship God would avoid disasters and suffering. Those who did not worship God would be injured by serpents and tigers. Those who worshipped God must not worship other deities: those who worshipped other deities would be committing a crime. (Curwin 1977:79)

Hong converted friends and relatives, and within a year a friend founded the Bai Shangdi hui (God Worshippers Society).

The *Quanshi liangyan* by Liang Afa, published in 1832, includes in English: "printed at the expense of the Religious Tract Society, Canton, China" (Teng 1962:2–3). An eclectic but primarily Christian work, it is the basic source for Hong's limited understanding of Christianity. In it we find the origin for Hong's terminology, including *shen* (spirit), as well as *shangdi* (God), *tianguo* (heavenly kingdom) meaning both Paradise and a kingdom on earth of Christian believers, and *taiping* (great peace), a perfect God–worshipping kingdom (Teng 1962:4). Hence, the title for Hong's nearly successful state, *Taiping tianguo*, derives from Liang's book.

Hong, however, did not slavishly follow the *Quanshi liangyan*. His movement adopted many Chinese religious practices specifically forbidden by the text. These practices included offering food and wine to God (see Chapter 2) as well as burning paper money and interpreting dreams and omens. By 1848, two of Hong's followers began to function as mediums (see Chapter 4) for God, the Heavenly Father, and Jesus, the Heavenly Elder Brother. Their descents and messages, especially preceding military crises, continued the revelation of Hong's initial vision (see Boardman 1952).

Hong's awareness of Christianity was further increased during the month or so he spent in 1847 with the Reverend Issachar T. Roberts, an American Southern Baptist, in Canton. However, Hong left or was forced to leave before becoming formally baptized.

Between 1847 and 1849, the economic and political situation in southern China continued to deteriorate. The God Worshippers Society began to arm and begin military training for its followers. By 1850, military clashes occurred between the Manchu government and the Society. Following a successful repulse of a major Manchu attack on the Society's forces at the end of 1850, at the beginning of 1851, Hong ceremoniously proclaimed himself the Tianwang (heavenly king) and declared the Taiping tianguo (heavenly kingdom of great peace). The Taiping armies continued on the whole to be successful, and in 1853 captured Nanjing. The old capital in central China was declared the Taiping capital.

Biblical Text

Hong probably encountered his first Bible during his stay with Roberts. Prior to being assigned to Canton, Roberts served as an assistant to Charles Gützlaff, one of the early Protestant translators of the Bible (Boardman 1952:44). Undoubtedly, Roberts was using the Medhurst-Gützlaff Chinese text version, the New Testament having been printed in 1835 and the Old Testament in 1838 (Meadows 1856:94).

It is this version of the Bible that the Taiping began to print in 1853 soon after capturing Nanjing and making it their capital. The first six books of the Old Testament (Genesis through Joshua) were published under the title *The Holy Book of the Old Testament Promulgated by Royal Order,* and the complete New Testament under the title, *The Holy Book of the Former Testament Promulgated by Royal Order* (J. C. Cheng 1963:81). That this Bible became important to Hong is evident in that it was substituted for the Classics as the text for the civil service examinations within the Taiping state (Meadows 1856:446).

The British Museum possesses a copy of the 1853 Taiping edition of the Bible, complete but for the fourth gospel (John), that must have been Hong's personal copy, for it has his handwritten annotations on the upper margins (the usual place for annotating Chinese books). These comments form the basis for the following analysis. Being marginalia, they are difficult to read and not always readily coherent to other than the writer. However, these difficulties are not likely to lead to any major errors in our understanding of Hong's thoughts since the commentary tends to be repetitive.

There have been two publications of these notes: a partial one by Xiao (1936:folio 1), and a complete text in Jin and Tian (1955:75–88). Translations are available in J. C. Cheng (1963) and Frederick Mote (in Michael 1971:2:224–37). Although I have consulted the above translations, the translations presented here are primarily my own.

Understanding the New Testament

Hong's comments on the New Testament fall into three recurring major themes and five minor points. The three major themes may be labelled (1) "Mediumism," (2) "The Trinity," and (3) "The Kingdom."

MEDIUMISM:

Hong understood the biblical Jesus as Christ mediumistically descended into Jesus rather than Jesus as Christ being an incarnation of God. Hence, the descent of the spirit of God in Matthew 3:16–17 is understood as a mediumistic experience. More important, he indicates that God and Christ have now also mediumistically descended to the earth:

> The Holy Ghost is God. Moreover, the Great Elder Brother [Christ] is God's Primary Son. So they came [into the world when Jesus was baptized by John]. Now in the present, God and Christ have descended into the ordinary world. Respect this [phrase used to conclude imperial documents].

The immediate presence of God and Christ is repeatedly emphasized:

> [Matthew 5:19—at the end of the commentary] Today, the Heavenly Father and Heavenly Elder Brother have descended into the ordinary world to begin the Heavenly Kingdom. Respect this.
> [The commentaries to both Matthew 10:32–33 and 13:30 contain this passage:] Now the Father and Elder Brother

have descended into the ordinary world to destroy evil and preserve the righteous.

That the above passages can only be understood as referring to mediumistic descent is certain from the commentary to 1 John 5:7, where in the midst of one of the longest commentaries is found explicit reference to the two individuals who are understood as the mediums for God and Christ:

> It is in the present time that God has descended into the ordinary world, descended from the spirit world into the Eastern King [Yang Xiuqing], descended from the spirit world into the person of the Eastern King as the Holy Spirit . . . The Father knows the New Testament has erroneous records. Therefore, he descended into the Eastern King to proclaim and certify that the Holy Spirit is God. . . . Also, He knows that ordinary people mistakenly understand Christ as God. Therefore, God descended into the Eastern King in order to make clear that the Divine Father indeed exists. Christ descended into the Western king [Xiao Chaoguei] in order to make clear that the Primary Son indeed exists.

The concept is repeated in the commentary to Revelations 11:19.

Mediumistic descent is understood according to the usual functions of mediumism, such as divine direction from above, healing, and divination. Jesus's healing in Matthew 8:3, 9:29–30, and Mark 2:12 are commented upon by Hong as mediumistic possession:

> [Matthew 8:3] God spiritually descended to reside in the head of the Great Elder Brother. A word from the Great Elder Brother was a word from God. Therefore, the leper was cleansed. Respect this.

Mediumistic guidance is referred to in Hong's comments to Romans 10:10 and Revelations 12:13–16 and 21:1–2.

THE TRINITY:

More commentary is devoted to explicitly arguing that the Christian understanding of the Trinity is mistaken than any other theme. As in the comment to Matthew 3:17 quoted above and repeated in Mark 1:11 and Corinthians 2:10–16, the Holy Ghost is God.

Even more important is the point that God and Christ are two different spiritual entities; father and son cannot be the same person. Indeed, both are present in two different possessed mediums as quoted in the commentary to 1 John 5:7 above. Hong's understanding of monotheism in some respects is closer to Judaism and Islam than to normative Christianity:

> [Mark 12:29 where Jesus speaks the "Shema"] The Great Elder Brother clearly proclaimed a single Supreme Lord. Why did later disciples erroneously consider Christ to be God? If this were true, then there would be two Gods. Respect this.

In the comment to the following passage concerning Jesus teaching in the temple, Hong continues the argument and points out the evidence of his vision:

> Furthermore, how can it be that at the time I ascended into Heaven, I met in Heaven God the Heavenly Father, Mom the Heavenly Mother, as well as the Great Elder Brother Christ and the Heavenly Elder Sister–in–law. Now [I] have descended into the ordinary world and there is still the Heavenly Father, the Heavenly Mother, the Heavenly Elder Brother and the Heavenly Sister–in–law! Respect this.

Further arguments that God and Christ are two different deities are to be found in Hong's comments to Luke 4:12, 7:16, and 12:8–10; Acts 4:24 and 7:55; Romans 1:4 and 9:5; and Corinthians 1:9 and 8:6.

Different from the Semitic understanding of monotheism is Hong's Chinese understanding of God as having a family; hence, we have in effect a single God-family. The vision described in the preceding quotation is repeated in the comments to 1 John 5:7 and Revelations 12:1–17.

Hong considered himself a member of this divine family, a younger brother of Christ:

> [Hebrews 7:1] This Melchizedek is myself [Hong uses the Chinese term for self used only by the emperor]. Previously in Heaven, Mom gave birth to the Great Elder Brother, myself and others of my generation. [Here follows a story of Hong blessing Abraham and a statement of Yang Xiuqing speaking as God that is understood as referring to Hong.]

> This statement is evidence that today I have descended to
> the ordinary world to be Lord. Respect this.

This commentary is repeated in but slightly different words in Hong's comments to Revelations 12:13–16. His "descent into the world as a human" is the subject of his commentary to Acts 2:22. In the first line of his commentary to Revelations 6:12–17, Hong writes, "I am the Taiyang; my wife is the Taiyin." Taiyang [Great *yang*] means the sun, but the sun as masculine, celestial power, humanized in the Chinese emperor, and Taiyin [Great *yin*] means the moon, but the moon as feminine, celestial power, humanized in the wife of the emperor. (See Chapter 8 for the background of this concept.)

That Hong is the Taiyang, in the sense of both the sun and the emperor, is reiterated in several commentaries to passages in Matthew:

> [Matthew 4:16–17] God is flame; the Taiyang is also
> flame. Therefore, God and the Taiyang have arrived
> together. Respect this . . . God is flame; therefore, he is Spiri-
> tual Light. The Great Elder Brother is flame; therefore, he
> is Great Light. I am the Taiyang; therefore, I am also
> light. Respect this.

In Matthew 24:27–29, Hong found reference to both himself and his wife:

> The Great Elder Brother feared to divulge it; therefore, he is-
> sued a secret proclamation that I am the Taiyang and have
> descended to the world to become a human. Hence, it [the
> sun] "darkened." My wife, the Taiyin, has descended to the
> world to become a human. Hence, it [the moon] "does not
> give its light."

In this regard, Hong also plays a Chinese word game:

> [Matthew 27:40] Three dots is Hong [referring to the first
> three strokes in the written character]. "Three days" is
> Hong/sun [day and sun are the same Chinese character].
> The Great Elder Brother secretly proclaimed Hong/sun will
> become Lord and rebuild the temple which God de-
> stroyed. Respect this.

THE KINGDOM:

From a Chinese standpoint, Heaven and Earth are equal; they are, respectively, the male and female procreative forces (see Chapter 8). Both were sacrificed to by the emperor:

> [Matthew 5:19] The unitary Great Kingdom includes Heaven above and Earth below, and one speaks of Heaven above as including the Heavenly Kingdom and Earth below as including the Earthly Kingdom. Heaven above and Earth below together compose the Divine Father's Heavenly Kingdom. Do not mistakenly assume it only refers to the Heavenly Kingdom in Heaven above. Therefore, the Great Elder Brother issued a proclamation stating "the Heavenly Kingdom is almost at hand," meaning the Heavenly Kingdom will come on the ordinary world. Today, the Heavenly Father and Heavenly Elder Brother descend to the ordinary world to establish the Heavenly Kingdom. Respect this.

The capture of Nanjing by Hong's movement was understood as the fulfillment of the promise of the second coming; hence, the establishment of the Taiping tianguo (heavenly kingdom of great peace). Hong understands the New Testament to be referring to future events that have now actually occurred:

> [Matthew 24:38–39] Now the Father and Elder Brother ascend to Heaven on clouds [see Chapters 3 and 6] and gather all the people, who come from the four quarters, from the boundaries of the sky [the horizon]. All has been fulfilled. Respect this.
>
> [Acts 15:15–16] Now God and Christ have descended to the ordinary world to rebuild God's temple in the Heavenly Capital. All the realm is united and seeks the Supreme Lord. Respect this.

Nanjing was declared the Taiping capital, the Heavenly Capital, and was understood as the New Jerusalem:

> [Revelations 3:12] The Heavenly Father, God, sent down from Heaven the New Jerusalem which is now our Heavenly Capital. It is fulfilled. Respect this.
>
> [Revelations 21:1–2] On Earth as it is in Heaven, what John saw was the Great Heavenly Palace. Heaven above and

Earth below are the same. The New Jerusalem is now our Heavenly Capital.

MINOR POINTS:

(1) SACRIFICE: The practice of sacrificial meals has been central to Chinese religious practices since the Neolithic period (see Chapter 2) although denied to Chinese Christians by missionaries since the end of the Rites Controversy. Hong disagreed with the Christian missionaries and allowed a shift of the normative sacrifices from ancestral spirits to God:

> [Matthew 9:12–13] The Great Elder Brother proclaimed his desire for mercy rather than sacrifice. This means people must have a good heart before sacrificing to God [a concept stressed in the *Lunyu* (Analects) of Kongfuzi (Confucius)]. [Christ] did not proclaim people should not sacrifice to God. Respect this.

This point is reiterated in Hong's commentary to Hebrews 10:8.

(2) CONFRONTING GOD AND CHRIST: Now that the Heavenly Kingdom is established, God and Christ are to be confronted as the emperor at an imperial audience:

> The character *hui* [to assemble] . . . now changed to the character *jin* [an inferior presenting himself to his superior]. Before the Father and Elder Brother descended to the ordinary world to reign, it was appropriate to gather and *hui*. Now that the Father and Elder Brother have descended to the world to reign, it is appropriate to *jin* at court. Respect this.

(3) MARY: Mary becomes understood as the mother of God from a mediumistic standpoint rather than from the normative Christian position:

> [Luke 1:35] It is said that the Holy Spirit, God, spiritually descended to her. It is not said that the Holy Spirit, God, entered her womb, was conceived and became a human. It is essential to understand [this]. Respect this.

(4) POLYGAMY: Contrary to the rulings of Christian missionaries in regard to common Chinese practices of the wealthy in the nineteenth century, Hong allowed the practice of polygamy, at least for the high officials:

> [Titus 1:6] Now God's holy directive is that high officials' wives are not limited [Hong's language here is unclear].

(5) CHINESE BUDDHIST INFLUENCE: In Hong's commentaries there are a few examples of minor influence from popular Chinese religion. For example, in Hong's commentary to 1 Corinthians 15:49, he mentions "thirty–three Heavens."

In Revelations, Abaddon is equated by Hong (e.g., 9:11) with Yenlo (Sanskrit: Yama), who in Chinese Buddhism is ruler of one or all of the Hells (there are regional variations). In Revelations 12:13–16, in the midst of a long commentary, Yenlo is conflated with the "dragon" of the New Testament text as Satan: "serpent Yenlo," "serpent-demon Yenlo," and "the great red dragon is Abaddon Yenlo supernatural creature." Hong saw his role in this regard as follows:

> Therefore, now the Father and Elder Brother have descended into the ordinary world making me the sovereign to especially destroy this serpent. Now the serpents and beasts have been destroyed and there is great peace [*taiping*] in the realm. Respect this.

Analysis

The analysis in this section is specific to Hong's commentary to the New Testament. Hence, the presentation of Hong's thought is limited and accordingly simplistic. Such a restricted presentation has the advantage of accentuating those points specific to biblical interpretation. A more general and thorough analysis of Hong's thought and Taiping ideology, and one that is relatively similar to my own, will be found in Shih (1967).

For the typical mid-nineteenth-century missionary in China, usually fundamentalist, Hong and his movement was anathema. Robert Forrest (1867:204), who translated a number of the above commentaries in the 1860s, wrote: "Considering the life of Hong-tsiu-tsuen [Hong Xiuquan], I am in no wise astonished at the grotesque monstrosity of his belief."

However Europeans more aware and understanding of Chinese culture, and of the fact that there are and have been many kinds of Christianity, took a more equable view. Thomas Taylor Meadows (1856:412), writing during the early part of the movement, noted:

> That a number of adult converts of a nation like the Chinese,
> which so long entertained, and is thoroughly imbued with,
> a particular set of fundamental beliefs, would, with or without express intention, considerably modify the Christianity
> which had attracted them was not simply probable—it was,
> humanly speaking, a certainty.

An analysis of Hong's commentaries to the New Testament but serve to confirm Meadows' initial insight into Taiping Christianity. All of the foci of Hong's remarks—mediumism, the Trinity, and the Kingdom—reflect basic aspects of Chinese religious ideology and practice with a longstanding history.

Both shamanism and mediumism can be traced back at least as far as protohistoric Chinese religion, and they continue in Chinese culture to the present (see Chapters 4 and 5). Hence, it is to be expected that Hong understood the healing of Jesus from the standpoint of mediumism. Nor for that matter is such an interpretation uniquely Chinese. Morton Smith (1978) has analyzed the early Christian understanding of Jesus's healing within the context of Near Eastern magic, similar to but not identical with shamanism and mediumism.

Furthermore, local Chinese deities develop out of specific individuals' mediumistic experiences (Jordan 1972:31–84). Illnesses, especially those in which the person experienced visions, are often understood as deities summoning individuals to become their mediums, a phenomenon virtually universal to mediumism, from Africa through Indonesia. This is, of course, how Hong eventually understood his initial vision which occurred during an illness. That two other persons became mediums for the Holy Spirit and Jesus confirmed Hong's understanding that he had become the medium for, that is, he himself was, the deity, Jesus's younger brother.

Monotheism is alien to the Chinese concept of the numinous, outside of the mystic or union trance experience of the Dao found in Daoist thought (see Chapter 5). Hence, the Christian struggle to maintain a monotheistic concept as a primary value, leading to the development of the idea of the Trinity, is incomprehensible within Chinese ideology.

The Christian terminology of Father and Son, however, is perfectly comprehensible within Chinese thought from two regards. Within elite ideology, the emperor, of semidivine status, is conceived of as the Son of Heaven. In popular Chinese religion, local deities are understood as related to other deities, the relationship of deities reflecting the overwhelming family concept of Chinese society and culture. Hence, Hong's understanding of himself as younger brother within a divine family is congruous with the Chinese ideological pattern.

Finally, the understanding of the Kingdom as taking place on earth reflects Chinese messianism and is virtually identical with Israelite and probably early Christian concepts. Messianism has a history in China as long as it does in the Near East. Even the term, *taiping*, can be found as describing the ideal state in Chinese texts dating from the third century B.C.E. For example, in *Zhuangzi* 13, we find the phrase, "This is called Da[=Tai]ping, the most perfect form of government."

Max Kaltenmark (1979:24), in discussing the *Taiping jing* of the late Han period (first to second century C.E.) points out the messianism of the period, which is indistinguishable from that of Hong nearly two millennia later:

> The Celestial Master presents himself as a "divine man" (*shen-jen*) sent by Heaven to save mankind [from the accumulated inheritance of sins (*ch'eng-fu*)] by means of a celestial scripture (*t'ien-shu*), which teaches how one can return to a method of ideal government and assist the immanent arrival of the "Breath of T'ai-p'ing."

In the *Taiping jing*, as well, Earth is explicitly the equal of Heaven:

> Father and mother are equally human beings, and Heaven and Earth are both "Celestial" (Kaltenmark 1979:37).

Hence, Hong's understanding of the Kingdom as the establishment of ideal government, of the millennium, on earth, and Earth as the equivalent of Heaven is the Chinese common understanding. Furthermore, the Chinese concept of the Mandate of Heaven, a concept which in its early form dates to at least the eleventh century B.C.E., assumès that the successful establishment of a new regime is one of ideal peace under a Son of Heaven. The Taiping capture of Nanjing was understood to signify that the millennium had actually begun.

Overall, Hong's religious understanding is closer to that of popular Chinese religion than that of the elite, especially in regard to mediumism, which came to be frowned upon in elite culture. This, combined with the Taiping communistic economic program, led to disfavor among the elite, one of the factors leading to their eventual collapse, as Meadows (1856:456–57,463) presciently observed.

A Contemporary Chinese Interpretation

For comparison, a contemporary Chinese interpretation was solicited. The commentator, from northern China, was brought up and educated in Taiwan and had lived in Canada for the decade preceding the writing of the interpretation. Although nominally a Catholic in Taiwan (on conversion of her mother) but not in Canada, she was unfamiliar with basic Christian theology. Her ideological background, typical of those from elite mainland families in Taiwan and reinforced by the Guomindang (Nationalist party), reflects a modernized later *rujia* (Neo-Confucian) orientation.

The commentator, unacquainted with Taiping ideology, was asked to write an interpretive commentary, from a Chinese perspective, to the Gospel of Mark (Revised Standard Version) from which the following brief extracts were selected (L. C. Paper 1985). As with the commentary of Hong, on analysis, the comments can be seen to focus on mediumism, the Trinity, and the Kingdom.

MEDIUMISM:

The commentator readily noted the similarity of descriptions in Mark to the behavior of mediums (local Red Hat "Taoist priests"). However, the author reflects modern elite Chinese values in disparaging such behavior and activities:

> [Mark 1:21–26] Jesus is similar to a Taoist [Daoist] priest who may function as a medium, divine, heal, as well as exorcise evil spirits from sick persons. However, Taoist priests are not highly regarded by the educated in Taiwan. . . . For this reason, Jesus' method of functioning as a healer would make him unacceptable to educated Chinese people.
> [14:22–23] The eating of the bread as Jesus' body and the drinking of wine as his blood...the god comes into one, allowing one to function as a medium for that deity. Hence, the disciples should then have been able to speak with the voice of Jesus and heal with his powers.

THE TRINITY:

As with Hong, the overriding concept of family informs the understanding of divinity. In China, local deities are understood as related to other deities according to the pattern of the Chinese hierarchical family. If Jesus is the Son of God, then there must be a Divine Family in which the Son would be a lesser member, separate from the Father. (The commentator differs from Hong in considering the Holy Ghost distinct from God.)

> [1:1] If Jesus is the Son of God, he should also have a father, mother, sisters, and brothers in Heaven. The father is the head of the family. He is an authority figure and his children are subject to him. Therefore, Jesus is subject to his father, God.
> [3:29] Since the Holy Spirit is not the Son, from a Chinese perspective, the term must refer to our ancestral spirits. In China, deceased members of the family are still part of the family and are sacrificed to as spirits.

THE KINGDOM:

The commentator, like Hong, understands the "Kingdom" to refer to what must come in this life and on the earth. Different from

Hong is the utilization of the later *rujia* view of man, extending from Mengzi (Mencius), that man is innately good, not sinful.

> [8:36–38] Here Jesus implies that there is life only after death. From a Chinese perspective, there is no single understanding of a next world . . . it is this life that is the important one, and the afterworld tends to be understood as a reflection of it. Furthermore, it is not assumed in Chinese culture that all people are "adulterous and sinful," rather it is assumed that people are innately good.
>
> [11:10] The ideal kingdom to come must be a kingdom for the living, not the dead.
>
> [13:31] Heaven will not pass away because that is where the deities live. Nor for that matter will the Earth pass away, as they are equal spiritual entities. Without Heaven and Earth, there will be no place for humans, because our abode is between the two. We have the expression, meaning forever: "Eternal Heaven, immortal Earth."

CRITICISMS IN REGARD TO CHINESE VALUES:

Aside from the above similarities with the commentary of Hong, the modern commentator criticizes the Gospels as antagonistic to Chinese values and concepts of deity. These criticisms are of interest because they are identical to seventeenth-century critiques of which the author was unaware.

Jesus is criticized in two regards. First, he is considered too temperamental to fit the Chinese concept of divinity, usually beneficent:

> [11:13–14, 21] Jesus is arrogant and selfish to kill a fig tree just because there were no figs when he wanted them; hence, he is imperfect.
>
> [11:15–16] A god should never lose his/her temper.

This wording is similar to an obscure mid–seventeenth century critique of Jesuit-imparted Christianity: "They say the overflowing of waters which occurred during the period of Yao [the biblical flood] was occasioned by the wrath of the Master of Heaven. . . . A being of perfect virtue does not lose his temper" (Xu Dashou, *Zuopi* 3A, in Gernet 1985:222). (*Master of Heaven* is the term the Jesuits created as a translation for *God*.)

Second, Jesus is considered too impotent to fit the Chinese understanding of deity:

[13:2] A real god would not let his or her temple be destroyed.

[15:24] If Jesus is a god, he should be able to end his suffering and avoid his crucifixion.

[16:6] If Jesus is a god, he will never die. Furthermore, it is incomprehensible that he died and then rose again. Why does he bother to die in the first place?

This criticism is again similar to another mid–seventeenth-century critique: "Not only was Yesu not able to save mankind as a whole, but he himself was sentenced to the most ignomini-ous of deaths. Can this be the Master who created Heaven?" (*Pixielun*, in Gernet 1985:228).

Conclusions

In comparing the two Chinese interpretations one finds consid-erable correspondence: the three major themes of Hong's com-mentary correspond to the primary foci of the modern interpretation. In both cases, there was difficulty in assimilating the combination of monotheism and a triune deity found in Christianity; instead there was substituted a concept of related deities as a divine patriarchal family. Salvation was understood to exist for all people in this world, and this life is given priority over a potential but uncertain next life. Finally, Jesus's functional behavior was interpreted as that of a medium, which had nega-tive connotations for the late traditional elite, with whose views the author of the contemporary interpretation is imbued.

In summary, between the two interpretations, separated by more than a century, a common Chinese predilection for understanding Christian scriptures can be ascertained. This com-monality is further strengthened in that the contemporary inter-pretation unknowingly expressed values and terminology found in the earliest Chinese critiques of Christianity written in the sev-enteenth century.

Given that Hong Xiuquan's interpretation of the New Testament coincides with an independent late-twentieth-century interpretation, we cannot consider his theology exceptional. Hong understood the New Testament from a parallel perspective, that of the *Taiping jing*, that is as old as the Gospels. He received from his interpretation an impetus to create a millenarian state that in a short time covered more than half of China proper. His movement failed in part because a positive understanding of the Christian scriptures from a Chinese perspective supported behavioral patterns (mediumism) of which the educated elite disapproved. Obviously, a Chinese understanding of Christian scriptures was also unacceptable to normative nineteenth-century Christianity. With the Chinese elite and the Western powers ranged on the side of the declining Manchu dynasty, the Taiping kingdom was doomed to failure.

Accordingly, there appears to be a predisposition toward a particular Chinese interpretation of the Christian scriptures. First, religious understanding is primarily experiential rather than analytical. Knowledge gained from trance visions is true; the Scriptures are used to explicate the visions. Second, deity is not understood as monotheistic. Rather, monotheism is understood as deities combined in either a divine family or as divine parents. Finally, the Kingdom of Heaven is understood to be a new sociopolitical order in this world, an order actually achieved by the Taiping movement for a short time.

In the early twentieth century, scholars of religion examined Christian-influenced, non–Western religions and found confirmation of monotheism as a primary and universal human value. However, examination of indigenized non–Western Christianity indicates the opposite. This is the case not only in China and other East Asian cultures (see Paper 1986,1989b), but in other cultures as well. For example, the raising of Mary's status from the divinized human mother of deity to the equal female spouse of deity, contiguous with either Earth or Moon, can be found in both North (see Merrill 1988) and South (see Silverblatt 1987) America. As in China, many native American forms of indigenized Christianity find a holy couple more congenial than a solitary supreme deity:

Return here again next Sunday, I say to you. Never fail to
come here and ask forgiveness of Our Father [Sun] and Our
Mother [Moon]. (From a church sermon delivered by a male
Rarámuri governor following prayers led by a Mestizo
woman, Merrill 1988:68)

Hence, an examination of Chinese Christianity not only assists in understanding relevant indigenous religions by analyzing the differences between the stimuli—alien religion—and the
resultant religious movements, but it also illuminates Western
religions. The Chinese adaptation of Christianity strips away the
veneer of ethnocentric values and makes possible a study of
Western religions from a genuinely comparative perspective.
Through the Chinese cultural viewpoint, we gain new insights
into the bases of Western culture. Such studies serve theology as
well as religious studies. Chinese Christianity, as well as Korean,
African, and native American indigenous responses, illustrates
the range of interpretations necessary for a realistically universal (catholic) Christianity.

postface

Comparative Approaches

Participant-observation and comparative religious studies are the bases of the studies incorporated in this work. The focus has been on behavior rather than ideology; that is, an emphasis on ritual activity over belief. Since stressing belief is perhaps one of the unique characteristics of Christianity, it is less suitable than behavior for comparative analysis. Such an approach is normative to cultural anthropologists studying religion, but not to historians of religions until recently, especially in regard to Chinese religion.

Participation-observation, however, is far from unusual among students of Chinese culture in general. For example, in the last two decades, some Western scholars have become initiated Daoist priests. This has allowed them to gain access to esoteric Daoist teachings. For a few scholars, this has led to the adoption of sectarian values, including the position that only Daoism is properly Chinese religion. This stance was apparent when some Western scholars who are Daoist priests canceled their participation in the International Conference on Chinese Religion discussed in Chapter 1. The cancellation was subsequent to a boycott of the conference by the Daoist churches which did not wish to be associated with popular Chinese religion. However, a sectarian perspective tends to lessen the possibilities of comparative studies.

Although the understanding that Chinese culture developed in isolation in its formative years (Ho 1975) has virtually become a truism, if not somewhat exaggerated given recent archaeological (Shaughnessy 1988) and linguistic (T. Chang 1988) studies, that does not negate the need for a comparative perspective to understand Chinese religion in regard to religion *sui generis*.

However, the years of preparation required for a student to analyze classical Chinese texts inhibits sinologists from also becoming familiar with the religions of other cultures. This necessary
training also tends to bias sinology toward literary texts, although
the bases of Chinese religion would have been an oral tradition
at some time, and popular Chinese religion remains in large part
an oral tradition. Comparison with selected contemporary oral
traditions may elucidate the process of religious development in
China. As but one of many examples, divination in several cultures is relevant to divination in China: scapulamancy is cir-·
cumpolar and East African Ifa is quite comparable to the Yi (e.g.,
see Murphy 1988:15–20, 62ff.).

Hence, comparative studies on China are few and far between. More important, until recently there has been little concern that terminology utilized in describing and analyzing
religion in China be applicable cross-culturally so that other
scholars can use their studies for comparative purposes. Chapter 5 is particularly concerned that the terminology utilized in
describing aspects of Chinese religion accords with the study of
other traditions in order that comparative analyses can be carried out.

Recently, there has been a growing interest among historians of religion in ethnocentrism in the study of religion. Both
Chapters 1 and 8 concern specific ways that our understanding
of Chinese religion has been skewed by Eurocentric values. Chapter 9 reverses the studies in the preceding chapters and exam-
ines how a Western religious complex, Christianity, is understood
from Chinese perspectives. This type of analysis not only enables
us to better understand the fundamentals of Chinese religion, but
also provides a comparative approach to Western religions from
a non-Western perspective.

Sinology and history of religions began to merge with the
increased secularization of graduate religious studies programs
approximately two decades ago. Prior to that time, classical
sinologists, when interested in religion at all, tended to adopt
popularized generalizations based on Eurocentric assumptions.
Increasingly these presuppositions have been challenged by
younger scholars, and the last several years have seen a virtual
explosion of revisionist studies. Among a number of examples,

Robert Eno has argued from the paleographic evidence that *di* cannot be understood as a high god, the hitherto normative interpretation. The usual interpretation was not based on analysis but on the assumption that all civilizations, at least those to be admired, had a high god, and the lack of worship of a high god was the mark of a barbarian or heathen (in its literal sense) culture. Eno (1990b:25) argues that

> the term *ti* [di] derived its corporate or generic dimensions from an early function of denoting, singly or collectively, the "fathers" of a lineage. If we allow that the sense of lineage "father" was extended in Shang religion to include the realm of nature spirits . . . we can account for the function of *ti* in Shang texts entirely without recourse to the concept of an abstract supreme deity.

One further methodological aspect of the preceding studies perhaps should be addressed. Several arguments are based on single case examples or analogies. All conclusions derived from such arguments are only tentative and meant to be suggestive for further studies and explorations. For example, in Chapter 4, the use of an unusual decor element on a single bronze provides the key for a potential interpretation that fits other relevant data. This key provides a clue to the type of cultural understanding that is rarely expressed because it is so common. Of course, such an argument is by its very nature highly speculative. Another example is found in Chapter 5, where the transition of a shaman in an unrelated culture separated by enormous distance, both geographically and chronologically, is used to explicate a terminological and behavioral shift described in the *Zhuangzi*. Here the conclusion is still tentative but less speculative. For if the transition in the modern case for which we have considerably more data is explicable by religio-ecological analysis and if this analysis, is relevant to the earlier Chinese context, then the analytical relationship is quite plausible although not definitive.

Needed Studies

Most of the chapters note in passing further work that needs to be carried out with regard to the respective subject areas. Several of the concerns addressed in this book have already become the focus of scholarly attention. As discussed in the relevant chapters, research in the area of ritual studies and women's studies is expanding. An interest in various aspects of ecstatic Chinese religious experience is also developing among scholars. While the studies in this book cover a number of major aspects of Chinese religion that tended to be ignored, there are other important issues that beg for further study. One glaring gap in our understanding of Chinese religion is the realm of mythology.

Because the Western concept of time is linear, with an absolute beginning, Western religions and correspondingly Western studies in mythology focus on creation narratives. The sparsity of these narratives in the Chinese tradition, excepting the well-known Pan Gu myth which originated in India, has led to the view that these narratives have, in the main, been lost. The assumption is that cosmogonic myths had not been recorded, because they were not of interest to the *rujia* scholars. Most studies of myths and legends to date, including those of mine prior to my applying religious studies methodologies to Chinese culture (Paper 1971, 1973b), are within the realm of literary studies.

However, while cosmogony was of philosophical interest, especially in interpreting creation in relation to the mystic experience, it may not have been of major mythic concern to Chinese culture. Instead, the focus of origin myths was on culture heroes, such as Nüwa, and the inception of the aristocratic clans, the ruling clans understood to originate from spirit beings. In other cultures, such as native American, the equivalent of cosmogonic myths may be migration myths, and clan origin myths are normative.

Origin myths of the Shang and Zhou ruling clans are summarized in the *Shi* and later texts, a subject brilliantly investigated by Sarah Allan (1981, 1991). Indeed, the descent of the ruling clans from spirit birds can be found in the earliest dynasties (see Chapter 4) as well as the last. However, in regard to the later Manchurian regime, it is difficult to separate Chinese influence from the predilection in northern Altaic-speaking cultures to conceive of ancestral spirits in avian form. Investigating Chinese mythology without imposing Western values and priorities would open up a rich lode of mythic material, as pioneered in

Western scholarship by Eberhard (1968) and Girardot (1983), among others.

Expanding the Notion of Religion

The study of Chinese religion compels a revised understanding of religion *sui generis*. The notion that religion minimally concerns supernatural entities or powers still persists among historians of religions, despite the broad definition of "religion" common among religionists based on a Tillichean, vague theological focus on "ultimate concern." As discussed in Chapters 2, 5, 6, and 7, Chinese religion presents clear evidence that major forms of religion can so develop that they lose their primary reference to superhuman or supernatural beings, assuming that the dead of one's family are not superhuman, although they are spirits, and nature in and of itself cannot be supernatural. Of course, deities play an important role in the religious life of many Chinese, but most are human ghosts become benevolent. These religious modalities have been the practice and understanding, from a relative standpoint, of many people for nearly two and a half millennia.

For the Chinese ruling elite, the focus of rituals per se as well as values was on society itself. Furthermore, those among the elite, outside of institutional Daoism, who valued the mystic experience tended to interpret the experience atheistically, in the literal sense of the word. The ultimate with which they merged or lost themselves was usually perceived as complete nothingness or the totality of mundane nature, the two experientially and conceptually the same.

Hence, incorporating Chinese religion into the general understanding of religion requires an expansion of the notion of civil religion, originally developed by Bellah (1967; Bellah and Hammond 1980). Rather than a quasi religion, Americanism and other similar developments could be understood as a religion like any other. The qualification of "civil" is not only unnecessary, but it renders comparison difficult. With regard to Chinese religion as discussed in Chapter 2, it is impossible to distinguish elite "civil" rituals from any other sacrificial ritual, including those oriented toward ancestral and nature spirits.

Furthermore, as suggested a decade and a half ago (e.g., Sinclair-Faulkner 1977, Paper 1977b), those rituals and arts which are at the center of attention of a culture cannot easily be distinguished as secular ("civil") or religious. Sports, popular entertainment, and political rituals in the modern Western context have been analyzed by a number of scholars over the last decade as essentially religious. This accords with our understanding of early civilizations; for example, an archery contest as part of early Chinese sacrificial rituals (see Chapter 2) or the ballgame rituals of native American religious traditions.

Only in Western culture, which explicitly separates religion from government, does the opposition of "secular" and "religious" make sense. For only in the West did priests lose the competition with warrior-rulers for sociopolitical authority, the papal state now reduced to a few hectares; hence, the difficulty of the West in understanding Islamic governments. In India, the competition between warriors and priests was resolved by each accepting that the other incorrectly understood they had won. China presents an entirely different situation. The priest and warrior class was one, with the ruler also being the chief priest of the society—secular and sacred cannot be meaningfully distinguished. Accordingly, from a comparative perspective, in modern Western "democracies," politics, along with sports, is the major religious ritual. Voting, and all the activities that lead to it, is the means by which the individual participates in cyclic renewal rituals (particularly in the American, nonparliamentary model).

Similarly, the contemporary Western tendency to remove aesthetic pursuits from what has been their normal religious context since the beginning of human culture at least thirty thousand years ago, has, in effect, deemed art irrelevant to most people. The public art museum, although in architecture often modeled on Greek and Roman temples, such as the National Gallery of Art in Washington, has become more mausoleum than temple. A reinterpretation of art as inherently religious regardless of its content, as was understood in traditional China (see Chapters 6 and 7), could have the opposite effect.

A second major lesson from the study of Chinese religion is that maintaining the notion of exclusiveness between religious forms considerably skews our understanding of any complex religious situation. In China, as discussed in Chapter 1, the interpretation of *sanjiao* as "Three Religions" rather than "Three Teachings" (Wechsler 1985:69) led to major misunderstandings. Although Western religions do practice exclusiveness, in the modern context, they exist in a complex religious environment. For example, while Americanism may be understood as primarily a Protestant development, Americanism is embraced by Catholics, Jews, and others. The congregants at an American Midwestern basketball game may include members of several religions, all ecstatically celebrating the communal ritual together.

In these regards, Hultkrantz's (1956) notion of "configurations of religious modalities" (my modification) may be valid for all complex cultures:

> A configuration of religious belief [modalities] implies that one complex of religious conceptions which occurs beside other complexes of religious conceptions, dominates and momentarily displaces these in the area of active belief [behavior]. The decisive factor for this domination is its fundamental association with a dominant social situation.

Certainly, Hultkrantz's concept, modified to change "belief" to "modality," is highly relevant to religion in China and would resolve many of the difficulties in analyzing religion in modern cultures.

A third area for potential revision is the value placed on rationalism, on only valuing knowledge gained from a logical analysis of sense perception. It is rather ironic that the skewed understanding of Chinese culture in this regard as expressed in the Jesuit *Relations* was a major factor in the development of the European Enlightenment, which in turn has been highly influential on modern China through Marx, Dewey, and others. As pointed out in Chapters 4 through 6, until relatively recently, ecstatic religious experience has been of considerable importance in Chinese religion throughout the ranges of class and education. In contemporary Western culture, ecstatic experience is kept

separate from recognized religious activities, except among Pentacostals, who tend to be disdained by the intelligentsia.

Finally, China provides yet another proof that the West has understood religion from an androcentric perspective. Only recently, with the growing influence of feminist scholarship, has the considerable importance of female spirits in Chinese religion become apparent to Western scholarship (see Chapter 8). The religious roles of females throughout Chinese history still virtually remain an unexamined question.

In summary, the study of non-Indo-European-speaking cultures in general and Chinese religion in particular requires us to expand our understanding of religion. Rather than attempting to understand such traditions with Western models, the analysis of religion in our own culture from a Chinese perspective reaps insights otherwise unobtainable. Applying a broad understanding of religion that includes Chinese culture without distorting it through Eurocentric perceptions could lead us to reinterpret and re-evaluate major aspects of modern Western culture rather than focus on what have become minor aspects.

appendix

Analysis of Bronze Vessels and Decor Relevant to Chapter 4

This Appendix contains a discussion of pre-dynastic and early Zhou bronze ritual vessels with an emphasis on their decor. It documents and analyzes the shift in iconography that is the subject of the second part of Chapter 4.

A *you* with facing birds, according to Umehara (1959), is from the second set found at Baoji Xian in Shansi Province. Other than the bird decor being the central design, its workmanship is typical of very late Shang pieces. Its reputed provenance is of interest, for it is the traditional home of the Zhou. Max Loehr (1968:98–100,pl.41) considered that it may have been manufactured by a Shang artisan for the predynastic Zhou. Stylistically related vessels would include *you* vessels at the Boston Museum of Fine Arts (Loehr 1968:pl.41), the Minneapolis Museum of Art (Loehr 1968:pl.40), the Metropolitan Museum of Art (W. Watson 1962a:pl.21a), and the Freer Gallery of Art (Pope 1967:1,no.50). In regard to the latter, the editors of the catalog consider that the vessel "might have been cast by Chou bronze artisans before the conquest of the Shang." Of similar appearance is the *you* excavated in Hunan Province in 1970. Although found to the south of the Zhou homeland, it was not associated with a tomb burial but was found alone filled with jade discs, indicating that it had been carried there at a later date (Fong 1980:pl.25). These vessels all have facing birds of the Shang type, normally found only on upper friezes or as lid handles, in the central frieze where the *taotie* would normally be found.

Also associated with the Baoji sets are vessels that are unquestionably of early Zhou type with non-Shang bird decor.

These vessels include a *gui* with the early Zhou inverted cup lid and high square foot (W. Watson 1962a:pl.32). Similar to this vessel is the Brundage *guang* (d'Argencé 1966:pl.21a) and an almost identical piece in the Princeton Art Museum that Loehr considers predynastic Zhou (Loehr 1968:pl.50). These vessels have early versions of the Zhou bird motif with large back-sweeping crest (see fig. 9a in Chapter 4). A third type of vessel that may be predynastic Zhou or transitional is the Brundage *ding* with bird-shaped legs, the body of the vessel itself retaining the *taotie* design (d'Argencé 1966:pl.5).

Among the earliest Zhou vessels datable by inscription, the Brundage square *ding*, excavated from a royal tomb near Fengxing of the Zhou homeland, has legs similar to the above-mentioned *ding*, but with crested bird design as well (d'Argencé 1966:pl.28). Its plastic decor is of the transitional type; that is, without the inscription, the piece might well have been considered late Shang. The bird decor on this vessel has a forward-pointed head of the Shang type; more typical of early Zhou bird decor is a back-turned head. Two examples of very early Zhou pieces with the typical Zhou bird decor are the *you* excavated in 1959 in Anhwei (*Trésors* 1973:no.95) and the Buckingham *zun* (Kelley and Ch'en 1946:pl.23).

A second relatively common type of early Zhou ritual decor motif is the elephant. Although vessels in the shapes of elephants were produced in the Shang period—for example, the Freer *zun* (Pope 1967:no.40) and the vessel excavated in 1975 (Fong 1980:pl.24)—only on early Zhou vessels do elephants take the place of the *taotie* as the main frieze decor. One early Zhou type is an elephant-headed figure with a spiral body; an example is the set of four vessels excavated in Shansi Province in 1971 (Fong 1980:pls.49–51). Although this design is not always considered to represent an elephant (as it has a clawed foreleg), the extension of the curled upper lip into a long protuberance with double curve and split, flared end is unquestionably meant to represent the trunk of a trumpeting elephant (see fig. 10a). The identification of the head as that of an elephant is confirmed by the Buckingham *gui* with shape and main decor similar to the *gui* of the above-mentioned set (Kelly and Ch'en 1946:pl.20).

Here, the design replacing the *taotie* on the high foot has raised-wing and feathered-body creatures with unmistakably realistic elephant heads ill fitting the bodies (see fig. 10b). A logical conclusion would be that the foot design is a more explicit version of the vessel-body design, that the spiral-bodied monster represents a flying elephant-headed bird, and that the spirals represent an abstraction of winged bodies.

Also supporting the elephant identification is a *gui* excavated near Peking in 1974 with clearly depicted full-bodied elephants as *taotie* replacement decor (Fong 1980:pl.57). This design has been related to the set excavated in 1971 (Fong 1980:212). The British Museum houses a similar vessel without the four feet (W. Watson 1962a:pl.39a). The vessel is supported by four legs representing elephant trunks protruding from animal mouths; two of these trunks descend from bird-shaped handles. An early Zhou *guang*, excavated in 1976, has a similar handle, except that the elephant trunk is upturned; the rest of the vessel is of Shang-like appearance with a normal *taotie* design (Fong 1980:pl.45). On a *gui* in the Pillsbury Collection, the head of a similar bird handle is replaced by an explicitly depicted elephant's head with raised trunk and protruding tusks (Karlgren 1952:pl.35). Another early Zhou *zun* in the Shanghai Museum with *taotie* design has four plastic elephant heads with upturned trunks on the shoulder of the vessel (*Zhongguo* 1976:pl.38). The clearly represented elephant trunks descending from the bird handles indicate that the bottom appendages to the bird handles, found in vessels as early as the predynastic Zhou period, are abstracted elephant trunks. For example, on the previously mentioned Princeton and Brundage *guang*, there are two appendages dropping from the bird handle. The forward one has a curled split end like an elephant trunk. The elephant-headed bird motif is on a square-footed *gui*, excavated at the proto-Zhou capital of Qishou, that is dated by inscription to the first year of King Wen's victory over the Shang (Cheng 1963:220,pl.16a).

The sweeping crest of the bird decor becomes lengthy and elaborate (e.g., Loehr 1968:pls.51–52), occasionally taking on circles that give the plumage the appearance of a peacock's tail feathers (Loehr 1968:pl.49). In this regard, a vessel excavated in

1955 in Liaoning Province and tentatively dated to the third Zhou reign is of particular interest to later discussion. Described as having "the motif of the crested dragon with a bird's body" (Fong 1980: 209,pl.53; the head may be that of an elephant as it is similar to the spiral-bodied figures), the crest ends in an anthropomorphic design in the exact shape of the early Zhou glyph *wang* (king), including the upturned ends of the bottom bar. The spread cheek pieces of the horned mask helmet form the upper bar; the extended arms form the middle bar; and the legs, in a nonanthropomorphic spread, form the lower bar (see fig. 11a). If only a human form were intended, the legs would have formed rather an inverted "V."

Within a century following the establishment of the Zhou reign, both related design motifs—the crested bird and elephant bird—disappear, to be replaced by other design motifs. Two unusual vessels (part of a four-vessel set), a square *yi* and square *zun* excavated in 1956 in Shansi Province and dated to the late tenth to early ninth centuries, have identical designs that maintain elements of the earlier decor (Fong 1980:pls.50, 60). (The square *yi* is quite similar, especially in handle shape, to one in the Shanghai Museum, although the central frieze decor is more ambiguous in import; this vessel is linked by inscription to the Shansi set but is more precisely dated to the reign of King Yi.) The main frieze consists of a large circular design reminiscent of Shang-period whorls that Ma Cheng-yuan identifies as "a pictorialization of the graph meaning 'brightness of fire'" (Fong 1980:8). However, rather than the six clockwise-spiraling inner circles of the Shang design, the large circle has four clockwise-spiraling circles, and the entire circle is surrounded by a flamelike design. Hence, this design probably represents the sun, and the subcircles represent the four directions. On each side of the circle design is a creature close in depiction to the elephant-headed bird motif, although the workmanship is relatively crude for precise identification. The large handles consist entirely of an upturned elephant trunk, with the lower flange being the abstract elephant-trunk design.

references

Aijmer, Goran. 1964. *The Dragon Boat Festival on the Hupeh-Hunan Plain, Central China.* Stockholm: Statens Etnografiska Museet.

Ahern, Emily. 1973. *The Cult of the Dead in a Chinese Village.* Stanford, Calif.: Stanford University Press.

———. 1975. "The Power and Pollution of Chinese Women." In *Women in Chinese Society.* Edited by Margery Wolf and Roxanne Witke. Stanford, Calif.: Stanford University Press.

Allan, Sarah. 1979. "Shang Foundations of Modern Chinese Folk Religions." In *Legend, Lore, and Religion in China.* Edited by Sarah Allen and Alvin P. Cohen. San Francisco: CMC, Inc.

———. 1981. "Sons of Suns: Myth and Totemism in Early China." *Bulletin of the School of Oriental and African Studies* 44: 290–326.

———. 1985–1987. "Myth and Meaning in Shang Bronze Motifs." *Early China* 11–12: 283–89.

———. 1991. *The Shape of the Turtle: Myth, Art, and Cosmos in Early China.* Albany: State University of New York Press.

Allen, Catherine J. 1988. *The Hold Life Has: Coca and Cultural Identity in an Andean Community.* Washington, D.C.: Smithsonian Institution Press.

Anati, Emmanuel. 1960. *La civilisation du Val Camonica.* Paris: Arthaud.

Anderson, E. N., Jr., and Maria L. Anderson. 1977. "Modern China: South." In *Food in Chinese Culture.* Edited by Kwang-chih Chang. New Haven, Conn.: Yale University Press.

Andritzky, Walter. 1989. "Sociopsychotherapeutic Functions of Ayahuasca Healing in Amazonia." *Journal of Psychoactive Drugs* 21: 77–89.

Arlington, L. C., and William Lewisohn. 1935. *In Search of Old Peking.* Peking. Reprinted New York: Paragon, 1967.

Armstrong, David. 1994. "Drinking with the Dead: Alcohol and Altered States in Ancestor Veneration Rituals of Zhou Dynasty China and Iron Age Palestine." Unpublished M.A. thesis. Toronto: York University.

Bachhofer, Ludwig. 1946. *A Short History of Chinese Art*. New York: Pantheon Books.

Bagley, Robert W. 1980. "The Rise of the Western Zhou Dynasty." In *The Great Bronze Age of China*. Edited by Wen Fong. New York: Metropolitan Museum of Art.

Bailey, Alfred G. 1969. *The Conflict of Europeans and Eastern Algonkian Cultures, 1504–1700*. 2nd edition. Toronto: University of Toronto Press.

Baker, Dwight Condo. 1925. *T'ai Shan*. Shanghai: Commercial Press.

Balázs, Étienne. 1950. "La crise sociale et la philosophie politique à la fin des Han." *T'oung Pao* 39: 83–131.

Barnard, Noel. 1961. *Bronze Casting and Bronze Alloys in Ancient China*. Monumenta Serica Monograph, no. 14. Canberra: Australian National University.

Barnstone, Willis, and Ko Ching-po. 1972. *The Poems of Mao Tse-tung*. New York: Harper & Row.

Bauer, Wolfgang. 1976. *China and the Search for Happiness*. Translated by Michael Shaw. New York: Seabury Press.

Bell, Catherine. 1989. "Religion and Chinese Culture: Toward an Assessment of 'Popular Religion'." *History of Religions* 29: 35–57.

Bellah, Robert N.. 1967. "Civil Religion in America." *Daedalus*. Winter: 1–21.

Bellah, Robert N. and Phillip E. Hammond, editors. 1980. *Varieties of Civil Religion*. San Francisco: Harper & Row.

Benedict, Ruth. 1923. "The Concept of the Guardian Spirit in North America." *Memoirs of the American Anthropological Association* 12.

Benn, Charles. 1987. "Religious Aspects of Emperor Hsüan-tsung's Taoist Ideology." In *Buddhist and Taoist Practices in Medieval Chinese Society*. Edited by David W. Chappell. Honolulu: University of Hawaii Press.

Berger, Pamela. 1985. *The Goddess Obscured: Transformation of the Grain Protectress from Goddess to Saint*. Boston: Beacon Press.

Berglie, Per-Arne. 1976. "Preliminary Remarks on Some Tibetan 'Spirit-Mediums' in Nepal." *Kailash: A Journal of Himalayan Studies* 4: 85–108.

Bharati, Agehananda. 1976. *The Light at the Center: Context and Pretext of Modern Mysticism*. Santa Barbara, Calif.: Ross Erickson.

Bilsky, Lester James. 1975. *The State Religion of China*. Taipei: Orient Cultural Service.

Biot, Éduard, translator. 1851. *Le Tscheou-li*. Paris: L'Imprimerie Nationale.

Birch, Cyril. 1965. *Anthology of Chinese Literature*. New York: Grove Press.

Black, Alison H. 1986. "Gender and Cosmology in Chinese Correlative Thinking." In *Gender and Religion: On the Complexity of Symbols*. Edited by Caroline Walker Bynum, Steven Harrell, and Paula Richman. Boston: Beacon Press.

Blacker, Carmin. 1971. "Millenarian Aspects of the New Religions in Japan." In *Tradition and Modernization in Japanese Culture*. Edited by Donald H. Shively. Princeton, N.J.: Princeton University Press.

Boardman, Eugene Powers. 1952. *Christian Influence upon the Ideology of the Taiping Rebellion, 1851–1864*. Madison: University of Wisconsin Press.

Boas, Franz. 1902. *Tsimshian Texts*. Bureau of American Ethnology, Bulletin 27. Washington, D.C.

———. 1916. *Tsimshian Mythology*. Bureau of American Ethnology, Thirty-first Annual Report (1909–1910). Washington, D.C.

Bodde, Derk. 1975. *Festivals in Classical China*. Princeton, N.J.: Princeton University Press.

Boehme, Jacob. 1958. *Six Theosophic Points and Other Writings*. Translated by J. R. Earle. Ann Arbor: University of Michigan Press.

Boltz, Judith Magee. 1986. "In Homage to T'ien-fei." *Journal of the American Oriental Society* 106: 211–32.

Brown, Joseph Epes. 1977. "The Question of 'Mysticism' within Native American Traditions." In *Mystics and Scholars: The Calgary Conference on Mysticism 1976*. Edited by Harold Coward and Terence Penelhum. SR Supplements 3. Waterloo, Ont.: Wilfrid Laurier University Press.

Bucke, R. M. 1901. *Cosmic Consciousness*. Philadelphia: Innes.

Bush, Susan. 1971. *The Chinese Literati on Painting*. Cambridge, Mass.: Harvard University Press.

Cahill, James. 1960. "Confucian Elements in the Theory of Painting." In *The Confucian Persuasion*. Edited by Arthur F. Wright. Stanford, Calif.: Stanford University Press.

———. 1976. *Hills beyond River; Chinese Painting of the Yüan Dynasty, 1279–1368*. Tokyo: Weatherhill.

———. 1978. *Parting at the Shore; Chinese Painting of the Early and Middle Ming Dynasty, 1368–1580*. Tokyo: Weatherhill.

Cahill, Suzanne E. 1984. "Besides the Turquoise Pond: The Shrine of the Queen Mother of the West in Medieval Chinese Poetry and Religious Practice." *Journal of Chinese Religions* 12 (1984): 19–32.

———. 1986. "Performers and Female Taoist Adepts: Hsi Wang Mu as the Patron Deity of Women in Medieval China." *Journal of the American Oriental Society* 106: 155–68.

———. I.p. *Transcendence and Divine Passion: The Queen Mother of the West in Medieval China*. Stanford, Calif.: Stanford University Press.

Cai Xianghui. 1989. *Beigang chaotiangung zhi*. Pei-kang, Taiwan: Ch'ao T'ien Kung.

Cammann, Schuyler. 1953. "Types of Symbols in Chinese Art." In *Studies in Chinese Thought*. Edited by A. F. Wright. Chicago: University of Chicago Press.

Cassirer, Ernst. 1924. *Philosphie des formes symboliques. 2: La pensée mythique*. Paris.

Chang Chu-kun. 1988. "An Introduction to Korean Shamanism." Translated by Yoo Young-sic. In *Shamanism: The Spirit World of Korea*. Edited by Chai-shin Yu and R. Guiso. Berkeley, Calif.: Asian Humanities Press.

Chang Chung-yüan. 1963. *Creativity and Taoism*. New York: The Julian Press.

Chang Kwang-chih. 1963. "Changing Relationship of Man and Animal in Shang and Chou Myths and Art," *Bulletin of the Institute of Ethnology, Academia Sinica* (Nankang) 16: 33–46.

————. 1976. *Early Chinese Civilization: Anthropological Perspectives*. Cambridge, Mass.: Harvard University Press.

————. 1977a. *The Archeology of Ancient China*. 3d edition. New Haven, Conn.: Yale University Press.

————. 1977b. *Food in Chinese Culture*. New Haven, Conn.: Yale University Press.

————. 1978. "*Tieh kan*: A Key to the History of the Shang." In *Ancient China: Studies in Early Civilization*. Edited by David T. Roy and Tsuen-hsuin Tsien. Hong Kong: Chinese Universities Press.

————. 1980. *Shang Civilization*. New Haven, Conn.: Yale University Press.

————. 1981. "The Animal in Shang and Chou Bronze Art." *Harvard Journal of Asiatic Studies* 41: 527–54.

————. 1983. *Art, Myth and Ritual: The Path to Political Authority in Ancient China*. Cambridge, Mass.: Harvard University Press.

Chang Tsung-tung. 1988. "Indo-European Vocabulary in Old Chinese: A New Thesis on the Emergence of Chinese Language and Civilization in the Late Neolithic Age." *Sino-Platonic Papers* 7: 1–56.

Chavannes, Edouard. 1910a. *Cinq cents contes et apologues*. Paris: Ernest Leroux.

————. 1910b. *Le T'ai Chan*. Annales du Musée Guimet. Paris: Ernest Leroux.

Chaves, Jonathan. 1976. *Mei Yao-ch'en and the Development of Early Sung Poetry*. New York: Columbia University Press.

————. 1977. "The Legacy of Ts'ang Chieh: The Written Word as Magic." *Oriental Art* 23: 200–15.

Ch'en, Jerome. 1965. *Mao and the Chinese Revolution*. Oxford: Oxford University Press.

Chen Meng-jia. 1936. "Shangdai de shenhau yu wushu," *Yenjing xuehbao* 20: 555–59.

Chen Yinko. 1983. "Tianshidao yu Binhai dicheng zhi guanxi." *Bulletin of the National Research Institute of History and Philosophy, Academia Sinica* (Beijing), 3: 462–66.

282   THE SPIRITS ARE DRUNK

Chen Zhungyu. 1969. "Yindai gu chi jung de long xing tu an zhi fen xi" (An analysis of the dragon design on the bone artifacts of the Shang dynasty). *Bulletin of the Institute of Philology, Academia Sinica* (Nankang) 41 (3): 455–96.

Cheng, J. C. 1963. *Chinese Sources for the Taiping Rebellion, 1850–1864*. Hong Kong: Chinese University Press.

Cheng Te-k'un. 1963. *Archeology in China*. 3: *Chou China*. Cambridge: W. Heffer & Sons.

Childs-Johnson, Elizabeth. 1984. "Relationships between Symbolism and Function in Ritual Bronze Art of the Shang: New Archaeological and Bone Inscriptional Evidence." Unpublished Ph.D. dissertation. New York: Institute of Fine Arts.

———. 1987. "The Ancestor Spirit and Animal Mask in Shang Ritual Art." Unpublished paper delivered at the International Symposium on the Yin-Shang Culture of China. Anyang.

Chou Ju-hsi. 1977. *The 'Hua-yü-lu' and Tao-chi's Theory of Painting*. Tempe: Arizona State University Center for Asian Studies.

Chow, Tse-tsung. 1978. "The Childbirth Myth and Ancient Chinese Medicine: A Study of Aspects of the *Wu* Tradition." In *Ancient China: Studies in Early Civilization*. Edited by David T. Roy and Tsuen-hsuin Tsien. Hong Kong: Chinese University of Hong Kong Press.

———. 1986. *Gu wuyi yu "liushi" kao*. Taipei: Lien Ching Publishing Co.

Clarke, Prescott, and J. S. Gregory. 1982. *Western Reports on the Taiping*. Honolulu: University Press of Hawaii.

Cohen, Alvin P. 1992. "Biographical Notes on a Taiwanese Red-Head Taoist." *Journal of Chinese Religions* 20: 187–201.

Concordance to Chuang Tzu, A. 1947. Harvard-Yenching Institute Sinological Index Series, Supplement No. 20. Cambridge, Mass.: Harvard University Press.

Consten, Eleanor von Erdberg. 1957. "A Terminology of Chinese Bronze Decoration I." *Monumenta Serica* 16:287–314.

———. 1958. "A Terminology of Chinese Bronze Decoration II." *Monumenta Serica* 17: 208–54.

Contag, Victoria, and Wang Chi-ch'üan. 1940. *Mader und Sammler-Stempel aus der Ming und Ch'ing Zeit*. Shanghai: Commercial Press.

Craven, Margaret. 1967. *I Heard the Owl Call My Name*. Toronto: Clarke, Irwin & Co.

Creel, Heerlee G. 1937. *The Birth of China*. New York: Frederick Ungar.

———. 1960. *Confucius and the Chinese Way*. New York: Harper & Row (reprint of 1949: *Confucius; The Man and the Myth*).

———. 1970. *The Origins of Statecraft in China*. 1: *The Western Chou Empire*. Chicago: University of Chicago Press.

Curwin, C. A. 1977. *Taiping Rebel, The Deposition of Li Hsiu-ch'eng*. Cambridge: Cambridge University Press.

d'Aquili, G., and Charles D. Laughlin, Jr. 1979. "The Neurobiology of Myth and Ritual." In *The Spectrum of Ritual, A Biogenic Structural Analysis*. Edited by G. d'Aquili, Charles D. Laughlin, Jr., and John McManus. New York: Columbia University Press.

d'Argencé, René-Yvon Lefebvre. 1966. *Ancient Chinese Bronzes in the Avery Brundage Collection*. Berkeley, Calif.: Diablo Press.

Dai Chiwei. 1973. *Xiao yueh lou yin xiang*. (From *Meishu congshu*.). Taipei: World Book Co.

David, Sir Percival. 1971. *Chinese Connoisseurship*. London: Faber & Faber.

de Bary, Wm. Theodore, editor. 1964. *Sources of Chinese Tradition*. New York: Columbia University Press.

de Groot, J. J. M. 1910. *The Religious System of China*. Leiden: E. J. Brill.

Deikman, Arthur J. 1963. "Experimental Meditation." *Journal of Nervous and Mental Diseases* 136: 329–373.

———. 1977. "Bimodal Consciousness and the Mystic Experience." In *Symposium on Consciousness*. Edited by Philip R. Lee et al. Harmondsworth, England: Penguin Books.

Despeux, Catherine. 1989. "Gymnastics: The Ancient Tradition." In *Taoist Meditation and Longevity Techniques*. Edited by Livia Kohn. Ann Arbor: Center for Chinese Studies, University of Michigan.

Detienne, Marcel, and Jean-Pierre Vernant. 1989. *The Cuisine of Sacrifice among the Greeks*. Translated by Paula Wissing. Chicago: University of Chicago Press.

Dewdney, Selwyn. 1975. *The Sacred Scrolls of the Southern Ojibway*. Toronto: University of Toronto Press.

DeWoskin, Kenneth J. 1983. *Doctors, Diviners, and Magicians: Biographies of "Fang-shih"*. New York: Columbia University Press.

Dohrenwend, Doris. 1975. "Jade Demonic Images from Early China." *Ars Orientalis* 10: 55–78.

Doolittle, Justus. 1865. *Social Life of the Chinese*. New York: Harper & Brothers.

Drinnon, Richard. 1980. *Facing West: The Metaphysics of Indian-Hating and Empire-Building*. New York: New American Library.

Duara, Prasenjit. 1991. "Knowledge and Power in the Discourse of Modernity: The Campaigns against Popular Religion in Early Twentieth-Century China." *Journal of Asian Studies* 50: 67–83.

Dudbridge, Glen. 1978. *The Legend of Miao-shan*. London: Ithaca Press.

Dun Lichen. 1936. *Yenjing suishi ji* (Annual customs and festivals in Beijing). Translated by Derk Bodde. Hong Kong: Henri Vetch.

Durkheim, Émile. 1910. *Formes élémentaires de la pensée religieuse*. Paris.

Eberhard, Wolfram. 1968. *The Local Cultures of South and East Asia*. Translated by Alide Eberhard. Leiden: E. J. Brill.

Ebrey, Patricia Buckley. 1991. *Chu Hsi's Family Rituals*. Princeton, N.J.: Princeton Universtiy Press.

Ecke, Yu-ho. 1971. *Chinese Calligraphy*. Philadelphia: Philadelphia Museum of Art.

Eliade, Mircea. 1960. *Myths, Dreams, and Mysteries*. Translated by Philip Mainet. New York: Harper & Row.

———. 1964. *Shamanism, Archaic Techniques of Ecstacy*. Translated by Willard R. Trask. New York: Bollingen Foundation.

———. 1965. *The Two and the One*. Translated by J. M. Cohen. New York: Harper & Row.

Elliot, Alan J.A. 1955. *Chinese Spirit Medium Cults in Singapore*. London: London School of Economics and Political Science.

Eno, Robert. 1990a. *The Confucian Creation of Heaven: Philosophy and the Defense of Ritual Mastery*. Albany: State University of New York Press.

1990b. "Was There a High God *Ti* in Shang Religion?" *Early China* 15: 1–26.

Erkes, Eduard. 1926. "Chinesisch-Amerikanische Mythenparallelen." *T'oung Pao* 24: 32–53.

Fehl, Noah. 1971. *Li: Rites and Propriety in Literature and Life.* Hong Kong: Chinese University of Hong Kong Press.

Fingarette, Herbert. 1972. *Confucius—The Secular As Sacred.* New York: Harper & Row.

Fisher, H. R., R. I. Simpson, and B. Kapur. 1987. "Calculation of Blood Alcohol Concentration (BAC) by Sex, Weight, Number of Drinks, and Time." *Canadian Journal of Public Health* 78: 300–4.

Fong Wen. 1976. "Archaism as a 'Primitive' Style." In *Artist and Traditions.* Edited by Christian F. Murck. Princeton, N.J.: Princeton University Press.

———. 1980. *The Great Bronze Age of China.* Editor. New York: Metropolitan Museum of Art.

Forrest, Robert J. 1867. "The Christianity of Hung Tsiu Tsuen, A Review of Taeping Books." *Journal of the North Branch of the Royal Asiatic Society* N.S. 4.

Fox, Cyril Fred. 1959. *Life and Death in the Bronze Age.* London: Routledge & Kegan Paul.

Frankel, Hans. 1952. "The Plum Tree in Chinese Literature." *Asiatische Studien* 6: 88–115.

Fraser, Douglas. 1968. *Early Chinese Art and the Pacific Basin.* New York: Intercultural Arts Press.

———. 1972. "Early Chinese Artistic Influence in Melanesia." In *Early Chinese Art and Its Possible Influences in the Pacific Basin.* Edited by Noel Barnard and Douglas Fraser. New York: Intercultural Arts Press.

Frazer, James. 1915. *The Golden Bough.* 3rd edition. London: Macmillan.

Freedman, Maurice. 1974. "On the Sociological Study of Chinese Religion." In *Religion and Ritual in Chinese Society.* Edited by Arthur P. Wolfe. Stanford, Calif.: Stanford University Press.

Freeman, Michael. 1977. "Sung." In *Food in Chinese Culture.* Edited by Kwang-chih Chang. New Haven, Conn.: Yale University Press.

Frodsham, J. D. 1967. *The Murmuring Stream*. Kuala Lumpur: University of Malaya Press.

Frozen Tombs: The Culture and Art of the Ancient Tribes of Siberia. 1978. London: British Museum.

Gao Zhao. 1968. *Guan shi lu*. (From *Meishu congshu*.) In *Yu shi gu chi pu lu yi*. Taipei: World Book Co.

Garner, H., and M. Medley. 1969. *Chinese Art*. New York: Asia Society.

Geertz, Clifford. 1966. "Religion as a Cultural System." In *Anthropological Approaches to the Study of Religion*. Edited by Michael Banton. London: Tavistock Publications.

Gernet, Jacques. 1970. *Daily Life in China*. Translated by H. M. Wright. Stanford, Calif.: Stanford University Press.

———. 1985. *China and the Christian Impact*. Translated by Janet Lloyd. Cambridge: Cambridge University Press.

Gimbutas, Marija. 1989. *The Language of the Goddess*. New York: Harper & Row.

Girardot, Norman. 1978. " 'Returning to the Beginning' and the Arts of Mr. Hun-tun in the *Chuang-tzu*," *Journal of Chinese Philosophy* 5: 21–69.

———. 1983. *Myth and Meaning in Early Taoism, The Theme of Chaos*. Berkeley and Los Angeles: University of California Press.

———. 1992. "Very Small Books about Large Subjects: A Prefatory Appreciation of the Enduring Legacy of Laurence G. Thompson's *Chinese Religion, An Introduction*." *Journal of Chinese Religions* 20: 9–15.

Graham, A. C. N.d. "Chuang-Tzu and the Rambling Mode." In *The Art and Profession of Translation*. Edited by T. C. Lai. Hong Kong: Hong Kong Translation Society.

———. 1961. "The Date and Composition of Liehtzyy." *Asia Major* N.S. 8: 139–98.

———. 1967. "Chuang-tzu's Essay on Seeing Things as Equal." *History of Religions* 9: 137–59.

———. 1979. "How Much of *Chuang Tzu* Did Chuang Tzu Write?" In *Studies in Chinese Classical Thought*. Edited by Henry Rosemont,

Jr., and Benjamin I. Schwartz. *Journal of the American Academy of Religion Thematic Issue* 47 (3S): 459–502.

Graham, David Crockett. 1961. *Religion in Southwest China.* Washington, D.C.: Smithsonian Press.

Granet, Marcel. 1929. *Fêtes et chansons anciennes de la Chine.* Paris: Libraire Ernest Leroux.

———. 1930. *Chinese Civilization.* London: Kegan, Paul.

Gulik, Robert Hans van. 1938. *Mi Fu on Inkstones.* Peking: Henri Vetch.

———. 1940. *The Lore of the Chinese Lute, An Essay in Ch'in Ideology.* Tokyo: Sophia University.

———. 1941. *Hsi K'ang and His Poetical Essay on the Lute.* Tokyo: Sophia University.

Hallowell, A. Irwin. 1955a. "Aggression in Saulteaux Society." In *Culture and Experience.* Philadelphia: University of Pennsylvania Press.

———. 1955b. "Some Psychological Characteristics of the Northeastern Indians." In *Culture and Experience.* Philadelphia: University of Pennsylvania Press.

———. 1976. "The Role of Dreams in Ojibwa Culture." In *Contributions to Anthropology.* Chicago: University of Chicago Press.

Handbook of the Cleveland Museum of Art. 1970. Cleveland.

Hanna, J.M. 1976. "Ethnic Groups, Human Variation, and Alcohol Use." In *Cross-Cultural Approaches to the Study of Alcohol: An Interdisciplinary Perspective.* Edited by M. Everett, J. Waddell and D. Heath. The Hague: Mouton.

Hansen, Valerie. 1990. *Changing Gods in Medieval China, 1127–1276.* Princeton, N.J.: Princeton University Press.

Hansford, S. Howard. 1968. *Chinese Carved Jades.* London: Faber & Faber.

Hardy, Alister. 1979. *The Spiritual Nature of Man.* Oxford: Clarendon Press.

Harrell, Steven. 1979. "The Concept of 'Soul' in Chinese Folk Religion." *Journal of Asian Studies* 38: 519–28.

———. 1986. "Men, Women, and Ghosts in Taiwanese Folk Religion." In *Gender and Religion: On the Complexity of Symbols.* Edited by

Caroline Walker Bynum, Steven Harrell, and Paula Richman. Boston: Beacon Press.

Harva, Uno. 1938. *Die religiösen Vorstellungen der altaischen Völker*. Folklore Fellows Communications no. 125. Helsinki.

Hawkes, Christopher. 1954. "Archeological Theory and Method: Some Suggestions from the Old World." *American Anthropologist* 56: 155–68.

Hawkes, David. 1959. *Ch'u Tz'u: The Songs of the South*. London: Oxford University Press.

Hay, John. 1985. *Kernels of Energy, Bones of Earth: The Rock in Chinese Art*. New York: China Institute in America.

Hayashi Minao. 1972. "The Twelve Gods of the Chan-Kuo Period Silk Manuscript Excavated at Ch'ang-Sha." Translated by Noel Barnard. In *Early Chinese Art and Its Possible Influences in the Pacific Basin*. Edited by Noel Barnard and Douglas Fraser. New York: Intercultural Arts Press.

Hentze, Carl. 1936. *Objets rituels, croyances et dieux antiques de la Chine et de l'Amérique*. Anvers: Éditions "de Sikkel."

Hickerson, Harold. 1962. "Notes on the Post-Contact Origin of the Midewiwin." *Ethnohistory* 9: 404–23.

———. 1963. "The Sociohistorical Significance of Two Chippewa Ceremonials." *American Anthropologist* N.S. 65: 67–85.

———. 1970. *The Chippewa and Their Neighbors: A Study in Ethnohistory*. New York: Holt, Rinehart and Winston.

Hightower, James R. 1954. "Ch'u Yüan Studies." *Silver Jubilee Volume of the Zinbun-Kagaku-Kenkyusyo*. Kyoto: Kyoto University.

———. 1970. *The Poetry of T'ao Ch'ien*. Oxford: Oxford University Press.

Hisayaki Miyakawa. 1979. "Local Cults and Mount Lu at the Time of Sun En's Rebellion." In *Facets of Taoism*. Edited by Holmes Welch and Anna Seidel. New Haven, Conn.: Yale University Press.

Historical Relics Unearthed in New China. 1972. Beijing: Foreign Languages Press.

Ho P'ing-ti. 1975. *The Cradle of the East*. Chicago: University of Chicago Press.

Ho Wai-kam. 1976. "Tung Ch'i-ch'ang's New Orthodoxy." In *Artists and Traditions*. Edited by Christian F. Murck. Princeton, N.J.: Princeton University Press.

Hoffman, Helmut. 1967. *Symbolik der Tibetischen Religionen und des Shamanismus*. Stuttgart: Anton Hiersmann.

Hoffman, W. J. 1891. *The Midéwiwin or "Grand Medicine Society" of the Ojibwa*. U.S. Bureau of American Ethnology Seventh Annual Report, 1885–1886. Washington, D.C.

Holzman, Donald. 1976. *Poetry and Politics: The Life and Works of Juan Chi, A.D. 210–263*. Cambridge: Cambridge University Press.

Hooke, S. H. 1933. "The Myth and Ritual Patterns of the Ancient East." In *Myth and Ritual*. Edited by S. H. Hooke. London: Oxford University Press.

Hsü, Cho-yun. 1965. *Ancient China in Transition, An Analysis of Social Mobility, 722–222 B.C.* Stanford, Calif.: Stanford University Press.

Huang Liu Hung. 1984. *A Complete Book of Happiness and Benevolence (Fuhui ch'üan-shu), A Manual for Local Magistrates in Seventeenth-Century China*. Translated by Djang Chu. Tucson: University of Arizona Press.

Hubert, M., and M. Mauss. 1899. "Essai sur la nature et la function du sacrifice." Reprinted in M. Mauss, *Oevres*. 1. Paris.

Hultkrantz, Åke. 1956. "Configurations of Beliefs among the Wind River Shoshoni." *Ethnos* 21: 194–215.

———. 1957. *The North American Orpheus Tradition*. Statens Museum Etnografisca Monograph 2. Stockholm.

———. 1965. "Types of Religion in the Arctic Hunting Cultures, A Religio-Ecological Approach." In *Hunting and Fishing*. Edited by Harold Hoarfner. Lulea, Sweden: Norrbttens Museum.

———. 1966. "An Ecological Approach to Religion." *Ethnos* 31: 131–50.

———. 1973. "A Definition of Shamanism." *Temenos* 9: 25–37.

———. 1979. "Ritual in Native North American Religions." In *Native Religious Traditions*. Edited by Earle II. Waugh and K. Dad Prithipaul. Waterloo, Ont.: Wilfrid Laurier University Press.

———. 1980. "The Problem of Christian Influence on Northern Algonkian Eschatology." *Studies in Religion* 9: 161–84.

Hurvitz, Leon. 1970. "Tsung Ping's Commentary on Landscape Painting." *Artibus Asiae* 32: 146–56.

Jacobsen, Thorkild. 1975. "Religious Drama in Ancient Mesopotamia." In *Unity and Diversity.* Edited by Hans Goedicke and J. J. M. Roberts. Baltimore: The Johns Hopkins University Press.

James, William. 1902. *The Varieties of Religious Experience.* Reprinted New York: New American Library, 1958.

Jameson, Anna Burwell. 1943. *Winter Studies and Summer Rambles in Canada.* Edited by James J. Talman and Elsie McLeod Murray. Toronto: T. Nelson and Sons (originally published 1837).

Jen Yu-wen. 1973. *The Taiping Revolutionary Movement.* New Haven, Conn.: Yale University Press.

Jenness, Diamond. 1935. *The Ojibwa Indians of Parry Island: Their Social and Religious Life.* Ottawa: National Museum of Canada.

Jilek, Wolfgang C. 1974. *Salish Indian Mental Health and Culture Change.* Toronto: Holt, Rinehart and Winston.

Jin Yufu and Tian Yuqing. 1955. *Taiping tianguo shiliao.* Beijing.

Jochim, Christian. 1988. " 'Great' and 'Little,' 'Grid' and 'Group': Defining the Poles of the Elite-Popular Continuum in Chinese Religion." *Journal of Chinese Religions* 16: 18–42.

———. 1992. "A Report on the 'International Academic Conference on Religion' Beijing, April 6–10, 1992." *Journal of Chinese Religions* 20: 221–24.

Johnson, Elizabeth L. 1988. "Grieving for the Dead, Grieving for the Living: Funeral Laments of Hakka Women." In *Death Ritual in Late Imperial and Modern China.* Edited by James L. Watson and Evelyn S. Rawski. Berkeley and Los Angeles: University of California Press.

Johnson, Marilyn E. 1978. "Shamanic 'Flight' Analysis and Comparison to the *Ch'u Tz'u.*" Unpublished paper. Toronto: York University. (Extract reproduced, with minor editing by J. Paper, by permission of the author.)

Jordan, David K. 1972. *Gods, Ghosts, and Ancestors, The Folk Religion of a Taiwanese Village.* Berkeley and Los Angeles: University of California Press.

Jordan, David K., and Daniel L. Overmyer. 1986. *The Flying Phoenix: Aspects of Chinese Sectarianism in Taiwan*. Princeton, N.J.: Princeton University Press.

Juan ke xue. 1973. (From *Meishu congshu*.) Taipei: World Book Co.

Kaltenmark, Max. 1953. *Le Lie-sien Tchuan*. Peking: Publications du Centre des Études Sinologiques de Pekin.

———. 1979. "The Ideology of the T'ai-p'ing ching." In *Facets of Taoism*. Edited by Holmes Welch and Anna Seidel. New Haven, Conn.: Yale University Press.

Karlgren, Bernhard. 1930. "Some Fecundity Symbols in Ancient China." *Bulletin of the Museum of Far Eastern Antiquities* (Stockholm) 2: 1–66.

———. 1936. "Yin and Chou in Chinese Bronzes." *Bulletin of the Museum of Far Eastern Antiquities* (Stockholm) 8: 9–156.

———. 1937. "New Studies on Chinese Bronzes." *Bulletin of the Museum of Far Eastern Antiquities* (Stockholm) 9: 1–118.

———. 1946a. "Legends and Cults in Ancient China." *Bulletin of the Museum of Far Eastern Antiquities* (Stockholm) 18: 199–366.

———. 1946b. "Once Again the A and B Styles in Yin Ornamentation." *Bulletin of the Museum of Far Eastern Antiquities* (Stockholm) 18: 367–82.

———. 1950. *The Book of Odes*. Stockholm: Museum of Far Eastern Antiquities.

———. 1951. "Notes on the Grammar of Early Bronze Decor." *Bulletin of the Museum of Far Eastern Antiquities* (Stockholm) 23: 1–80.

———. 1952. *A Catalogue of the Chinese Bronzes in the Alfred E. Pillsbury Collection*. Minneapolis: University of Minnesota Press.

———. 1957. *Grammata Serica Recensa. Bulletin of the Museum of Far Eastern Antiquities* (Stockholm) 29.

Kelleher, Theresa. 1987. "Confucianism." In *Women in World Religions*. Edited by Arvind Sharma. Albany: State University of New York Press.

Kelley, Charles, and Ch'en Meng-chia. 1946. *Chinese Bronzes from the Buckingham Collection*. Chicago: Art Institute Press.

Kendall, Laurel. 1985. *Shamans, Housewives, and Other Restless Spirits, Women in Korean Ritual Life*. Honolulu: University of Hawaii Press.

Kennedy, Allison Bailey. 1982. "*Ecce Bufo*: The Toad in Nature and in Olmec Iconography." *Current Anthropology* 33: 273–90.

Kessell, John L. 1978. "Diego Romero, the Plains Apaches, and the Inquisition." *The American West* 15 (3): 12–16.

Kirkland, Russell. 1992. "Person and Culture in the Taoist Tradition." *Journal of Chinese Religions* 20: 77–90.

Kluckhohn, Clyde. 1942. "Myths and Ritual: A General Theory." *Harvard Theological Review* 35: 45–79.

Kohn, Livia. 1989a. "Guarding the One: Concentrative Meditation in Taoism." In *Taoist Meditation and Longevity Techniques*. Edited by Livia Kohn. Ann Arbor: Center for Chinese Studies, University of Michigan.

———. 1989b. "Taoist Insight Meditation: The Tang Practice of *Neiguan*." In *Taoist Meditation and Longevity Techniques*. Edited by Livia Kohn. Ann Arbor: Center for Chinese Studies, University of Michigan.

———. 1991. *Taoist Mystical Philosophy, The Scripture of Western Ascension*. Albany: State University of New York Press.

———. 1992. *Early Chinese Mysticism: Philosophy and Soteriology in the Taoist Tradition*. New Haven, Conn.: Yale University Press.

Küng, Hans, and Julia Ching. 1989. *Christianity and Chinese Religions*. New York: Doubleday.

La Barre, Weston. 1970. *The Ghost Dance: The Origins of Religion*. New York: Doubleday.

Lai, T. C. 1976. *Chinese Seals*. Seattle: University of Washington Press.

Laing, R. D. 1967. *The Politics of Experience*. New York: Pantheon Books.

Lame Deer, John Fire, and Richard Erdoes. 1972. *Lame Deer, Seeker of Visions*. New York: Simon and Schuster.

Landes, Ruth. 1968. *Ojibwa Religion and the Midéwiwin*. Madison: University of Wisconsin Press.

———. 1970. *The Prairie Potawatomi: Tradition and Ritual in the Twentieth Century*. Madison: University of Wisconsin Press.

Laski, Marghanita. 1961. *Ecstasy.* Bloomington: Indiana University Press.

Lau D. C. 1963. *Lao Tzu: Tao Te Ching.* Baltimore: Penguin Books.

———. 1979. *Confucius: The Analects.* Baltimore: Penguin Books.

Leacock, Eleanor. 1978. "Women's Status in Egalitarian Society: Implications for Social Evolution." *Current Anthropology* 19: 247–76.

Ledderose, Lothar. 1977. "Some Taoist Elements in Six Dynasties Calligraphy." Unpublished paper delivered at the Yale University Conference on Chinese Calligraphy. New Haven, Conn.

———. 1979. *Mi Fu and the Classical Tradition of Chinese Calligraphy.* Princeton, N.J.: Princeton University Press.

Legge, James, translator. 1885. *Li Ki* [Liji]. Edited by F. Max Müller. *Sacred Books of the East.* Oxford: Clarendon Press.

Levenson, Joseph. 1968. *Confucian China and Its Modern Fate.* Berkeley and Los Angeles: University of California Press.

Levine, Paul. 1982. "The Daily Life and Year Cycles as Observed in Nanjing, PRC, 1979–81." Unpublished paper presented to the Midwest Regional Seminar. Chicago.

Levy, Howard S. 1967. *Chinese Footbinding, the History of a Curious Erotic Custom.* New York: Bell Publishing.

Lewis, I. M. 1971. *Ecstatic Religion, An Anthropological Study of Spirit Possession and Shamanism.* Harmondsworth, England: Penguin Books.

Li Chi. 1957. *The Beginnings of Chinese Civilization.* Seattle: University of Washington Press.

Lin Yutang. 1947. *The Gay Genius.* New York: John Day.

Liu, James. 1966. *The Art of Chinese Poetry.* Chicago: University of Chicago Press.

Lo Fuyi. 1963. *Yin jang gai shu.* Peking.

Loehr, Max. 1956. *Chinese Bronze Age Weapons.* Ann Arbor: University of Michigan Press.

———. 1968. *Ritual Vessels of Bronze Age China.* New York: Asia Society.

Loewe, Michael. 1979. *Ways to Paradise.* London: George Allen & Unwin.

Lommel, Andreas. 1967. *Shamanism: The Beginnings of Art.* Translated by Michael Bullock. New York: McGraw-Hill.

————. 1970. *Masken: Gesichter der Menschheit*. Zurich: Atlantis Verlag.

Lou, Dennis Wing-sou. 1957. "Rain-Worship among the Ancient Chinese and the Nahua-Maya Indians." *Bulletin of the Institute of Ethnology, Academia Sinica* (Nankang) 4: 31–108.

Lowie, Robert H. 1934. *An Introduction to Cultural Anthropology*. New York: Farrar & Rinehart.

Lü Zongli and Liu Chun. 1986. *Zhungguo minjian zhushen* (Chinese folk deities). Shijiazhuang: Hebei renming chupanshe.

Ludwig, Arnold M. 1966. "Altered States of Consciousness." *Archives of General Psychiatry* 15: 225–34.

Luomala, Katherine. 1940. *Oceanic, American Indian and African Myths of Snaring the Sun*. Bernice P. Bishop Museum Bulletin 168. Honolulu.

Ma Cheng-yuan. 1980. "The Splendor of Chinese Bronzes." In *The Great Bronze Age of China*. Edited by Wen Fong. New York: Metropolitan Museum of Art.

Ma Xisha. 1984. "Lüelun Ming Qing shidai minjian zongjiao de liangzong fazhan chushi" (Briefly on two tendencies in the development of the folk religions in the Ming and Qing dynasties). *Shijie zongjiao yanjiu* (1): 22–33.

Mair, Victor H. 1990. "Old Sinitic *Mʸag, Old Persian Maguš, and English Magician." *Early China* 15: 27–48.

Major, John. 1978. "Research Priorities in the Study of Ch'u Religion." *History of Religions* 17: 225–43.

Mandell, A. J. 1980. "Towards a Pyschobiology of Transcendence: God in the Brain." *The Psychobiology of Consciousness*. New York: Plenum.

Mao Chiling. 1968. *Hou guan shi lu. Meishu congshu* edition. In *Yu shi gu chi pu lu yi*. Taipei: World Book Co.

Mao Tse-t'ung Poems. 1976. Peking.

Maslow, Abraham. 1971. *The Farther Reaches of Human Nature*. New York: Viking Press.

Maspero, Henri. 1950. *Le Taoïsme*. Publications du Musée Guimet Bibliothèque de Diffusion. Paris.

Mastromattei, Romano. 1989. "Shamanism in Nepal: Modalities of Ecstatic Experience." In *Shamanism: Past and Present*. Edited by Mihály Hoppál and Otto von Sadovsky. Budapest: Ethnographic Institute, Hungarian Academy of Sciences.

Mather, Richard B. 1969. "The Controversy over Conformity and Naturalness During the Six Dynasties." *History of Religions* 9: 159–80.

Meadows, Thomas Taylor. 1856. *The Chinese and Their Rebellions*. London: Smith Elder. Reprinted Stanford, Calif.: Academic Reprints, 1953.

Merkur, Daniel. 1985. *Becoming Half Hidden: Shamanism and Initiation among the Inuit*. Stockholm: Almqvist & Wiksell.

———. 1989. "Unitive Experiences and the State of Trance." In *Mystical Union and Monotheistic Faith, An Ecumenical Dialogue*. Edited by Moshe Idel and Bernard McGinn. New York: Macmillan.

Merrill, William L. 1988. *Rarámuri Souls: Knowledge and Social Process in Northern Mexico*. Washington, D.C.: Smithsonian Institution Press.

Meyer, Jeffrey F. 1991. *The Dragons of Tiananmen: Beijing as a Sacred City*. Columbia: University of South Carolina Press.

Michael, Franz. 1966. *The Taiping Rebellion: History*. Seattle: University of Washington Press.

———. 1971. *The Taiping Rebellion: Documents*. Seattle: University of Washington Press.

Michaud, Paul. 1958. "The Yellow Turbans." *Monumenta Serica* 17: 47–127.

Michihara Ito. 1975. *Chūgoku kodai ōchō no keisei-shutsudo shiryō chūshin to suru inshūshi no kenkyū* (Structural kingship in ancient China). Tokyo: Sobunsha.

Miller, Alan L. 1989. "Internalization of Kami: Buddhist Affinities in Kurozumi-kyō." In *Kurozumi Shinto: An American Dialogue*. Edited by Willis Stoesz. Chambersburg, Pa.: Anima Press.

Ming-fu. 1976. " 'Huachan' yu 'Chanhua.' " *Fojiao wenhua xuebao* (Taiwan). Oct.

Mizuno Seiichi. 1959. *Bronzes and Jades of Ancient China*. Tokyo: Nihon Keizai.

Monberg, Torben. 1991. *Bellona Island Beliefs and Rituals*. Honolulu: University of Hawaii Press.

Monroe, Thomas. 1965. *Oriental Aesthetics*. Cleveland: Western Reserve University Press.

Morrison, Hedda. 1987. *Travels of a Photographer in China, 1933–1946*. Hong Kong: Oxford University Press.

Mote, Frederick. 1960. "Confucian Eremitism in the Yüan Period." In *The Confucian Persuasion*. Edited by Arthur F. Wright. Stanford, Calif.: Stanford University Press.

———. 1971. *Intellectual Foundations of China*. New York: Alfred A. Knopf.

———. 1977. "Yüan and Ming." In *Food in Chinese Culture*. Edited by Kwang-chih Chang. New Haven, Conn.: Yale University Press.

Mu Xhongjian. 1986. "Zhongguo zongjiao de lishi tedian" (The historical characteristics of Chinese religion). *Shijie zongjiao yanjiu* (2): 36–40.

Mungello, D. E. 1989. *Curious Land, Jesuit Accommodation and the Origins of Sinology*. Honolulu: University of Hawaii Press.

Murematsu, Yuji. 1960. "Some Themes in Chinese Rebel Ideologies." In *The Confucian Persuasion*. Edited by Arthur F. Wright. Stanford, Calif.: Stanford University Press.

Murphy, Joseph M. 1988. *Santerí, An African Religion in America*. Boston: Beacon Press.

Nakamura Hajime. 1964. *Ways of Thinking of Eastern Peoples*. Translated by Philip P. Wiener. Honolulu: East-West Center Press.

Naquin, Susan. 1976. *Millenarian Rebellion in China: The Eight Trigrams Uprising in 1813*. New Haven, Conn.: Yale University Press.

Needham, Joseph. 1956. *Science and Civilization in China* 2. Cambridge: Cambridge University Press.

———. 1959. *Science and Civilization in China* 3. Cambridge: Cambridge University Press.

Neihardt, John G. 1932. *Black Elk Speaks*. Lincoln: University of Nebraska Press.

Noll, Richard. 1985. "Mental Imagery Cultivation as a Cultural Phenomena: The Role of Visions in Shamanism." *Current Anthropology* 26: 443–61.

Norman, Jerry. 1988. *Chinese.* Cambridge: Cambridge University Press.

Osborne, Harold. 1968. *Aesthetics and Art Theory.* London: Harlow, Longmans.

Overmyer, Daniel. 1976. *Folk Buddhist Religion: Dissenting Sects in Late Imperial China.* Cambridge, Mass.: Harvard University Press.

Paper, Jordan. 1971. "The *Ch'un meng so yen* (Trifling tale of a spring dream): An Erotic Literary Chinese Tale." *Nachrichten* 109: 69–85.

———. 1973a. *Guide to Chinese Prose.* 1st edition. Boston: C. K. Hall.

———. 1973b. *An Index to Stories of the Supernatural in the "Fa yüan chu lin."* CMRASC Occasional Series No. 19. Taipei.

———. 1974. "The Early Development of Chinese Cosmology." *Chinese Culture* 15 (2): 15–25.

———. 1977a. "Dating the *Chuang tzu* by Analysis of Philosophical Terms." *Chinese Culture* 18 (4): 33–40.

———. 1977b. "A Shaman in Contemporary Toronto." *Religion and Culture in Canada/Religion et Culture au Canada.* Edited by Peter Slater. Waterloo, Ont.: Wilfrid Laurier University Press.

———. 1983a. "The Forgotten Grandmothers: Amerindian Women and Religion in Colonized North America." *Canadian Woman Studies* 5: 48–51.

———. 1983b. "The Post-Contact Origin of an American Indian High God: The Suppression of Feminine Spirituality." *American Indian Quarterly* 7 (4): 1–24.

———. 1986. "The Divine Principle: The Bible from a Korean Perspective." *Studies in Religion* 15: 450–60

———. 1987a. "Cosmological Implications of Pan-Indian Sacred Pipe Rituals." *Canadian Journal of Native Studies* 7(2): 297–307.

———. 1987b. *The "Fu-tzu": A Post-Han Confucian Text.* Leiden: E. J. Brill.

———. 1988. *Offering Smoke: The Sacred Pipe and Native American Religion.* Moscow: University of Idaho Press.

———. 1989a. "Fu Hsüan as Poet, A Man of His Season." In *Wen-lin* 2. Edited by Chow Tse-tsung. Hong Kong: Chinese University of Hong Kong Press.

————. 1989b. "The Normative East Asian Understanding of Christian Scriptures." *Studies in Religion* 18: 451–65.

————. 1990a. "The Persistence of Female Spirits in Patriarchal China." *Journal of Feminist Studies in Religion* 6: 25–40.

————. 1990b. " 'Sweat Lodge': A Northern Native American Ritual for Communal Shamanic Trance." *Temenos* 26: 85–94.

————. 1990c. "Through the Earth Darkly: The Female Deity in Native American Religions." *Religion in Native North America*. Edited by Christopher Vecsey. Moscow: University of Idaho Press.

————. 1991. "Religious Studies: Time to Move from a Eurocentric Bias?" In *Religious Studies: Issues, Prospects and Proposals*. Edited by Klaus K. Klostermaier and Larry W. Hurtado. Atlanta: Scholars Press: 73–84.

————. 1992. "Further Notes on Contemporary Chinese Religion— 1992." *Journal of Chinese Religions* 20: 215–20.

————. 1993a. "Religious Transformations and Socio-Political Change: A Western Eurocentric Paradigm?" In *Religious Transformations and Socio-Political Change: Eastern Europe and Latin America*. Edited by Luther H. Martin. Berlin: Walter de Gruyter: 61–72.

————. 1993b. "Wai lai zongjiao yu zhongguo wenhua: Bijiao moshi" (Foreign religions and Chinese culture: Comparative paradigms). Translated by Zhou Guoli. *Shijie zongjiao ziliao* 1993/(1): 15–20.

————. 1994. "Slighted Grandmothers: The Need for Increased Research on Female Spirits and Spirituality in Native American Religions." In *Annual Review of Women in World Religions* 3. Edited by Arvind Sharma and Katherine Young. Albany: State University of New York Press: 88–106.

Paper, Jordan, and Li Chuang Paper. 1994a. "Chinese Religion." In *Population and the Environment: Population Pressures, Resource Consumption, Religions and Ethics*. Edited by Harold Coward. Albany: State University of New York Press: in press.

————. 1994b. "Matrifocal Rituals in Patrilineal Chinese Religion: The Story of an Early 20th Century Chinese Feminist." *International Journal of Comparative Religion*: in press.

Paper, Li Chuang. 1985. "The Interpretation of the Gospel According to Mark from a Modern Chinese Perspective." Unpublished paper presented at Eastern Interpretation of Scriptures symposium. Martinique.

Parker, Seymour. 1960. "The Wiitiko Psychosis in the Context of Ojibwa Personality and Culture." *American Anthropologist* N.S. 62: 603–23.

Parrish, William L., and Martin King Whyte. 1978. *Village and Family in Contemporary China*. Chicago: University of Chicago Press.

Pas, Julian. 1984. "Temple Oracles in a Chinese City." *Journal of the Hong Kong Branch of the Royal Asiatic Society* 24: 1–45.

———. 1989. "Journey to Hell: A New Report of Shamanistic Travel to the Courts of Hell." *Journal of Chinese Religions* 17: 43–60.

Patterson II, E. Palmer. 1972. *The Canadian Indian: A History Since 1500*. Toronto: Collier-Macmillan.

Paul, Diana. 1985. "Kuanyin: Savior and Savioress in Chinese Pure Land Buddhism." In *The Book of the Goddess, Past and Present*. Edited by Carl Olson. New York: Crossroad.

Pelletier, Kenneth R., and Charles Garfield. 1976. *Consciousness: East and West*. New York: Harper & Row.

Pelletier, Wilfrid, and Ted Poole. 1973. *No Foreign Land: The Biography of a North American Indian*. Toronto: McClelland and Stewart.

Peng Yue and Zheng Tianxing. 1988. "Guowai zongjiao shehuixue guankui sikao." *Shijia Zongjiao Yanjiu* 2: 143–51.

Pettazoni, Raffaele. 1956. *The All-Knowing God*. London: Methuen & Co.

Phanke, Walter N. 1966. "Drugs and Mysticism." *The International Journal of Parapsychology* 8: 295–313.

Pilgrim, Richard B. 1977. "The Artistic Way and the Religioaesthetic Tradition in Japan." *Philosophy East & West* 27: 285–305.

Pope, John, et al. 1967. *The Freer Chinese Bronzes*. Washington, D.C.: Freer Gallery of Art, 1967.

Porée-Maspero, Eveline. 1962–1969. *Étude sur les rites agraires des Cambodgiens*. 3 vols. Paris: Mouton & Co.

Potter, Jack M. 1974. "Cantonese Shamanism." In *Religion and Ritual in Chinese Society*. Edited by Arthur P. Wolf. Stanford, Calif.: Stanford University Press.

Potter, Sulamith Heins, and Jack M. Potter. 1990. *China's Peasants: The Anthropology of a Revolution.* Cambridge: Cambridge University Press.

Prip-Møller, J. 1937. *Chinese Buddhist Monasteries.* Copenhagen: G. E. C. Gad.

Radin, Paul. 1914. "An Introductive Enquiry in the Study of Ojibwa Religion." *Papers and Records of the Ontario Historical Society* 12.

———. 1936. "Ojibwa and Ottawa Puberty Dreams." In *Essays in Anthropology Presented to A. L. Kroeber.* Edited by R. H. Lowie. Berkeley and Los Angeles: University of California Press.

Rasmussen, Knut. 1925. *Thulefahrt.* Frankfurt-am-Main.

Redsky, James. 1972. *Great Leader of the Ojibway: Mis-quona-queb.* Edited by James R. Stevens. Toronto: McClelland and Stewart.

Ricci, Matteo. 1953. *China in the Sixteenth Century: The Journals of Matthew Ricci, 1583–1610.* Translated by Louis J. Gallagher. New York: Random House.

Robinet, Isabelle. 1979. *Méditation taoïste.* Paris: Dervy Livres.

———. 1989. "Visualization and Ecstatic Flight in Shanqing Taoism." In *Taoist Meditation and Longevity Techniques.* Edited by Livia Kohn. Ann Arbor: Center for Chinese Studies, University of Michigan.

Rogers, Edward S. 1962. *The Round Lake Ojibwa.* Toronto: Royal Ontario Museum.

———. 1969. "Natural Environment–Social Organization–Witchcraft: Cree Versus Ojibwa—A Test Case." In *Contributions to Anthropology: Ecological Essays.* Edited by David Damas. Ottawa: National Museums of Canada.

[ROM] Royal Ontario Museum, Toronto: unpublished artifact number.

Rostovtzeff, Mikhail. 1929. *The Animal Style in South Russia and China.* Princeton, N.J.: Princeton University Press.

Rouget, Gilbert. 1985. *Music and Trance, A Theory of the Relations between Music and Possession.* Translated by Brunhilde Biebuyck. Chicago: University of Chicago Press.

Sakanashi, Shio. 1935. *Kuo Hsi, An Essay on Landscape Painting.* London: John Murray.

Sallot, Lynne, and Tom Peltier. 1977. *Bearwalk*. Don Mills, Ont.: Musson Book Co.

Sangren, P. Steven. 1983. "Female Gender in Chinese Religious Symbols: Kuan Yin, Ma Tsu, and the 'Eternal Mother.' " *Signs* 9: 4–25.

Saso, Michael. 1978. *Teachings of the Taoist Master Chuang*. New Haven, Conn.: Yale University Press.

———. 1990. *Blue Dragon White Tiger, Taoist Rites of Passage*. Washington, D.C.: The Taoist Center.

Schafer, Edward H. 1961. *Tu Wan's Stone Catalogue of Cloudy Forest*. Berkeley and Los Angeles: University of California Press.

———. 1973. *The Divine Woman, Dragon Ladies and Rain Maidens in T'ang Literature*. Berkeley and Los Angeles: University of California Press.

———. 1977. "T'ang." In *Food in Chinese Culture*. Edited by Kwang-chih Chang. New Haven, Conn.: Yale University Press.

Schipper, Christopher. 1978. "The Taoist Body." *History of Religions* 17: 355–86.

Schmidt, Wilhelm. 1912. *Der Ursprung des Gottesidee* 1. Munster: Aschendorff.

Schram, Stuart. 1966. *Mao Tse-tung*. Baltimore: Penguin Books.

Scwitters, S.Y., Ronald C. Johnson, Gerald E. McClearn, and James R. Wilson. 1982. "Alcohol Use and the Flushing Response in Different Racial-Ethnic Groups." *Journal of Studies on Alcohol* 43: 1259–62.

Seidel, Anna K. 1969. *La divinisation de Lau Tseu dans le Taoisme des Han*. Paris: École Française d'Extrême-Orient.

Seiwert, Hubert. 1985. *Volksreligion und nationale Tradition in Taiwan: Studies zur regionalen Religionsgeschichte einer chineischen Provinz*. Stuttgart: Franz Steiner Verlag.

Seiwert, Hubert, et al. 1989. "The Institutional Context of the History of Religions in China." In *Marburg Revisited, Institutions and Strategies in the Study of Religion*. Edited by Michael Pye. Marburg: Diagonal Verlag.

Seligman, C. G. N.d. "Shilluk." *Hastings Encyclopedia of Religion and Ethics*, 1st edition. New York: Charles Scribner's Sons.

Shaughnessy, Edward. 1988. "Historical Perspectives on the Introduction of the Chariot into China." *Harvard Journal of Asiatic Studies* 48: 189–237.

Shen Fu, 1983. *Six Records of a Floating Life.* Translated by Leonard Pratt and Chiang Su-hui. Harmondsworth, England: Penguin Books.

Sherman, Spencer. 1972. "Brief Report: Very Deep Hypnosis." *Journal of Transpersonal Psychology* 4: 87–91.

Shi Xingbang. 1962. "Youguan Majiawenhua di yixieh wenti." *Kao qu* 6.

Shih, Vincent Y. C. 1967. *The Taiping Ideology, Its Sources, Interpretations, and Influences.* Seattle: University of Washington Press.

Sholem. Gershom C. 1954. *Major Trends in Jewish Mysticism.* 3d. edition. New York: Schocken Books.

Siikala, Anna-Leena. 1978. *The Rite Technique of the Siberian Shaman.* Helsinki: FF Communications.

———. 1991. "Siberian and Inner Asian Shamanism." In *Studies on Shamanism.* Edited by Anna-Leena Siikala and Mihály Hoppál. Budapest: Akadámiai Kiadó.

Silverblatt, Irene. 1987. *Moon, Sun, and Witches: Gender Ideologies and Class in Inca and Colonial Peru.* Princeton, N.J.: Princeton University Press.

Sinclair-Faulkner, Tom. 1977. "A Puckish Look at Hockey in Canada." In *Religion and Culture in Canada/Religion et Culture au Canada.* Edited by Peter Slater. Waterloo, Ont.: Wilfrid Laurier University Press.

Siven, Nathan. 1978. "On the Word 'Taoist' as a Source of Perplexity: With Special Reference to the Relations of Science and Religion in Traditional China." *History of Religions* 17: 303–30.

Skinner, H. D. 1923. *The Morioris of the Chatham Islands.* Bernice P. Bishop Museum Bulletin 9 (11). Honolulu.

Smith, Arthur H. 1899. *Village Life in China.* New York: F. H. Revell.

Smith, Morton. 1978. *Jesus the Magician.* San Francisco: Harper & Row.

Smith, W. Robertson. 1894. *Lectures on the Religion of the Semites.* London: A. & C. Black..

Snow, Edgar. 1961. *Red Star over China*. New York: Grove Press.

Söderbom, Georg. 1940. Unpublished manuscript. Stockholm: Etnographisca Museet.

Soothill, W. E. 1913. *The Three Religions of China*. London: Hodder & Staughton.

Staal, Fritz. 1975. *Exploring Mysticism*. Harmondsworth, England: Penguin Books.

Stace, W. T. 1961. *Mysticism and Philosophy*. Philadelphia: Lippincott.

Stanley-Baker, Joan. 1977. "The Development of Brush-Modes in Sung and Yüan." *Artibus Asiae* 39: 13–59.

Steele, John. 1917. *The I-li: Book of Etiquette and Ceremonial*. London: Probsthain & Co.

Steinmetz, Paul B. 1984. "The Sacred Pipe in American Indian Religions." *American Indian Culture and Research Journal* 8(3): 27–80.

Stoller, Paul. 1989. *Fusion of the World: An Ethnography of Possession among the Songhay of Niger*. Chicago: University of Chicago Press.

Stoller, Paul, and Cheryl Oakes. 1985. *In Sorcery's Shadow: A Memoir of Apprenticeship among the Songhay of Niger*. Chicago: University of Chicago Press.

Stover, Leon E. 1974. *The Cultural Ecology of Chinese Civilization: Peasants and Elites in the Last of the Agrarian States*. New York: New American Library.

Strickmann, Michael. 1979. "On the Alchemy of T'ao Hung-ching." *Facets of Taoism*. Edited by Holmes Welch and Anna Seidel. New Haven, Conn.: Yale University Press.

Sullivan, Michael. 1974. *The Three Perfections, Chinese Painting, Poetry and Calligraphy*. London: Thames and Hudson.

Sun Haipo. 1963. *Jiaquwen bien*. Taipei: I Wen Book Co.

Swanton, John R. 1909. *Tlingit Myths and Texts*. Bureau of American Ethnology, Bulletin 39. Washington, D.C.

Tart, Charles T. 1970. "Transpersonal Potentialities of Deep Hypnosis." *Journal of Transpersonal Psychology* 2: 27–40.

Taylor, Rodney L. 1978. "The Centered Self: Religious Autobiography in the Neo-Confucian Tradition." *History of Religions* 17: 266–83.

Tedlock, Barbara. 1982. *Time and the Highland Maya*. Albaquerque: University of New Mexico Press.

Teiser, Stephen F. 1986. "Ghosts and Ancestors in Medieval Chinese Religion: The Yü-lan-p'en Festival as Mortuary Ritual." *History of Religions* 26: 47–67.

Teng, Ssu-yü. 1962. *Historiography of the Taiping Rebellion*. Cambridge: Cambridge University Press.

———. 1971. *The Taiping Rebellion and the Western Powers*. Oxford: Clarendon Press.

Thiel, P. Jos. 1968. "Schamanismus im Alten China." *Sinologica* 10: 149–204.

Thomas, Northcote W. N.d."Animals." *Hastings Encyclopedia of Religion and Ethics*. 1st edition. New York: Charles Scribner's Sons.

Thompson, Laurence. 1989. *Chinese Religion*. 4th edition. Belmont, Calif.: Wadsworth Publishing.

Thompson, S. E. 1988. "Death, Food, and Fertility." In *Death Ritual in Imperial and Modern China*. Edited by James L. Watson and Evelyn S. Rawski. Berkeley and Los Angeles: University of California Press.

Trésors d'art Chinois. 1973. Paris: Petit Palais.

Tsien Tsuen-hsuin. 1962. *Written on Bamboo and Silk*. Chicago: University of Chicago Press.

Turner, Victor. 1969. *The Ritual Process*. Chicago: Aldine Publishing.

Umehara, Sueji. 1959. "Sensei-shō Hōkeiken shutsudo no dai ni no henkin." *Tōhōgaku Kiyō* 1.

Underhill, Evelyn. 1955. *Mysticism*. New York: New American Library.

Underhill, Ruth. 1948. *Ceremonial Patterns in the Greater Southwest*. Reprinted Seattle: University of Washington Press, 1966.

Vastokas, Joan, and Romas Vastokas. 1973. *Sacred Art of the Algonkians*. Peterborough, Ont.: Mansard Press.

Visser, M. W. de. 1913. *The Dragon in China and Japan*. Amsterdam: Johannes Muller.

Volker, T. 1950. *The Animal in Far Eastern Art*. Mededelingen van het Rijksmusseum voor Volkenkunde (6, 7). Leiden.

Wakeman, Frederick, Jr. 1988. "Mao's Remains." In *Death Ritual in Late Imperial and Modern China*. Edited by James L. Watson and Evelyn S. Rawski. Berkeley and Los Angeles: University of California Press.

Waley, Arthur. 1918. *One Hundred and Seventy Chinese Poems*. London: Constable & Co.

———. 1955. *The Nine Songs*. London: Allen & Unwin.

———. 1960. *The Book of Songs*. New York: Grove Press.

Wallos, W. D. 1919. "The Sun Dance of the Canadian Dakota." *Anthropological Papers of the American Museum of Natural History* 16: 317–80.

Wang Sung-hsing. 1974. "Taiwanese Architecture and the Supernatural." In *Religion and Ritual in Chinese Society*. Edited by Arthur P. Wolfe. Stanford, Calif.: Stanford University Press.

Ward, J. A. 1975. "The Wikwemikong Suicide Epidemic, A Psychiatric Analysis." Unpublished presentation to Coroner's Jury, December 11–12, 1975.

Ward, J. A., and Joseph Fox. 1977. "A Suicide Epidemic on an Indian Reserve." *Canadian Psychiatric Association Journal* 22 (8): 423–26.

Waterbury, Florence. 1942. *Early Chinese Symbols and Literature*. New York: E. Weyhe.

———. 1952. *Bird Deities in China*. Ascona, Switzerland: Artibus Asiae.

Watson, Burton. 1968. *Chuang Tzu*. New York: Columbia University Press.

Watson, James L. 1985. "Standardizing the Gods: The Promotion of T'ien Hou (Empress of Heaven) Along the South China Coast, 960–1960." In *Popular Culture in Late Imperial China*. Edited by David Johnson, Andrew J. Nathan, and Evelyn S. Rawski. Berkeley and Los Angeles: University of California Press.

———. 1988. "The Structure of Chinese Funerary Rituals: Elementary Forms, Ritual Sequence, and the Primacy of Performance." In *Death Rituals in Late Imperial and Modern China*. Edited by James L. Watson and Evelyn S. Rawski. Berkeley and Los Angeles: University of California Press.

Watson, William. 1960. *Archaeology in China*. London: Max Parrish.

———. 1962a. *Ancient Chinese Bronzes*. London: Faber & Faber.

———. 1962b. *Handbook to the Collections of Early Chinese Antiquities*. London: British Museum.

———. 1974. *Styles in the Arts of China*. Harmondsworth, England: Penguin Books.

Waugh, Earle H., and K. Dad Prithipaul, editors. 1979. *Native Religious Traditions*. Waterloo, Ont.: Wilfrid Laurier University Press.

Wechsler, Howard J. 1985. *Offerings of Jade and Silk: Ritual and Symbol in the Legitimization of the T'ang Dynasty*. New Haven, Conn.: Yale University Press.

Weller, Robert P. 1987. *Unities and Diversities in Chinese Religion*. Seattle: University of Washington Press.

Wen wu (Beijing). 1965. (6).

Wen Yido. 1948. *Wen Yido chuanji*. 2d edition. Shanghai.

Werblowsky, R. J. Zvi. 1990. "The Western Perception of China 1700–1900—From Leibnitz to De Groot." *Dialogue and Alliance* 4 (2): 60–70.

Werner, E. T. C. 1961. *Dictionary of Chinese Mythology*. New York: Julian Press.

White, William. 1945. *Bone Culture of Ancient China*. Toronto: University of Toronto Press.

———. 1956. *Bronze Culture of Ancient China*. Toronto: University of Toronto Press.

Whyte, Martin King, and William L. Parrish, 1984. *Urban Life in Contemporary China*. Chicago: University of Chicago Press.

Williams, S. W. 1883. *The Middle Kingdom*. New York.

Wills, John E., Jr. 1979. "State Ceremony in Late Imperial China." *Bulletin, Society for the Study of Chinese Religions* 7: 46–57.

Wolf, Arthur P. 1974. "Gods, Ghosts, and Ancestors." In *Religion and Ritual in Chinese Society*. Edited by Arthur P. Wolfe. Stanford, Calif.: Stanford University Press.

Wolff, Peter H. 1972. "Ethnic Differences in Alcohol Sensitivity." *Science* 175: 449–50.

Wright, Peggy Ann. 1989. "The Nature of Shamanic State of Consciousness: A Review." *Journal of Psychoactive Drugs* 21 (1): 25–34.

Wu Bingan. 1989. *Shenmi de saman shijie.* Shanghai: Sanlien shudien.

Wu, G. D. 1938. *Prehistoric Pottery in China.* London: Kegan, Paul, Trench, Truebner & Co.

Wu, Nelson I. 1962. "Tung Ch'i-ch'ang: Apathy in Government and Fervor in Art." In *Confucian Personalities.* Edited by Arthur F. Wright and Dennis Twitchett. Stanford, Calif.: Stanford University Press.

Wu Shichi. 1988. "Zhongguo xinshiqishidai de taoshuo yishu." *Zhongguo wenwu shijie* 36 (September): 16–24.

Xian banpo. 1963. Beijing.

Xiao Yishan. 1936. *Taiping tianguo congshu.* Shanghai.

Yang, C.K. 1967. *Religion in Chinese Society.* Berkeley and Los Angeles: University of California Press.

Yang Hsien-yi, and Gladys Yang. 1957. *The Courtesan's Jewel Box.* Beijing: Foreign Language Press.

Yang, Martin C. 1945. *A Chinese Village: Taitou, Shantung Province.* New York: Columbia University Press.

Yang Shuda. 1933. *Handai hun sang li su kao* (Research on Han dynasty marriage and funeral rites). Reprint Taipei: Hua-shih Publishing Co., 1976.

Yeh Ch'iu-yüan. 1940. "The Lore of Chinese Seals." *T'ien Hsia Monthly* (Shanghai) 10, 1: 9–22.

Yen Changyu. 1986. " 'Meiguo guomin zongjiao' guanxi" (A bird-eye [sic] view of American civil religion). *Shijie zongjiao yanjiu* (3): 102–10.

Yen Iping. 1962. *Chuan ke ru men.* Taipei: I Wen Publishing Co.

Yetts, W. Percival. 1912. *Symbolism in Chinese Art.* China Society Lecture, January 18, 1912.

———. 1925. *Chinese Art.* London: B. T. Batsford.

————. 1939. *The Cull Chinese Bronzes.* London: University of London Press.

Yip Wai-lim. 1976. *Chinese Poetry: Major Modes and Genres.* Berkeley and Los Angeles: University of California Press.

Yoshikawa Kojiro. 1967. *An Introduction to Sung Poetry.* Translated by Burton Watson. Cambridge, Mass.: Harvard University Press.

Yu, Anthony C., translator. 1977–1983. *The Journey to the West.* Chicago: University of Chicago Press.

Yü Chün-fang. 1990. "Feminine Images of Kuan-yin in Post-T'ang China." *Journal of Chinese Religions* 18: 61–89.

Yü Ying-shih. 1964. "Life and Immortality in Han China." *Harvard Journal of Asiatic Studies* 25: 80–122.

Yuan Ko. 1957. *Zhongguo gudai shen hua* (Ancient Chinese deities). Shanghai: Commercial Press.

Zaehner, R. C. 1957. *Mysticism, Sacred and Profane.* New York: Oxford University Press.

Zhang Yingwen. 17th cent. *Qing mi cang.*

Zhen Zhiming. 1988. *Zhongguo shanshu yu congjiao* (Chinese "Good Books" and religion). Taipei: Hsüeh Sheng Shu Chü.

Zhu Xiangxian, editor. 1778. *Yin tian. Siku chuanshu* edition.

Zhongguo gudai chingtung chi ji (A selection of ancient Chinese bronzes). 1976. Beijing: Wenwu.

Zimmer, Heinrich. 1946. *Myths and Symbols in Indian Art and Civilization.* Edited by Joseph Campbell. Princeton, N.J.: Pantheon Press.

Zürcher, E. 1959. *The Buddhist Conquest of China.* Leiden: E. J. Brill.

index